How to Coach Teachers Who *Don't* Think Like You

Using Literacy Strategies to Coach Across Content Areas

Bonnie M.
DAVIS

CORWIN PRESS
A SAGE Company
Thousand Oaks, CA 91320

For information:

Corwin Press
A SAGE Company
2455 Teller Road
Thousand Oaks, California 91320
www.corwinpress.com

SAGE Ltd.
1 Oliver's Yard
55 City Road
London EC1Y 1SP
United Kingdom

SAGE India Pvt. Ltd.
B 1/I 1 Mohan Cooperative
   Industrial Area
Mathura Road, New Delhi 110 044
India

SAGE Asia-Pacific Pte. Ltd.
33 Pekin Street #02–01
Far East Square
Singapore 048763

Printed in the United States of America.

Library of Congress Cataloging-in-Publication Data

Davis, Bonnie M.
How to coach teachers who don't think like you : using literacy strategies to coach across content areas / Bonnie M. Davis.
      p. cm.
Includes bibliographical references and index.
ISBN 978-1-4129-4909-5 (cloth)
ISBN 978-1-4129-4910-1 (pbk.)
   1. English language—Composition and exercises—Study and teaching (Elementary)
2. English language—Composition and exercises—Study and teaching (Secondary)
3. Teachers—In-service training. I. Title.

LB1576.D2372 2008
372.6′044—dc22   2007029947

This book is printed on acid-free paper.

07   08   09   10   11   10   9   8   7   6   5   4   3   2   1

Acquisitions Editor:	Dan Alpert
Editorial Assistant:	Tatiana Richards
Production Editor:	Eric Garner
Copy Editor:	Barbara Coster
Typesetter:	C&M Digitals (P) Ltd.
Proofreader:	Theresa Kay
Indexer:	Sheila Bodell
Cover Designer:	Rose Storey
Graphic Designer:	Karine Hovsepian

Contents

Introduction

HOW TO READ THIS BOOK

As a coach, you encounter teachers who think like you and teachers who don't think like you. Often, those who don't think like you do so because of the "mental models" of their content. Whether they teach math or mechanics, they use a different set of mental models. Good coaches bridge this divide by successfully supporting teachers who do not think like them by using literacy strategies that improve instruction, no matter the content area. In addition, as a coach, you must first create the space to work with teachers who do not think like you. Therefore, this book includes both the process and content of coaching blended in the narratives of practicing coaches; in other words, these are real stories set in the real world of coaching.

Written for both the beginning coach and the practicing coach, this book has some parts more applicable to your work than others. If you are a beginning coach, much of the information may be new. However, if you are a practicing coach, you may want to skip sections that repeat what you already know. The book includes the work of school-based coaches, district coaches, and independent coaches. If you coach in a single building, feel free to skip the sections written for independent coaches and district coaches. In other words, pick and choose what sections suit your needs. The subtitles offer you a road map to guide your reading.

This is not a novel, and it is not intended to be read as one. The book relies heavily upon reflective questions to support your navigation through the text. It is a coaching book that emphasizes writing instruction, and the information contained within refers to coaches who coach across the content areas. Read and digest it in small bites. Since each chapter can be read independently, examine the table of contents and choose what works for you.

Acknowledgments

In 1983 the words of one woman, Elizabeth Krekeler, changed my life. She was the Language Arts Curriculum Director (today she might be called a literacy coach) for the large district in which I taught. She said to me, "Why don't you think about your teaching as a profession?" Perhaps peculiar words today, but this was long before I had heard of professional development plans, professional learning communities, and lifelong learning. Her words caused me to reflect upon my teaching and make the necessary changes from one who taught with no goals in mind to a teacher who designed a professional development plan for herself. I now live that plan, and these are the people who helped me realize my dream. Thank you, Beth, you continue to provoke me to change and grow.

I owe so much to Sue Heggarty, my coworker and friend, who makes working a discovery and a joy each year we continue together. Thank you, Sue. Thanks to all those at Cooperating School Districts, especially our International Education Consortium division with Dennis Lubeck, Sheila Onuska, Megan Moncure, Michael Grady, and John Robinson. Thanks also for the leadership and support of Dennis Dorsey, Sandy Blanco, and the folks of CharacterPlus. We owe much to Doug Miller of the Missouri Department of Elementary and Secondary Education (DESE), who has supported our work for more than 20 years. Thank you, Doug.

I am grateful to all the administrators and teachers working hard in the schools where I coached for more than a decade, especially Cheryl Compton, Gerry Kettenbach, Michael Ebert, Linda Henke, Nancy Saguto, Todd Benben, Beverly Nance, Barbara Kohm, Mary Jo Lieberstein, Sarah Riss, Sue McAdamis, Chauna Williams, and all those credited below in the Contributors list. Your work is reflected in this book. I hope you're proud!

This book would not be complete without the writings of the coaches—Nan Starling, Lola Mapes, Susie Morice, Sue Heggarty, and Mary Kim Schreck—whose work resides within its covers. Thank you, coaches, for sharing your professional struggles and victories. Hopefully, your words will positively influence the coaching and instruction of many professionals.

Thanks to the teachers—Gloria Brazell, Robyn Haug, Stephanie Hughes, Julie Pallardy, Derek Rowley, Erin Groff, and Dorcas Wanner—for your writings. Thank you, Kim Gutchewsky, for sharing your winning National Council of Teachers of English (NCTE) article. A special thanks to you, John Hefflinger; your journey is a metaphor for the growth and change we see in teacher instruction as we continue our coaching work. Thanks also to the many teachers who participated in my workshops and whose evaluative comments are found within the book.

Thank you, Mary Kim Schreck, for your stunning poetry that graces the pages of this book. May the poems included within spur readers to seek out *Pulse of the Seasons* (2004), *The Red Desk* (2005), *and Crystal Doorknobs* (2006)—your books of poetry that expose the loamy layers of an educator's life.

Thanks and love to you, Dorothy Kelly; your life work continues to inspire me to stay strong. Thanks to Kim Anderson, who has guided my work since 2000 and continues to Webmistress my professional life.

Without the support and help from my family, my work would not exist. My love and thanks to my father, Homer Schnurbusch, for our special relationship and your unfailing support. This book is in memory of my mother, my first teacher and enthusiastic supporter of all of my work. Special love and thanks to my sisters and their families: Susan Welker for your phone calls and encouragement; Ruth Dambach for your editing advice, guidance, and eternal help with everything; Mary Aldredge for thrashing through life with me and your ongoing support. Loads of love to my children and future grandchildren: my daughter, Leah, a brave woman who dares speak the truth against injustice in difficult situations; and my son, Reeve, a special soul and a kind man with a generous heart.

Thanks and love to Dr. Joseph "Fred" Baugh, my noncritical partner who continues to encourage my work and share my dream. Living with a passionate musician turned physicist continues to open my mind to the possibilities of the imagination and of the universe.

Thanks also to the Corwin Press team: Acquisitions Editor Dan Alpert, Editorial Assistant Tatiana Richards, Production Editor Eric Garner, Copy Editor Barbara Coster, Typesetter C&M Digitals (P) Ltd., Proofreader Theresa Kay, Indexer Sheila Bodell, Cover Designer Rose Storey, and Graphic Designer Karine Hovsepian.

The contributions of the following reviewers are gratefully acknowledged:

Jim De Laney
Lab Extension Specialist
Mid-Atlantic Regional Educational Laboratory
Fairfax, VA

Terry A. Green, Ph.D.
Founder
Literacy Initiatives, Inc.
Richardson, Texas

Lori L. Grossman
Instructional Coordinator
Professional Development Services
Houston Independent School District
Houston, TX

Cindy Harrison
Independent Consultant
Past President of NSDC
Broomfield, CO

Kathryn Kee
Leadership Coach and Consultant
Coaching School Results, Inc.
Shady Shores, TX

Dale Moxley
Principal
Lake County Schools
Mount Dora, FL

Marti Richardson
Executive Director
Tennessee Staff Development Council
Knoxville, TX

Contributors

The following educators contributed writings to this book:

Coworker and Coach: Sue Heggarty

Coaches
   Mary Kim Schreck
   Nan Starling
   Susie Morice
   Lola Mapes

Teachers
   Dorcas Wanner
   John Hefflinger
   Erin Groff
   Julie Pallardy
   Robyn Haug
   Derek Rowley
   Gloria Brazell
   Stephanie Hughes
   Kim Gutchewsky

Principals
   Gerald Kettenbach
   Michael Ebert

Students
   Alex Blodgett
   Megan Illy

Additional teacher evaluative comments are attributed in the text.

About the Author

Bonnie M. Davis, PhD, is the author of the best-selling Corwin Press book *How to Teach Students Who Don't Look Like You: Culturally Relevant Teaching Strategies* (2006), recommended by the National Education Association. She currently serves as a consultant on literacy coaching, writing across the content areas, and culturally proficient instruction to schools, districts, and professional organizations.

For 30 years, she taught English in middle schools, high schools, universities, homeless shelters, and a men's prison. She is the recipient of several awards, including Teacher of the Year, the Governor's Award for Teaching Excellence, and the Anti-Defamation League's World of Difference Community Service Award.

She holds a PhD in English from Saint Louis University, an MA in English from the University of Mississippi, an MAI in communications from Webster University, and a BS in education from Southeast Missouri State University.

She has presented for the National Staff Development Council, Association for Supervision and Curriculum Development, National Education Association, National Council of Teachers of English, and National Association of Multicultural Education, among others.

Her publications include *African-American Academic Achievement: Building a Classroom of Excellence* (2001) and numerous articles on literacy and cultural instruction, such as "A Cultural Safari," an NCTE Paul Farmer Writing Award runner-up winner. Recently, she authored the cover article in the Missouri National Education Association's (MNEA) publication, *Something Better* (Winter, 2006). She appears in the School Improvement Network's video program *No Excuses! How to Increase Minority Student Achievement* (2006), along with experts James Comer, Kati Haycock, Sonia Nieto, Gary Howard, Beverly Tatum, and Jaime Almazen, and she is a coauthor, along with Curtis Linton, of the book *No Excuses! How to Increase Minority Student Achievement* (2007).

In addition to her writing, she spends her professional life coaching and presenting to educators. Because she spent 30 years in the classroom, she considers herself first a teacher, and she relates to staffs in a lively, interactive manner. When she works with educators, she is passionate, funny, and energetic, modeling instructional and relationship strategies to "close the achievement gap" by improving instruction.

A former Midwesterner, she currently lives in Southern California and is available for keynotes, presentations, workshops, and consultation. You can reach her at a4achievement@earthlink.net or view her Web site at www .a4achievement.net.

Moving From Teaching Students to Coaching Teachers

How far you go in life depends on your being tender with the young, compassionate with the aged, sympathetic with the striving, and tolerant of the weak and the strong. Because someday in life you will have been all of these.

—George Washington Carver
(agricultural chemist, former slave)

In Frank Smith's chapter called the "Myths of Writing" (1983), he discusses commonly held beliefs about writing and then exposes them as myths. Several are especially applicable to this book.

For example, he states that a commonly held belief is that "writing involves transferring thoughts from the mind to paper." However, the reality is that "thoughts are created in the act of writing, which changes the writer and changes emerging text" (n.p.). This book exemplifies that reality. Its earliest origins sprang from a decade of work by coaches in a variety of school districts from rural to urban. Yet writing it changed both the writers and the emerging text.

This is a descriptive work that illuminates the coaching of a handful of colleagues as they interacted with hundreds of educators. Our goal was and still is to support teachers in improving classroom instruction and, in turn, improve student achievement. Even though my name appears on the title page, this book is a collective effort of several coaches who have used literacy strategies to support teachers across the content areas.

However, just as important is our goal of supporting teachers to find their writing voices—creating spaces where they will view themselves as writers, no matter what discipline they teach. We believe that writing is a powerful vehicle teachers can use to develop ways to customize their own learning in order to meet the needs of the students. Frank Smith (1983) also states that unless teachers *write* and are writers themselves, they will not teach students how to write.

How do we, as coaches, create spaces for teachers to release the writer within, risk writing in order to learn what they think, and reflect upon those thoughts in order to improve instruction? How do we give voice to teachers' writings? Even more challenging, how do we encourage and support teachers who do not think like us and do not have a background in writing?

This book shares how we meet that challenge at the elementary and secondary levels. Included also are the writings of several teachers with whom we've worked. As you read these teachers' writings, you enter their minds and classrooms and begin to understand how the power of coaching creates an environment of safety for their writing voices to emerge. The final chapter in the book describes the transformative power of a writer's workshop. When teachers find their writing voices and become writers themselves, they model the act of writing for their students, embedding writing as an integral piece of classroom instruction.

In addition, each of the coaches described in this book is a writer immersed in a social consciousness of equity. We believe that each human being is a unique individual with a unique cultural lens who has the fundamental right to grow to his or her potential. We believe writing offers individuals a vehicle to reach that potential.

Smith (1983) also dispels the myth that "writing should be the same for everyone," and he tells us that "each of us develops an idiosyncratic set of strategies we're comfortable with for us" (n.p.). This book offers you myriad ways in which to reach the teachers you coach with an "idiosyncratic set of strategies" to match the individuals with whom you work.

Whether you are a beginning coach or one with several years of experience, you will find in this book suggestions and avenues for exploration, reflection, inspiration, and application.

THE CHAPTERS

Chapter 1 defines coaching, including questions to assess qualifications, readiness, and desire. Chapter 2 examines the "inner coaching" life and offers you tools to use as you coach. It also includes information we *wish* we would have known before we began coaching. Chapter 3 discusses how to coach teachers who don't think like you and the qualities you need to develop in order to do that. Chapter 4 consists of several narratives by working literacy coaches that include concrete strategies for your work world. Chapter 5 gives you the time structures we used throughout a decade of coaching and ideas for how you can find time to coach. Chapter 6 offers you scenarios to test your coaching savvy. Chapter 7 presents a demonstration lesson and professional development workshop outlines. Chapter 8 outlines the coaching we did in a district to improve student achievement on state assessments. Chapter 9 describes a decade of coaching teams of teachers using a year-long professional development model that ends in teachers having their work published. Chapter 10 outlines how to support teachers as writers using an action research model. Chapter 11 gives you an outline for a writer's workshop to use in your work. The appendices include multiple resources to support your coaching work, including frequently asked questions as well as classroom and workshop resources.

FOR THE TEACHER CONSIDERING COACHING OR FOR THE NEW COACH

Are you considering moving from teaching to coaching? Are you a beginning coach currently coaching staff in your building or district?

If these descriptions fit, read on.

Why coaching rather than teaching? Are you at a place in your career where perhaps you need the challenge coaching provides? Do you think knowing how to teach qualifies you to be a coach? If so, think again. Although coaching shares similarities with teaching, coaching is not the same as teaching. Coaching requires additional skills.

If you are a classroom teacher, you hold the power to create the learning environment. As a coach, we support the work of the teacher, but we can't force change. With coaching, we need weapons. This book tells you about those weapons. It tells you how to arm yourself. It gives you battle plans. It even gives you strategies for cleaning up your messes. Gee, why all the war talk? Don't know, it just slipped in. Let's try another metaphor.

Let's try gardening. This book tells you how to enrich the soil to set the stage for change, how to plant seeds for future growth by giving teachers new strategies to implement, and how to nurture new growth as teachers use strategies to harvest improved student achievement.

Whether you resonate to the war or gardening metaphor, as a coach you need a plan and multiple strategies to carry out that plan. This book offers you several plans as well as multiple success stories to prove their effectiveness.

In this book, you will find coaching strategies and models for individual teachers, teams of teachers, and entire schools. All the strategies presented have been used over the past 10 years and with documented success. (Also included are strategies that didn't work and common pitfalls to avoid.) Many of the classroom strategies are literacy strategies—reading, speaking, writing, thinking, listening, viewing—that are applicable across the disciplines. However, there is an emphasis on writing: writing to learn, writing to express, writing to improve student test scores. The reason we emphasize writing is that the coaches included are all writing teachers. We may have started out years ago as teachers of "literature." However, as we progressed in our teaching careers, we became writers ourselves (though never abandoning our teaching and love of literature).

As we implemented more writing, we witnessed its transformative power: classroom community improved as students shared their writing with their peers, and student achievement improved as our students saw themselves as writers. In *Results Now: How We Can Achieve Unprecedented Improvements in Teaching and Learning*, Mike Schmoker (2006) underscores the importance of students writing along with the challenges associated with its instruction. He states that "writing, combined with close reading, is among the most valuable, but least understood elements of schools" (p. 63). It is often misunderstood because so many teachers were not taught how to teach writing or how to use writing to learn across the disciplines; therefore, writing instruction suffers in the classroom. Yet, students need teachers who are writers themselves and can deliver powerful and effective writing instruction.

How does this happen? One way is through the use of a coach to support teachers as they work to improve their instruction. We build upon teacher strengths. This book is full of numerous examples, anecdotes, strategies, and narratives that use writing to learn and improve thinking. Teachers like these because they work. Students like them, once they understand and use them, because they work. You'll like them because they work. And because they work, everyone is happy and will thank you for helping them make a difference in their classrooms.

Think of This Book as a Buffet of Choices for Coaching

How do you enjoy a buffet? Do you eat everything? Of course not. You usually choose some familiar foods you know you like. You also may choose some you do not eat often but plan to taste and digest. Finally, you may be willing to try one or two "exotic" foods you never thought about trying before, but something convinces you to sample them. This book is like that buffet: taste and digest the familiar, pass by what does not fit your style or mood, and try a few things you've never tried before. We hope you enjoy the buffet!

WHAT IS COACHING?

Coaching has been defined in many different ways by many different people. Now that is as innocuous as you can find. However, it is true. Coaching means something similar but not exactly the same to myriads of people, some of whom are educators.

In the field of education, one seminal definition comes from cognitive coaching concept, founded by Arthur Costa and Robert Garmston. In *Cognitive Coaching: A Foundation for Renaissance Schools* (2002), they define coaching as "a nonjudgmental, developmental, reflective model derived from a blend of the psychological orientations of cognitive theorists and the interpersonal bonding of humanists" (p. 5). In an article titled "School-Based Coaching: A Revolution in Professional Development—Or Just the Latest Fad?" Alexander Russo (2004) states that school-based coaching "generally involves experts in a particular subject area or set of teaching strategies working closely with small groups of teachers to improve classroom practice and, ultimately, student achievement" (n.p.).

In this book, Russo's definition most closely aligns with ours. We define school-based coaching as a collegial practice where experienced educators work with teachers in order for teachers to improve classroom instruction. Notice the wording "work with teachers in order for teachers to improve," which denotes it is not the coaches improving instruction but rather the teachers themselves. It is not possible to make another person change, and the role of the coach in the classroom is like the coach on the football field. The football coach teaches the plays, coaches the players on their implementation, and gives positive feedback. However, the players execute the moves, not the coach. Likewise, coaches coach teachers about their instruction; they do not implement the instruction. They may model the instruction, but in the classroom, it is the teacher who must teach the students.

The National Council of Teachers of English (NCTE; 2006) defines a literacy coach as someone who

- Is a highly trained and qualified individual
- Assists teachers in developing strategy to improve student literacy
- Forms long-term partnerships with teachers and school districts
- Provides assistance to help students read content effectively
- Allows students to engage in critical thinking to improve literary skill
- Helps students engage in discussion about literature that is relevant to real experiences (n.p.)

On NCTE's Web site (www.ncte.org), you will find links to standards developed for middle and high school literacy coaches. They also include numerous other sites to support your work as a literacy coach.

In this book, we define coaching as an elastic term, one that continues to evolve. In addition, unlike many of the available books on coaching, we have focused on coaches who emphasize writing to learn.

Are you qualified to be a coach?

The following questions are useful in determining your readiness:

- Do you have an advanced degree in literacy?
- Do you enjoy working with adults?
- Are you familiar with adult learning theory?
- Have you taught literacy for a number of years in order to have gained proficiency in the classroom?
- Are you willing to listen more than talk?
- Have you had adequate training in how to coach?
- Have you read the leading books on coaching?

There are several excellent books on coaching to guide your work, and this book offers you an opportunity to learn and reflect on your coaching. Included is the work of several school-based coaches who worked with groups of educators, both teachers and teacher trainers, in hopes of improving classroom practice and, as a result, student achievement. Much of the work was designed to improve state test scores.

Coaching should meet the standards for effective staff development as set forth by the National Staff Development Council (NSDC), the nation's largest professional development association dedicated to professional development. These standards exemplify the best in professional development and guide us as we improve our practice, knowing that no longer can we abide the "sit and get" and the one-shot workshop.

In the past, teachers may have left a workshop with 50+ strategies for implementation, all of which might be useful. But long before their next class, teachers get back to their usual business and all the new strategies sit in the workshop folder. Coaching eliminates this. With a good coaching model in place, teachers learn a new strategy from the coach and then are observed and given specific feedback for the implementation of that strategy in the classroom.

Using these strategies with feedback from the coaches, teachers have the opportunity to observe change in themselves, their practices, and the students. Once teachers try the strategy and see a change in their own classrooms, they are much more willing to buy into future strategies that you present. Some strategies are more efficacious than others, and all depend upon the personalities of the teachers involved. That is why this book offers you several models and many strategies, and in these pages you will find the strategies that changed classroom practice and improved student achievement.

This book is an authentic show-and-tell that has resulted from years of classroom teaching of English and reading and more than a decade of literacy coaching. The coaches in this book coached in inner-city schools, suburban schools, and rural schools. They share their stories complete with frustrations, failures, and successes. The book offers several different models for coaching and offers a workbook format to guide you through your coaching experiences as you navigate the world of coaching.

QUESTIONS FOR THE BEGINNING COACH

Knowing yourself is a powerful first step to becoming a coach. Consider the following questions as you begin your coaching journey.

Describe yourself and include the strengths you believe you bring to the coaching role.

_____

_____

_____

How do you define the role of a coach?

_____

_____

_____

Do you like to read and write? What kinds of reading and writing do you do?

_____

_____

_____

What literacy books have you read and used in your work?

_____

_____

_____

How much time up front do you believe needs to be spent building relationships with those you will coach? How much time will you spend to maintain an ongoing relationship with those you coach?

_____

_____

_____

How comfortable are you when going to a strange place and meeting strangers?

_____

_____

_____

How comfortable are you when meeting with a group of teachers who may not think like you and may not want to meet with you?

_____

_____

_____

What grade level teachers would you be most comfortable coaching?

_____

_____

_____

After you have responded to the above questions, take a few moments and process your thoughts.

Describe the coach you want to be.

_____

_____

_____

_____

_____

_____

_____

_____

_____

Hopefully, by processing the above questions in writing, you have clarified some aspects of the coaching role you want to assume or currently hold. The more clear you are about your role, the easier it will be to explain it to others.

Coaching is not an easy role. It demands a multitude of qualifications and experience. Coaches need to be

- Excellent classroom teachers of literacy
- Excellent presenters to large groups
- Knowledgeable about literacy acquisition
- Capable of modeling lessons for teachers in front of students they have never met
- Capable of working with teachers they do not know on instructional practices
- Excellent facilitators
- Excellent one-on-one communicators
- Capable of building trusting relationships
- Empathetic and sympathetic without lowering expectations for growth

HOW TO PREPARE TO BECOME A COACH

Do you still want to be a coach? If so, the following suggestions can help.

- Read books on coaching such as this one and the ones listed in the bibliography.
- Attend workshops at your local assistance center or university to network and build your repertoire.

- Build your own network. We hold a luncheon four times a year for literacy coaches. If funds are tight, hold them at different school sites and ask everyone to bring his or her lunch.
- Find a mentor in your district or outside your district, if necessary.
- Consider upgrading your professional dress to set you apart when you are functioning as a coach.
- Remember that you must maintain the privacy of your teacher observations, even when you talk with your closest friends in the district. This is a challenge, since you now know information about others that might be titillating to share; however, confidentiality is imperative.
- Spend a large percentage of your time nurturing the administrator directly above you. The relationship you create with this person will carry you through many challenges.*

---

*Some bright, competent coaches have been sabotaged in their positions without the support from the administrator above them. As soon as you take the position, begin sharing with your "boss" your challenges, concerns, successes, and victories. Keep this line of communication open and honest. Schedule weekly coffees, daily e-mails, and frequent phone calls to nourish this relationship. When times become tough, your greatest ally is your immediate supervisor. Keep him or her as your professional friend.

ATTAINING THE COACHING POSITION

Are you a classroom teacher who wants to coach in your district? The following suggestions may help you attain that position.

- Teach the best you can. Administrators look for good teachers to coach and model lessons for others.
- Go to as many trainings as possible.
- Network with educators in other districts.
- Stay on the radar screen of administrators and those in positions to appoint you to a coaching position.
- Stay in contact through e-mail.
- Send handwritten thank-you notes to administrators or professional developers after training.
- Write grants for your classroom.
- Apply for teaching grants and awards—this will get you noticed.
- Ask colleagues to nominate you for Teacher of the Year and other awards.
- Become active in professional organizations—e.g., NCTE, International Reading Association (IRA), NSDC.
- Join an administrator professional organization for networking— Association for Supervision and Curriculum Development (ASCD), Phi Delta Kappa (PDK).

Do you have a plan to attain the position you desire? Brainstorm a plan below.

_____

_____

_____

_____

_____

_____

_____

_____

_____

MISTAKES

We all make mistakes. We make them more often when we are learning a new position. From the spilled cup of coffee to the missed appointment to the incorrect assessment of a situation, mistakes have a way of coming full circle to self-sabotage us unless we attend to them immediately. First, admit when you make a mistake and apologize. If you attempt to cover errors, you may find yourself embroiled in a situation that festers and worsens. However, if you immediately admit your error even when it is extremely uncomfortable to do so, you will usually find others willing to forgive you and move on.

Coaching begins with you taking the first step. If you have answered the questions and know you have what it takes to be a coach, it is time for you to take the next step.

SUMMARY

In this chapter, you read definitions of coaching along with reflective questions to assess your qualifications and readiness for coaching. Tips are included to help you prepare to become a coach and how to attain a coaching position.

❖   ❖   ❖

THE NEXT STEP

After you have decided you want to be a coach, you can begin gathering the materials you need, both physical and mental needs. Chapter 2 offers you a guide to prepare your outer and inner self for the coaching role.

2

Organizing to Save Stress, Time, and Mistakes

Your Personal Tool Kit

First organize the inner, then organize the outer. . . . First organize yourself, then organize others.

—Zhuge Liang

Rather than focusing on the process or content of coaching, this chapter focuses on you—it includes the "what I wish someone had told me before I became a coach" information. Because coaching is usually about the needs of the teachers you are coaching, you might lose sight of your own needs as a coach—and that can cause problems. The following addresses

- Your organizational style
- The accoutrements you need when you coach (whether you are based in a building or travel)
- Suggestions for maintaining your health
- A plan for collaborating with other coaches
- Ideas for connecting to teachers
- Books to guide your reflection and rejuvenation

The following reflections and suggestions help to manage stress, to utilize time, and to avoid mistakes.

YOUR ORGANIZATIONAL STYLE

What are your organizational strengths?

_____

_____

_____

What are your organizational challenges?

_____

_____

_____

How good are you at organization? What is your learning style? Circle one of the following:

I like to jump into projects. I usually don't read instructions before beginning tasks. I work toward goals and closure.

I like to philosophize and talk about the big picture and goals before I begin a task.

I need everything spelled out and concrete before I begin a task; I want to do things in a sequential order.

I think relationships are the key to coaching. I spend a lot of time building relationships before I get to the task at hand.

Even though these are generalizations, they connote different approaches to work. There are several style assessments, and using one is a powerful way to understand your style as you begin your work. You can take the Myers-Briggs personality test online to learn more about yourself. The book _Differentiated Coaching_, by Jane Kise (2006), uses the Myers-Briggs to learn about those you are coaching as well as yourself before you begin the differentiation of your coaching. Ultimately, the more you know about yourself, the more you can adjust to the needs of those you coach.

WHAT YOU NEED BEFORE YOU COACH

For the Coach Who Travels Between Schools or Districts

Suggested Car Needs for a Traveling Coach

Whether you are renting a car or driving your own, the car can become your office on wheels. Therefore, equipping this office with the following items—before you begin your first coaching position—can pay off for you in saved time and errors.

- Good maps for the area in which you will travel
- Insurance papers and emergency phone numbers
- A kit with your special needs
  - Replacement contacts/glasses
  - Contact fluid
  - Makeup
  - Hand sanitizer; paper towels or napkins
  - Hand lotion
  - Comb/Brush
  - Other personal needs
- Briefcase: Include *all of the following:*
  - Contact info of administrators and teachers
  - Buildings to visit
  - Teachers to visit
  - Sample lessons
  - Charts, graphs
  - Graphic organizers to fit a variety of needs
  - Markers, overheads, highlighters, paper clips, stamps, envelopes, ziplock bags (I label the bags and use them to keep all my receipts together)
- Food: Note about food and cups. Don't count on lunch at the school, and you may not be close to a restaurant. Consider keeping healthy food in your car. Easy selections include dried fruit, protein bars, bananas. Bottled water is important. You need to keep your brain hydrated and may not find a working water fountain. If you are a coffee or tea drinker, you may want a thermos full of your favorite brew. Sometimes a quick break to your car for a cup of tea is a wonderful brain-friendly way to prepare you for your coaching session. There may not be cups available—the coffee cup ritual is an entrenched one, and usually each person has his or her own. So if you are looking for a clean cup for that coffee you really want, you may be out of luck. Instead, pack a cup in your briefcase and you will always be prepared.
- A notebook for ideas that stays in the car
- An auto/travel/business log for recording expenses for taxes
- Lots of business cards

Fill the car up whenever you have some downtime so you won't be caught without enough gas to reach a faraway school or in an area where you cannot find a gas station.

List below what you need to carry in your car:

_____

_____

_____

_____

For the Coach Who Gets Outside an Office (That's Most of Us, Right?)

Your Carrying Case

You may pack all you need into a briefcase; however, if you find that you need something larger, a bag on wheels is often a good choice. Consider one with file sections where you can file your materials and with one section large enough to pack other needs. Some materials you may want to include are the following:

- Handouts for instruction
- Graphic organizers to fit a variety of needs
- Several pens, markers, and highlighters
- Observation logs
- Phone numbers, e-mail addresses, and contact information for all involved educators
- Your own personal needs (Consider a large ziplock plastic bag to hold these and transfer them from the car to your carrying case)
- Snacks for yourself

List below what you need to carry with you when you coach:

_____

_____

_____

_____

_____

Your Cell Phone

Consider programming the important school numbers into your cell phone before you begin coaching. That way you'll have them with you. Be sure to include a car charger for emergencies.

Food

Food is important to the teachers we coach. You may not agree with our food philosophy, but we take food to the team meetings and individual conferences with teachers. We find supplying food honors the teachers who are spending long hours in the classroom with few breaks. We try to match preferences with teachers. Once we find what kinds of snacks teachers enjoy, we attempt to provide them. One teacher always comments that we remember to bring the pretzels stuffed with peanut butter because that is what she likes. Another person comments about the trail mix with the spicy nuts because her team prefers it. This gesture involves a small expenditure on our part but gives us a big payback.

We purchase snacks at a store such as Trader Joe's in an attempt to buy healthy snack food and include a variety of sweet and salty snacks. These snacks also become an icebreaker, as staff can talk about what they like to eat, where they purchase snacks, and so on. The food list includes foods such as nuts/trail mixes, dried fruit, pretzels, peanut butter, chips, chocolate, and cookies.

Invariably, when we return, someone will remark that we remembered his or her favorite snack and beam smiles our way. This tells us we have connected on one level with that teacher—teachers believe that we care about their basic needs and empathize with their need for a break (we usually meet during teachers' planning sessions, so we are taking up a portion of their time). This also signals to the teachers that they are not invisible to us and that the coaching isn't about us but about them.

Information Needed for Contact

It is important to confirm and reconfirm schedules. Even though we have things on our calendars, we are all busy people and make mistakes. Too often you might find yourself arriving for a meeting that others have forgotten, or missing a meeting that you had cancelled but others still believed was on. Even though we may send most of our communications through e-mail, sometimes e-mails do not go through. We have become so dependent upon electronic communication that we may falsely believe that we can always count on it to work.

Reconfirming meetings the day before they are scheduled is important. Some schools make it more difficult to do this than others. Some schools limit access through a central receptionist who may deliver the message, but not in time. These same schools may not have voice mail, or if they do, the teachers may not check their voice mail several times a day—the same with their e-mail. We cannot count on our e-mails to reach staff. Some schools even today do not foster a technological culture that promotes teachers communicating through e-mail. This is one of the most frustrating aspects of working in schools where a culture of communicating with coaches has not been developed.

If possible, try to get some cell phone numbers of teachers, at least one per team. This way you can leave a message on a cell phone as well as call the office.

Out-of-Town Coaching

When you fly to your destination, you may want to consider the following tips. Also included are some terrific organizational strategies from Nan Starling (her coaching narrative appears in Chapter 4), whose organizational skills far exceed my own.

Tips for Traveling Out of Town

- Carry on everything you need for your presentation. Just when I thought it was safe to no longer do this, I checked it at the last minute. That happened to be the trip of the big snowstorm. I had to take a car for the final leg of the trip, and my luggage wasn't delivered until 11:00 P.M. after the next day's presentation. That day I presented in running shoes, jeans, and with none of my materials. Luckily, the middle and high school teachers were wonderful, and we spent a fruitful day discussing and practicing research-based instructional strategies. Had my presentation been solely dependent upon my overheads and materials, it would have been a bust. I learned that I need to carry important items on the plane with me, but in addition, I need, like an actor, to have the entire presentation in my head.
- In addition, be sure to carry on one change of clothes and your toiletries; luckily I found a 24-hour drugstore on the snow-jinxed trip!
- Be sure to pack an alarm clock that does not rely upon electricity and some kind of light source. Having experienced being in a hotel with no electricity, I found out the importance of both of these items.

Nan's Tips

I keep a loose-leaf binder for each city. Each binder has a clear sleeve on the cover in which I insert the name of the city and school. For each school I retain copies of the following:

- The school address and general telephone number (I also store the telephone numbers in my cell phone, which is valuable after I've been circling the neighborhood trying to find the school)
- Yahoo! maps or other directions to the school
- The principal's name and other administrators' names and phone numbers
- Schedules for regular school days and special schedules (early release, etc.)
- A list of the teachers I coach and their schedules, including their class schedules and their planning times
- Course outlines and sequencing schedules
- Copies of my reports on my recent service to the schools (used as a reminder of what I recommended in the past)

- Copies of the agendas, which include the materials I have used, for professional development (I need these so that I don't repeat activities and materials. Schools and presentations quickly become hard to distinguish after multiple trips)
- Telephone numbers of taxi drivers I can depend on when I don't have a car
- Lists of my favorite restaurants near the school and hotel

Other Tricks/Tools I've Found Useful in Schools

- A rolling computer bag, as small and lightweight as possible (I store my wallet and personal items in this bag instead of carrying a handbag so that I have less to keep track of and don't have a purse to tempt thieves. I also take a bottle of water in a plastic bag so that if it leaks, it won't dampen my papers)
- 3M luggage tag "makers" (laminate for business cards with pre-punched slots and plastic loops for attaching tags to luggage; cards laminated back-to-back attached with this product create official-looking identification)
- Name tags to wear for official-looking identification while working in schools. If your organization does not provide a name tag, having one made is worthwhile. Wearing name tags eases entry to schools and helps people remember your name. I found a local company that made tags for me quickly for under $10 each. I had one made to hang on a lanyard (two-sided so the "front" is always in front) and one made with a magnetic back for a lapel label.

Tricks/Tools I've Found Useful for Traveling

- Brightly-colored baggage tags to use on the outside of luggage (I use my cell phone number on my luggage so that no one will be able to use my home phone number to determine my home address, find my house, and enter while I'm away)
- My name, address, and telephone numbers inside my luggage (in case the identification on the outside becomes detached. I include my cell number, home phone number, and another contact number, just in case I become separated from my baggage, my cell doesn't work, no one is home, and I want my bags back)
- TSA locks to secure luggage on flights and in hotel rooms (even though I take locks, I don't take my best jewelry or my favorite clothes on most trips. If I would be upset if I lost it, I try not to take it)
- Comfortable shoes (my shoes determine what else I wear. Working in many schools requires distance walks from parking lots, between classrooms and buildings, and up and down stairs. I find my feet are the locus of my energy, which I try to conserve)
- Clothing that matches the "climate" of the weather in the city and of the dress practices of the school staff helps establish position (duplicate travel supplies such as cosmetics and underwear, which remain in frequently

(Continued)

(Continued)

> used luggage or are replenished after each trip, make packing less time-consuming and help prevent forgotten essentials. One such essential is a duplicate cell phone charger, which, when I've forgotten mine, my ability to communicate was limited)
> - Dollar bills for vending machines, tips, and so on
> - Antibacterial wipes for airplane and school restrooms

Reprinted with permission from Nan Starling.

List below your specific travel needs:

_____

_____

_____

_____

Building an Office

Building your office, whether it is school based or home based, is an evolving process. As you add to your professional library, you grow your resources. You can find several suggested books on coaching throughout this book and in the Bibliography and the suggested readings below. Consider the following items for your office:

- Computer
- Printer/scanner/fax
- Large wall calendar or desk calendar
- White erasable board
- Planner system
- Library of books
- Supplies: permanent markers, pens, paper, thank-you notes, Post-its, folders, chart paper, and so on (take a stroll through an office supply store and note what you need)
- Wastebasket, comfortable chair, desk or flat surface, lamp
- Filing cabinet
- Phone, directories
- Mailing materials
- Coffeepot, teapot, water, food
- Cleaning supplies
- Jacket or sweater
- Toiletries
- Medicinal needs

The more complete your office, the less time you will waste running around searching for what you need.

The Workshop or Presentation

When presenting to a group, you need certain things. We include the following in a rolling case:

- Computer
- PowerPoint materials
- Presentation outline on a hard copy
- Handouts
- Overheads and markers
- Books (when you suggest a book, you can hold up a copy for participants)
- Snacks for breaks such as trail mix, bananas, or apples
- Coffee/tea if none is provided
- Water
- Keys (you may want to have a second set of car keys if you are driving to a presentation)
- Personal needs

Even though these lists may seem simplistic, it can be the simple things that keep you from being your best. By checking a list to ensure you take everything you need, you may be saving yourself headaches later on.

THE WHO OF COACHING

The who of coaching pertains to who you are first as a person, then as a coach. We often connect to others because of who we are rather than what we know. Parker Palmer's (1997) book *The Courage to Teach: Exploring the Inner Landscape of a Teacher's Life* applies also to coaching. He discusses the who of teaching. There is also a who of coaching. The who of coaching refers to "Who are you?" It is not what we coach; rather, it is who we are.

To remain connected to the who we are, we need tools. Parker Palmer's (2004) book *A Hidden Wholeness: The Journey Toward an Undivided Life* functions as a tool to continue our journey toward truth, integrity, and wholeness. Another resource we use is Jim Burke's (2006) book *Letters to a New Teacher: A Month-by-Month Guide to the Year Ahead.* In it he describes how poetry sustains him in his daily life. Among others, he suggests the book *Teaching With Fire: Poetry That Sustains the Courage to Teach,* edited by Sam M. Intrator and Megan Scribner (2003). We couldn't agree more. We share poems with teachers.

When I finish a coaching session, I must always come back to this essential question: What could I have done differently to get different results? When I do a coaching session and it doesn't feel right or didn't go just right, I have to reflect. If I merely ask what's wrong with these teachers, I am placing blame outside myself. When I ask what I could have done differently, then the cause lies inside me, and I can search for answers. If the cause lies outside me, I probably have little power to influence it.

After each coaching session, you might ask the following questions:

> - How did the teacher(s) respond?
> - What indications did I receive that we are making progress?
> - What behaviors did I observe as reactions to the workshop?
> - What evidence did I receive that teachers are implementing the coaching suggestions?

We find it works best for us to immediately process our coaching visits. You may want to take a laptop with you and, as soon as you finish the sessions, find a quiet room and process what you did and the response to it. These can later be edited and e-mailed as feedback to those you coached. Also, a follow-up e-mail or note to the lead administrator lends a nice touch.

Handwritten Thank-You Notes

One appreciated act of gratitude is the handwritten thank-you note. A simple gesture, this never fails to make an impression. If you buy a bunch of thank-you notes at a store such as Target or Tuesday Mornings, you can write several in 30 minutes while traveling by plane or watching television and send them on their way. This ritual offers an honorable closure to the work.

YOUR HEALTH

Most of these suggestions are obvious ones you can read about in several sources; the important point is whether or not you practice them. Since coaching involves giving out so much energy to others, both physical and emotional, you must take care of yourself.

Consider engaging in some physical program to maintain your health, whether that be yoga, Pilates, aerobic exercise, walking, hiking, running, and so on. Since most coaches are mature adults, we need to protect our health by exercising to maintain physical health. You can support your mental health through your choice of healthy practices, such as frequent mental breaks, meditation, journaling, and leisure activities.

In addition to exercise, you need healthy food, lots of water, and a good night's sleep. Your body will only run so long on poor fuel.

What do you do for yourself to ensure you stay healthy?

_____

_____

_____

How can you improve your self-care plan?

_____

_____

_____

COACHING COLLEAGUES

We all need colleagues to process our work with, and fortunately I have found a group of women who share a passion for this work. The women who share their educational narratives in Chapter 4 started out as colleagues and now are friends. We try to meet once a month, depending on our schedules. We used to be English teachers—now we are coaches. In our travels to diverse school districts across the United States—some inner-city, some suburban, some rural and everything in between, including one school with 38 spoken languages—we encounter much diversity. We share a wide variety of experiences with each other as we process our roles as coaches.

Our lessons learned provide a spectrum for coaching that is applicable throughout the United States. We know that the number one lesson we must learn is how to connect to the teachers with whom we work in order to coach them to improve their instructional practices.

CONNECTING TO TEACHERS

How do we connect to teachers, both those who think like us and those who don't think like us? If you've been one of those teachers who could always connect to students and now it's time to connect to teachers, isn't it the same? No and yes.

No, because in the classroom you are in a position of power as the teacher in charge. Even if you are a teacher who uses facilitation as your main delivery system with students, you still hold more power as the adult in the room. But as a coach, you are assuming a "coaching" or parallel role, not a power role.

The challenge is that as a teacher, we are so used to being able to call the shots, but while coaching, you may frame the event but you can't really control the outcome. You cannot determine the actions of the other adults. To complicate the situation, you may be coaching teachers whose mental models differ from yours. You not only have to build relationships with these teachers, you must bridge content areas with powerful strategies that support their instruction within their mental models.

However, yes, it is the same because you use many of the same relationship strategies when you connect with teachers as you coach. How do we make teachers, especially those who don't think like us, believe that coaching matters? Once again, we have to make that personal connection.

Sharing something about yourself is a first step to connecting with others. Tell the teachers about your family, your career, and your dreams. Keep it short, but be honest. Ask for feedback from the teachers, and just as you try to remember their personal preferences in snacks, take notes about their families and personal comments. The more you know about your teachers, the easier it is to connect when you see them the next time.

You can also connect with teachers through their students. Teachers usually care about their students, and if you can ask them about their students, you often find a point of intersection.

Connecting with those you coach is the important second step in the process. Connecting with yourself is the first. This chapter gives you several suggestions for organizing your outer and inner lives to ready yourself for the coaching life.

Listed below are several books you may consider for further reflection.

FURTHER SUGGESTED READING TO SOOTHE YOUR INNER SELF

Burke, J. (2006). *Letters to a new teacher: A month-by-month guide to the year ahead.* Portsmouth, NH: Heinemann.

Intrator, S. M., & Scribner, M. (Eds.). (2003). *Teaching with fire: Poetry that sustains the courage to teach.* San Francisco: Jossey-Bass.

Palmer, P. (1998). *The courage to teach: Exploring the inner landscape of a teacher's life.* San Francisco: Jossey-Bass.

Palmer, P. (2004). *A hidden wholeness: The journey toward an undivided life.* San Francisco: Jossey-Bass.

Roizen, M., & Oz, M. (2005). *You: The owner's manual: An insider's guide to the body that will make you healthier and younger.* New York: HarperResource.

Tate, M. (2004). *"Sit and get" won't grow dendrites: 20 professional learning strategies that engage the adult brain.* Thousand Oaks, CA: Corwin Press.

Wiggins, G., & McTighe, J. (2006). Examining the teaching life. *ASCD Educational Leadership, 63*(6), 26–29.

List below what you wish to include in your coaching tool kit:

_____

_____

_____

_____

_____

_____

SUMMARY

This chapter examined your coaching needs: your organizational style, the nitty-gritty things that coaching often requires you to acquire—whether you sit in an office or travel the country—and your inner self (the who of coaching).

Since we do better work when we're immersed in a culture of collegiality, tips are included for finding coaching colleagues with whom to share the work. Helpful lists are included for when you plan your presentations and travel, along with suggested books to expand your coaching repertoire.

❖   ❖   ❖

In Chapter 3 you will find ways to connect with teachers who don't think like you and mistakes to avoid during your coaching work.

MORNING ANNOUNCEMENTS

Attention Teachers:
There is no magic bullet!
You are
the magic
you are
the power, the strength
of the bullet
sent out to strike chords
and change forever
young minds.

Teachers:
Let go
of your hope
that some time, somewhere—
if only
you go to enough workshops,
read enough journals
collect enough lessons—
you'll find
the right answer.

Teachers:
You are the answer.
You are
the silver bullet.

Embrace
the beauty, the power
that is your legacy . . .
Relax,
enjoy, go within—
dip into your own private well
for meaning—
then teach!

—Mary Kim Schreck

3

Coaching Teachers Who Don't Think Like You

We are all learners. As coaches, we want to learn as well as support the professional growth of others. The work begins with us, and earlier chapters include tips for looking within. Now, how do we look outside ourselves and support teachers to improve their instruction? This chapter is about the how-to of coaching, the process in which we engage when we work with others.

How do we move teachers to look within rather than externalize issues and place the blame onto students, administration, and the school district? This is a huge challenge, not one easily met by a single coach. But we can make a difference with a faculty, one teacher at a time, through powerful coaching strategies.

This chapter examines the list below as a way to support teachers who don't think like you as we build the necessary relationships for the work.

- Cultural proficiency
- Learned helplessness in educators and students
- A veteran teacher's perspective
- Suggestions for working with teachers

"Each person is a unique individual" can be a guiding principle to focus our work as we coach. It is important to see each teacher as a unique individual, not a generalization (even though the title of this book generalizes about teachers who "don't think like you"). Yet as soon as we generalize about any group, someone interrupts the pattern and reminds us that we each possess a unique brain with a unique lens with which to view the world.

Seeing and respecting the uniqueness of each individual ensures that we coach with cultural proficiency. Cultural proficiency is the "policies and practices of a school or the values and behaviors of an individual that enable the person or school to interact effectively in a culturally diverse environment" (Lindsey, Nuri Robins, & Terrell, 2003, pp. xix–xx).

Cultural proficiency is the key to success when coaching. In *Blended Coaching,* Bloom, Castagna, Moir, and Warren (2005) state that almost all school issues contain cross-cultural and emotional intelligence issues (p. 23). Not being able to recognize these can pose a serious threat to the effectiveness of a coach. In order to recognize cross-cultural and emotional intelligence issues, coaches and teachers need to engage in talk that supports their learning about each other. In *How to Teach Students Who Don't Look Like You* (Davis, 2006), Chapter 1 offers you a template for establishing the cultural lens of those you coach.

Consider using the following prompts to establish cultural awareness and build cultural proficiency.

Think about the way you view your world. What factors contribute to the lens?

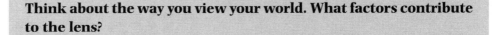

_____

_____

_____

Below are several major factors that influence the way we see our world and contribute to the many cultures we weave in and out of each day:

- Family
- Gender
- Race
- Age
- Sexual orientation
- Language
- Disabilities
- Friends
- Religion
- School
- Geography
- Income of family/social class
- Political views
- Ethnicity
- Electronic media
- Social organizations
- Others

Examine the list on page 26. Which ones do you share with your colleagues? For example, your district may be comprised largely of Protestants and you are Protestant; therefore, you share religion in common with your staff and students.

_____

_____

_____

Which ones do you differ from your colleagues?

_____

_____

_____

    The more differences you find, the more bridges you may need to build to reach those in your daily work lives. When we interact with our colleagues, we bring the baggage of our past experiences, our prejudices, our preferences, as well as those of our families and other factors that influence the lens through which we view the world. This is your cultural lens. The students we face bring the same.

What have you learned as a result of defining your culture?

_____

_____

_____

_____

Reprinted with permission from *How to Teach Students Who Don't Look Like You: Culturally Relevant Teaching Strategies* (Davis, 2006), pp. 7–8.

Chapters 2–6 of *How to Teach Students Who Don't Look Like You* (Davis, 2006) give you additional strategies to implement as you respect cultural differences in the teacher and student populations with whom you work. In addition, consider reading Lindsey, Roberts, and CampbellJones's (2005) *The Culturally Proficient School: An Implementation Guide for School Leaders* and Glenn Singleton and Curtis Linton's (2006) *Courageous Conversations About Race* as you plan your work.

RACIAL/CULTURAL HISTORIES

Another tool to learn about others and become more culturally proficient is to share personal histories. In *How to Teach Students Who Don't Look Like You*

(Davis, 2006, pp. 44–54), there is a template for sharing your racial history with others. We used this strategy with teams of teachers (described in Chapter 9). This powerful strategy built and cemented relationships between the 10 teams of teachers and the coaches working with them. After we spent an evening sharing our racial histories, we truly felt we were sisters and brothers in a community devoted to improving the teaching instruction for *all* children.

Learned Helplessness

Not only do individuals have cultural lenses, but entire schools develop cultures that may or may not support student learning. Coaching is usually much easier in a school culture where staff and students are efficacious and engaged with learning. Coaching is less easy and, in fact, downright difficult in a culture where "learned helplessness" and despair have wound around the roots of the school structures.

In *Differentiated Coaching: A Framework for Helping Teachers Change*, author Jane A. G. Kise (2006) discusses the concept of "learned helplessness" (pp. 46–47), "the giving-up reaction, the quitting response that follows from the belief that whatever you do doesn't matter" (Seligman, cited in Kise, 2006, p. 46). Learned helplessness functions like a building-wide negative osmosis if not held in check and rebalanced by both staff and administrators.

Eric Jensen (1998) identifies three conditions for learned helplessness: trauma, lack of control, and decision. In schools where learned helplessness is pervasive, the culture must be changed. In *How to Teach Students Who Don't Look Like You* (Davis, 2006), school culture is examined through the use of three scenarios you can use with coaches and teachers to examine their school cultures. School culture often contributes to the degree of empowerment or learned helplessness that a staff experiences.

Schools where learned helplessness is rampant can be found in rural, suburban, and urban areas. However, when your basic needs are met, you are supported by colleagues and administrators, and you have students who come from supportive environments, you are less likely to find cultures of learned helplessness. Contrasted to this, when students live in poverty, are not supported physically, emotionally, and mentally, and attend a school that is in physical and emotional disrepair, it becomes so much more difficult to succeed. But not impossible, and there are examples of schools that have survived in dire circumstances and improved classroom instruction to close the achievement gap, such as those found on the DVD kit *No Excuses! How to Increase Minority Student Achievement* (School Improvement Network, 2006).

When teachers feel hopeless, they may project the reasons for the failure of their instruction outside themselves. I have done this after a workshop. If things did not go exactly as I wanted, my first reaction is to place the blame on the building space, the time of day, the lighting, or other such things. It takes courage to look inward and dissect the reasons a presentation has not gone well, whether it is a classroom lesson or a professional development presentation. But when we look inward, we work from a perspective of power to analyze more thoughtfully the outcomes of our work.

How does learned helplessness look if you are coaching in an environment where the teachers may not welcome you and where teachers teach in a low-achieving, high-poverty school? After working in an inner-city school over a period of days and facing a culture worn down by years of neglect, I had to steel myself daily to prevent my mind from lowering my expectations for the teachers and the students. The first days I was passionate and positive, but soon I felt whittled away by the school culture and began to doubt myself, the students, and the teachers. Hour after hour, I witnessed too many students who were off-task, not exhibiting bad behavior but not "doing" class work. I witnessed too many teachers "assigning" seat work, not teaching concepts. I witnessed students expected to know how to do something they had never been taught.

One day a teacher wrote the assignment for a 15-page research paper on the board with a due date two weeks in the future. When the students asked him how to do it, he told them they were juniors in high school who should know how and should "just do it." Did this teacher feel helpless because he didn't know how to teach the research paper? Or did he not want to make the effort? These questions were never answered, because the teacher was resistant to coaching and failed to ask me to return for future support.

Why does coaching fail to reach teachers who are resistant to coaching? Articles on coaching may treat teachers as if they are the cause of the problem, just as teachers may blame students, rather than examining the coach and implementation of the coaching strategies.

This lays a heavy burden on the coach, similar to the one placed on every teacher in the classroom. Unless I know the individual well enough to understand his or her learning style, personal perspective, and cultural differences, I may flounder as I try to reach and teach this person. The coaching structure mirrors the classroom situation in so many ways, and this is key. Unless the relationship is built between the coach and those being coached, teachers may not care enough to learn from the coach they perceive does not care enough about them.

Once again, each of us is a unique individual, driven by different motivations. With the teacher cited above, I had neither the relationship nor the understanding of what he needed to succeed. I had a long way to go to learn that I didn't know what I didn't know about this teacher and how to meet his needs.

How might you mediate learned helplessness in the teachers you coach?

_____

_____

_____

Strategies for coaching in a culture of learned helplessness:

- Stay positive
- Take small steps to success
- Use models (videos, student work, anecdotes, articles) of teachers and schools that have improved student achievement in spite of the odds
- Work with the teachers who are most efficacious
- Build a cadre of proactive teachers
- Foster relationships
- Practice kindness
- Celebrate successes

VETERAN TEACHER'S PERSPECTIVE

Knowing the school culture and the history of those we coach may not be enough. When we neglect to remember that coaching is a collegial task based upon mutual respect, we may find that a teacher decides not to enter the coaching relationship. Dorcas, a veteran teacher, is such an educator. Dorcas's story describes it best:

When I was first told that we were going to have to attend meetings with a consultant hired by the district, I was both puzzled and aggravated. I had no idea why the district thought we would benefit from these additional meetings, and I felt that my time could be spent more usefully doing what I knew was necessary to prepare to teach. We were not actually informed of the rationale for this extra duty, other than to say that Bonnie Davis was going to tell us ways that we could improve preparation for the MAP [the Missouri state assessment]. Ah, yes, the MAP again! Everything revolves around that dreaded test that forces us to teach in ways that are not necessarily best for the students. As an experienced teacher of 20 years with a master's degree and special education experience, I was rather arrogantly irritated that someone thought I needed help. It wasn't that I was not willing to learn or try new things. It wasn't that I believed that I had no room for improvement. It was more that I felt that the district failed to recognize that I too had much to contribute. I resented the additional drain on my valuable time and waited rather impatiently for Bonnie Davis to prove her worth. I truly tried to hide my attitude, and I did indeed connect with Bonnie after the first few visits. I did try the strategies that were suggested and made a point of sharing my results in the meetings. I am not opposed to being given new ideas. I certainly want to be the best teacher I can be. I do want to educate excellent future citizens. I suppose my issue must have been that I needed someone to recognize my value and contributions to the education environment of my long-time school assignment.

Reprinted with permission from Dorcas Wanner.

As you read what Dorcas has to say, what are your thoughts?

_____

_____

_____

If you were Dorcas's coach, how might you best mediate the relationship between Dorcas and yourself?

_____

_____

_____

Dorcas taught me that our work is a collegial task based upon mutual respect for what each of us can bring to the table. Perhaps her story will save a future coach from the same errors. Had I listened to Dorcas from the onset, her story may have read differently.

Consider using these steps to listening when you work with teachers:

- Put away all of your things.
- Sit quietly, facing the person who is speaking.
- Consider mirroring his or her body language.
- Do not interrupt! Wait until he or she has completely finished speaking before you respond.
- Give nonverbal feedback throughout the conversation, such as nodding your head and eye contact.
- Paraphrase what you heard to ensure you are correctly receiving the information.
- Ask questions to probe for additional information.
- Resist the urge to give "the answer"; rather, offer powerful questions to stimulate further thinking on the part of the speaker.
- After the conversation, reflect in writing so that you will not only have a record of the conversation but will continue to reflect on your own process as a listener.

Listening is a powerful skill. You might consider discussing your listening skills with your coaching colleagues in order to do a check on how well you listen. One coach could sit out the conversation and time the minutes each of the other coaches speaks. You could process the activity as a group.

Do you talk more than you listen? If so, why do you think that is?

_____

_____

_____

What might you do to improve your listening skills?

_____

_____

_____

_____

_____

SUGGESTIONS FOR WORKING WITH TEACHERS WHO DON'T THINK LIKE YOU

Suggestion #1: Learn About Body Language

Pay careful attention to the "hidden rules" of the school culture and of the individuals. First, meet and greet each individual, looking the person straight in the eye and shaking hands in a professional manner while taking the handshake cues from that person. For example, if a person vigorously shakes your hand, do the same back to him or her; however, if someone lightly holds your hand and shakes, reciprocate in kind. Handshakes differ according to gender, culture, and, most important, individuals. Don't assume a small woman will have a weak handshake. Take your cues from the other person.

When you receive a signal from the other person, you know you've made a connection. This may come in the form of a nod, a meeting of the eyes, a personal comment, or an openness of body language. Try not to move on to the next person until you've seen the connection, because when you invest this personal energy to form a connection, you know the person will probably pay attention at the onset of the presentation. After that, you have to grab the person with the content. If you fail to do this, you may find teachers talking during your presentation,* failing to do the exercises, or otherwise not engaged. Making that initial contact ensures engagement.

In _Cognitive Coaching_ (2002), Costa and Garmston write that "recent explorations in cognitive neurology characterize the body as the theatre of the mind" (p. 106). If you are cognizant of your own body language as well as the body

---

*A good strategy to handle participants talking to each other during a presentation is to stop it before it begins by stating clearly norms and boundaries. One you may consider using is the following: "Listen deeply. Do not interrupt anyone who is speaking by talking. This includes the presenter and your colleagues." Then if someone begins to talk, simply stop presenting and wait for that person to finish. Or simply move near the talkers, which usually works to quiet them. Allowing talk to continue during a presentation diminishes the presentation for everyone involved.

language of those you coach, you hold a great advantage. Consider reading the following books on body language:

- *Telling Lies* by Paul Ekman (2001). New York: W. W. Norton.
- *Emotions Revealed* by Paul Ekman (2003). New York: Henry Holt.
- *The Silent Language* by Edward Hall (1990). New York: Random House.

Your passion is expressed through your body language as well as through your words. It contributes immensely to your connecting with those you coach. Teachers feel your passion through your energy output and react to it. Just as students must believe that their teachers are passionate about and engaged with their subject matter in order to learn at optimal levels, so teachers need to be facilitated by coaches who are passionate about their subject to fully engage. Authenticity is key. When we approach others with our authentic selves and our body language is congruent with our words, we tend to win them over. Then we connect as human beings who respect each other as unique individuals.

Do you make snap judgments about people based on their body language? How do you take body language into consideration as you coach?

_____

_____

_____

_____

_____

Suggestion #2: Set Behavior, Role, and Goal Expectations (or Make Explicit "the Hidden Rules")

In *Cognitive Coaching,* Costa and Garmston (2002) state that "nearly all relationship difficulties are rooted in conflicting or ambiguous expectations surrounding roles and goals" (p. 102). Unless we set behavior, role, and goal expectations with the teachers with whom we work, "we can be certain that unclear expectations will lead to misunderstanding, disappointment, and decreased trust" (p. 102). Establishing behaviors, roles, and goal expectations of the coaching/teacher relationship at the onset diminishes the probability of misunderstanding. We find that we need to revisit these periodically as we coach. Throughout this book, you will read how the coaches set behavior, roles, and goal expectations.

Suggestion #3: Learn What "Respect" Means to the Teachers You Coach

Clearly stating expectations is one step to establishing respect in workshops. In fact, having a discussion about what respect looks like is often a good way to work with a new group. Not doing so can uncover differences in the definitions for respect. In a painful episode, I learned this the hard way when I broke a hidden rule of respect. A participant in a workshop taught me that her definition for respect differed from mine during an all-day workshop for new teachers at an urban secondary school. Following lunch and a morning focused on how to use writing in the classroom, a teacher looked at me and said, "Why are you White people so rude?" Surprised, I asked her to help me understand what she meant by her remark. She shared the following:

She and another teacher were talking in an otherwise empty classroom. A first-year White male teacher entered the room, grabbed a notebook he had left in the room during the previous hour, and left quietly without speaking.

What did you see?

_____

_____

_____

_____

_____

When we discuss this scenario in workshops, we hear a variety of responses. Invariably, some of the educators will see the young White male as a respectful teacher who did his best not to interrupt the other two adults in the room who were deep in conversation.

Others will see the young White male as a rude individual who entered others' space and did not acknowledge the human beings in that space, thus relegating them to invisibility.

Sometimes reactions break down according to racial lines; other times, they break down according to demographics. One lady said it was "Southern"; she would never enter a room where another human being was without nodding to them and saying, "Excuse me" or "Good morning."

No matter how you define it, respect means different things to different people, depending upon their age, sex, race, demographics, class, culture, and so on, and if you don't know what respect looks like to the educators you are attempting to coach, you may get yourself into big trouble. Had I taken the time to learn what respect meant to Dorcas, I may have gained her respect at the onset.

Establishing the norms of respect early on in our relationships with the educators you coach may spare you such experiences as the one described above.

Teachers can do the same thing with students or with those who differ greatly in age. When we coach new teachers in their 20s, their version of respect may differ from ours. This exercise can give a faculty and its administration good insights into the variety of interpretations that respect might have in any given circumstance. Understanding our audience is key.

What does respect look like to you?

_____

_____

_____

_____

_____

How has the above discussion changed your views on the importance of respect in your work?

_____

_____

_____

_____

_____

Suggestion #4: Learn About Each Individual You Coach

How much do you need to know about the teachers you coach? Coaches differ in their opinions. Some feel you should be aware of individual preferences; others believe you need to focus on student work and not as much on personalities. You must decide, based on your style of coaching. However, learning about the personal preferences of those you coach can lead to a deepening of the relationship. If you simply share your interests as the occasion arises, others will often share theirs. Monitor the body language of those you coach. Some teachers might feel you are getting "in their business" if you ask personal questions; instead, share something about yourself and allow others to share what they want. Then remember what they have shared. Take notes!

If someone has shared an interest in a topic and you run across an article on the topic, why not clip it for the teachers? For example, John, a math teacher, is interested in math (yes!) and just about anything healthy. He petitioned and got the lights in his room changed to full-spectrum lighting, he pays attention to what he eats, and he consistently attempts to enlighten his students about healthy choice decisions. If I find an article that matches his interests (and those of the others I coach), I simply put it in a folder for the next team meeting. When John gets the article, he knows someone cared enough to think about him.

This was a strategy I used successfully in the classroom. Students appreciated knowing their teacher knew enough about them to be on the lookout for items that interested them.

What strategies might you use to learn the personal preferences of those you coach?

_____

_____

_____

_____

_____

_____

_____

Suggestion #5: Learn and Expand Your Background Knowledge About Coaching

These coaching books build background knowledge and expand your repertoire in the growing field of coaching:

Blended Coaching: Skills and Strategies to Support Principal Development by Gary Bloom et al. (2005). Thousand Oaks, CA: Corwin Press.

Cognitive Coaching: A Foundation for Renaissance Schools by A. L. Costa & R. J. Garmston (2002). Norwood, MA: Christopher-Gordon.

Collaborative Analysis of Student Work by Georgea M. Langer, Amy Colton, & Loretta Goff. (2003). Alexandria, VA: Association for Supervision and Curriculum Development.

Creating Dynamic Schools Through Mentoring, Coaching, and Collaboration by Judy F. Carr, Nancy Herman, & Douglas E. Harris (2005). Alexandria, VA: Association for Supervision and Curriculum Development.

Differentiated Coaching: A Framework for Helping Teachers Change by Jane A. G. Kise (2006). Thousand Oaks, CA: Corwin Press.

Individualized Professional Development: A Framework for Meeting School and District Goals by Vicki R. Husby (2005). Thousand Oaks, CA: Corwin Press.

Professional Learning Communities at Work: Best Practices for Enhancing Student Achievement by Rick DuFour & R. Eaker (1998). Alexandria, VA: Association for Supervision and Curriculum Development.

Quality Teaching in a Culture of Coaching by Stephen G. Barkley (2005). New York: Rowman & Littlefield.

Schools as Professional Learning Communities: Collaborative Activities and Strategies for Professional Development by Sylvia M. Roberts and Eunice Z. Pruitt (2003). Thousand Oaks, CA: Corwin Press.

Teacher-Centered Professional Development by Gabriel Diaz-Maggioli (2004). Alexandria, VA: Association for Supervision and Curriculum Development.

SUMMARY

This chapter outlined strategies and suggestions for coaching teachers who don't think like you. There was a focus on cultural proficiency and understanding learned helplessness. A veteran teacher provided critical information about what coaches need to do in order to really listen to those we coach. The following suggestions for working with teachers were listed and expanded upon:

- Learn about body language.
- Set behavior, role, and goal expectations.
- Learn what "respect" means to the teachers you coach.
- Learn about each individual you coach.

An extensive book list on coaching was included at the end of the chapter to expand your background knowledge of coaching.

❖   ❖   ❖

In Chapter 4 you will read about the experiences of several expert coaches as they share their coaching at the elementary, middle, and high school levels where they use literacy strategies to coach teachers to improve instruction.

BODY LITERACY

Streams of information
travel at the speed of sight
through the body language pipelines.

Flick of an eye,
turn of a head
hand playing with a curl,
shoulders slouched or arched in the chair.

Strong language
each
and all of it speaks
to a place in the brain
unfettered by syllables or vowel sounds.

The strongest speaker—the eye—
with its glance,
its roll,
its sustained contact.

We blast open
the privacy of another's self
with one deep gaze.

Then there's the smile—
the open face offering acceptance—
or
the cold chiseled face
of indifference and a tinge of distrust.
all shouts from the person within.

There is a literacy here
that needs respect,
recognition.
a true literacy—
reading the flow of feeling
just beneath the surface.

Reading
the language
the body speaks so well.

—Mary Kim Schreck

4

Coaching in a Variety of Settings

*Experienced Coaches
Share Their Success Stories*

Coaches need colleagues who practice as coaches and share their work. In this chapter several coaches share their experiences of coaching in elementary, middle, and high schools where they work throughout the United States. Their narratives combine the process and the content of coaching—the how-to with the what-if. And they offer you an opportunity to examine what coaching looks like in a variety of settings. In most cases, these coaches work with teachers who don't look like them and who may or may not think like them. They are as follows:

- **Mary Kim Schreck**—a literacy coach who shares her work as a coach in an inner-city high school
- **Nan Starling**—a literacy coach who shares her work with teachers in several high schools across the country
- **Susie Morice**—a coach who shares her work with an entire middle school staff to build community and improve student achievement in a suburban setting
- **Lola Mapes**—a coach who shares her work with a grade-level staff in an elementary school

For years, I taught high school students in isolation behind a closed door. Students learned and wrote about literature and usually left my classroom liking English more than when they entered the room. However, what I didn't know was what my colleagues were up to and what they knew to do that I didn't know. Only after teaching for 18 years did I observe a colleague teach, and that was due to my participating in Teacher Expectation, Student Achievement (TESA) training, a professional development program that focuses on 15 teacher behaviors. For the first time in my career, I was having conversations about instruction with colleagues.

Things are different now. Teachers meet to discuss instruction in many school districts with coaches often facilitating their discussions. Recently after coaching such a team discussion, a teacher said, "I always enjoy when you come because we talk about our instruction." Before coaching was added to their school, the teachers in this building seldom discussed instruction. However, as a result of embedding coaching within the culture of the school, there has been a gradual shift in the culture of school dialogue. Where we find coaching, we hope to find culture change.

The following narratives describe coaches who attempt to change school culture through the practice of coaching. The coaches who share their narratives are all former English teachers, having taught students ranging in levels from kindergarten to university. Now they coach teachers across the disciplines. The reason we share these narratives is so you can (a) read about the similarities and the differences you might encounter in your role as a coach and (b) reflect upon their experiences in order to inform your own.

MARY KIM SCHRECK

This narrative describes an onsite coaching position implemented with federal grant funds. The following are professional development suggestions for using Mary Kim's narrative:

> - Coaches read and discuss Mary Kim's narrative for suggestions for working in an inner-city high school. Mary Kim discusses important things every coach should know.
> - Literacy coaches read and discuss concrete, specific literacy strategies to use in reading and writing lessons.
> - Individual coaches read and reflect upon the experiences to inform their practice.
> - Administrators disseminate this narrative to a staff to discuss at a department meeting or faculty meeting to illustrate powerful instructional strategies.

Mary Kim Schreck, a 30-year classroom teacher, 12-year department chair, now serves as a "teacher of teachers" through literacy coaching and literacy academies in Missouri, Texas, and Maryland. She is a frequent presenter at both the state and national levels for the International Reading Association (IRA), National Council of Teachers of English (NCTE), National Education Association (NEA), the Missouri Writing Project, and other state conferences. Over the past five years, Mary Kim has published three books of poetry: Pulse of the Seasons *(2004),* The Red Desk *(2005), and* Crystal Doorknobs *(2006). She currently serves as the editor for the Missouri Association of Teachers of English literary publication,* Missouri Teachers Write. *Mary Kim graciously allowed her poems to be published throughout this coaching book. Her work inspires my work, and I owe her a big thank-you and a great debt!*

The Urban Experience

By Mary Kim Schreck

A Literacy Coach in the Inner City: Great Expectations

Dickens's world and the world of the inner-city schools hold much in common—beauty amidst the rubble; hope and courage and vulnerability amidst the cynicism; the outrage; the grinding backdrop of poverty. So as literacy coaches we walk into an environment of the best and the worst with "great expectations" and hopefully we carry Dickens's compassion, purpose, and clarity of vision with us through which to funnel our efforts. For the last two years, I have seen those efforts translate into real strides in literacy growth.

I have been serving as a literacy coach under a federal Small Learning Communities grant at a large high school in the heart of downtown St. Louis. The inner-city school environment is a magnified version of all the school climates I had experienced in my career within suburban and rural settings. For all the roughness associated with street kids, I saw an unbelievably vulnerable and sensitive population. Everything is set on high: the anger turns to fights, the appreciation turns to tears. Laughter, song, and friendly bantering can swell to ear-splitting proportions in seconds. Here the rules are different.

Stepping into this world, I quickly learned that body language is the first literacy. Survival on the streets demands proficiency at correctly reading body language. Where verbal abilities are lacking, body language fills in. I needed to master this before my reading and writing literacy could be acceptably packaged and utilized.

My personal desegregation process has been one of the most profound experiences in my life. My years of teaching had been with White populations of 95% or higher. Not much diversity in my classrooms. Although I thought I came equipped for the job through book learning, I found my senses bombarded with a world completely foreign to the one I left. I knew that if I intended to meet the teachers and students "with a curriculum grounded in these students' lives," I needed to learn fast! My most effective tools were humility, a sense of humor, and some advice my daughter who teaches in a racially mixed high school gave me. She told me to look at everyone. Don't follow your first impulse to look down or away when you walk up to a group of students in the halls, especially the boys. Look, greet, smile. This advice moved me light years ahead in my desegregation process. The next piece of advice was to ask questions. Don't let anything go by that you don't understand or didn't hear correctly.

Armed with these strategies, I began. Slowly, my eyes opened, and what was once a blur of faces and sounds became individuals and conversations. Soon

(Continued)

(Continued)

I was amazed at the beauty around me, the exquisitely shaped eyes with curly lashes, the unlimited variety of skin colors, the graceful hands, and the smiles, the magnetism of the smiles.

My job did not provide an office, a desk, a room, anything. This was a true godsend. I've witnessed literacy coaches who ended up isolating themselves from the teachers and student body by spending more time at their computers or at their desks than in the halls and classrooms. Having no such false luxury, I was either in the halls, or classrooms, or the library, where I made a sign advertising "Reading and Writing Help of All Kinds."

I was amazed at how well teachers controlled their classes. Contrary to urban myths perpetuated by the media, the majority here had orderly classrooms. These are effective teachers within a dysfunctional system perpetrating archaic procedures that provide the greatest obstacle to providing a quality education. In my two years' time, I never had one experience of a student being less than polite and courteous to me. Yes, there were behavior problems, but none I hadn't witnessed in my years of teaching in affluent suburban districts.

As a literacy coach I set my goals at promoting an environment where reading was "cool" and writing was for everyone. Reading was to be seen as a source of freedom, power, escape, and self-confidence, and writing as a tool for learning and thinking as well as communication.

The Fortune-Telling Strategy

The school's bookroom holdings provided a limited number of titles or leveled materials, so I bought a class set of Steinbeck's *Of Mice and Men* to use with an American literature teacher. I worked with this teacher to build a unit utilizing the book as content and providing activities, writing prompts, and a guided example of planning with "the end in mind."

For a front-loading activity to spark student curiosity, I used my fortune-telling strategy. I came up with wigs, fluorescent paper for name signs, a bedroll or bindle, a boa, and a play mouse, among other things from my box of props. Then I asked for volunteers to take the parts of main characters, promising that this was a student-friendly activity and they wouldn't have to do much more than sit, look good, and repeat a few lines. I distributed sheets with the characters' names plus the open-ended statements "Your Dream Is . . ." and "Be Sure You Don't . . ." typed below each character. I billed myself as a famous fortune-teller brought here to introduce the people they will meet in *Of Mice and Men* using my $1.29 over-sized gold sphere Christmas ornament from Wal-Mart as my crystal ball.

One by one I playacted with the students, telling Curley's wife not to go into the barn, cautioning Lennie not to disobey George, revealing Candy's dream to end his days on a place of his own in dignity, and so forth. By the end of the activity, everyone in class was equipped with a visual image of each character, an inkling of potential conflicts, and the underlying motivations that would move characters to action. In one class, while the students were reading Chapter 5, a girl shouted out, "Oh no, she's going in the barn!"

The School Counselor Strategy

Certainly the most effective lessons for students highly dependent on visual clues for understanding are those that involve active participation, varying the delivery, and creatively enticing the students to look, think, act, and react in a new manner. So I constantly helped teachers build units that placed students in roles. The novel *The Friends* by Rosa Guy was one both freshmen and sophomores enjoyed. For this book, I wrote a series of activities where the students took the roles of school counselors who dealt with the characters' problems and provided alternative ways to handle conflicts common to most teenagers. They wrote reports, letters to parents, summaries of behavior, case studies, and simulated group counseling sessions. They discussed scenarios of situations where so-called friends acted any way but friendly and then judged them against a chart of what they had decided earlier were qualities of true friendship. A final assignment involved analyzing a short story by Rosa Guy with similar characters and themes. Students molded these papers into good thesis essays with strong support from the text for the assertions they were making. One of my aims was to show teachers how much better their students could write and think given the right stimulus—in other words, lift up their expectations of student ability a couple of notches.

After my fledgling efforts with these novels took root, I worked with teachers to incorporate books such as Guy's *The Friends*, Lee's *To Kill a Mockingbird*, Myers's *Bad Boy*, Bradbury's *Fahrenheit 451*, Haley's *Malcolm X*, and Davis, Jenkins, and Hunt's (2002) *The Pact*, an autobiography of three young doctors with inner-city roots. My participation was becoming more and more advisory as teachers got the feel for developing activity-based units.

Besides my work in the actual classrooms, I began four projects aimed at bringing reading and writing to the forefront of both student and faculty minds:

- A bookmaking project with the teen mothers who had children in the school's daycare center as well as with the girls who were pregnant and expecting to deliver during the year
- A writing contest
- A student book club
- An adult book club

Three of these projects plus additional activities are described below.

Baby's First Book: A Bookmaking Project

Now everything I read about literacy stresses the importance of early home training for setting the mental stage to be receptive to language. I had recently gone to Ruby Payne's training on the impact of poverty on learning and wanted to pour everything I had heard into the heads of the young mothers and fathers who were still children themselves. I wanted to preach!

(Continued)

(Continued)

I know better, though, so I set up an ongoing activity that allowed me to make my points while keeping them actively involved. I bought over 40 hardcover blank books from a Waldenbooks store plus a variety of felt suns, moons, balls, flowers, bugs, multicolored tissue paper, feathers, glue, scissors, magazines, markers, and black pens. We made Baby's First Book with numbers, primary colors, the alphabet, and shapes for content. Each page was a new number or letter all decorated and colorful. I had them write dedications to their children plus save beginning pages for pictures. While they worked, I talked about the importance of words and language to their children's later success in school. They listened, they worked, and they greeted me in the halls with "When are we going to meet again to work on our books?"

The Writing Contest

One of my duties as the grant literacy coach was to run a writing contest in concert with the coaches at the two other comprehensive high schools. This contest would yield six winners from each school whose essays would be published in booklets and distributed throughout the district.

To get students involved in the contest, I visited language arts classes and gave my pitch, solicited promises of extra credit from teachers, then made a sign and staked out my territory at a library table. Gradually a trickle of students willing to brainstorm the topic with me began to show up. For many, the total focus of one-on-one attention was the trigger to get them writing and returning with drafts. I had my laptop and a cheap $29.95 printer with me. I urged them to just bring me material and we could work from there. No draft was too rough not to provide a starting point.

The drafts came in and I typed them as is into the computer. On the following visit, I went over what was now typed up as well as the added questions I had included within the text. After each of these questions, I left spaces for the students to answer the question and add more information. I then printed out the essay for the student to take away and fill in the spaces I had added. This system worked really well with students who needed a little coaxing to write more: "Tell me how you felt," "What happened next?" "Explain what you mean here; give me some examples." These are some of the questions an active, curious reader would like answered, I told them.

When the student returned, I typed in the additional material with the student next to me and read through the essay out loud for word choice, phrasing, correct construction, and logic. What I actually was doing was modeling for these students just what "real" writers do when they are composing a piece. We changed sentences around, added punctuation—I always explained why the semicolon goes here, the comma there in terms of clarity and reader understanding. Then we worked on a cool ending, a unifying beginning, and a title. When the student agreed that it said exactly what he or she wanted it to say, we quit and printed out a copy to show his or her teachers and parents.

After the first year's contest, in spite of our school winning the first place prize, I felt bad that all the students who entered didn't get enough recognition for their efforts. So the second year I made booklets of all our school's entries and added a full-page picture of the student in front of his or her essay. Getting those booklets prepared was a labor of love for me. In these books all students are published, honored, and recognized, and there are no losers or winners in this collection.

Because I was becoming a familiar figure at my library table, I attracted seniors who needed help with scholarship essays and college applications; I attracted special education students working on Black History Month reports; I attracted students just interested in how I thought about things. Few of these students had any contact with White people other than the sprinkling of Caucasian teachers in their all-Black school and community. One young man brought me a magazine and turned to an ad that featured a man, woman, and a fancy car. He asked me if I considered the man handsome. I replied that the man would be called "tall, dark, and handsome" by most White women. The boy looked at me in disbelief and blurted out, "But he's not dark at all; he's a White guy!"

One 16-year-old boy came to my table not so much interested in the essay contest as in having me read the sheet upon sheet of folded up essays, stories, and rap songs he had written. His was a raw talent untouched by any formal instruction that was fresh and vital and just Waiting to be nudged into being.

Another such student brought me a rough draft essay of over five sides of that tiny, tiny handwriting we have all experienced a few times in our teaching careers. I told him he could use only 750 words out of his thousands in order to be eligible for the contest. I told him to leave it with me and I'd try to thin it out without losing any of his ideas. This paper was amazing in its redundancy. As his language arts teacher noted later when I went to talk to him about this student, "He always writes in this biblical fashion where you feel you're reading the genealogy section." But his ideas were tremendous and thought provoking. I spent over two and one-half hours pulling out phrases and juggling clauses just for the heck of it, just because I had the time to do it for once in my teaching career. The resulting essay took my breath away. Here were all his words, phrasing, and intended ideas but now pared down and edited. When I gave it back to him, I was rambling like a crazy lady trying to explain what I had done and why, wanting his approval and wanting him to see what his thoughts can look like when all cleaned up! He politely said thank you and left.

A couple of months later he stopped me in the hall and asked if I'd seen his report card. He proudly showed it to me—all A's and B's. I went back to his language arts teacher, who filled me in. It seems this senior never got any grade other than a C or D or worse, but that crazy essay put a fire in him. His writing dropped that biblical redundancy style, he showed an interest in completing all his assignments, and he was asking about college information. Oh, the power of a few hours of attention and guidance!

The Student Book Club

Most of us are aware of the inequity in resources that is prevalent in so many inner-city schools. Ours is no different. But we do have our share of benefactors also. One of my goals was to begin a student book club.

(Continued)

(Continued)

By the second year, I had found an organization that was willing and able to underwrite the cost of the books. This organization is composed of businesspeople from the community, politicians, and residents whose purpose is to improve the neighborhood and its schools.

The creation of the book club was similar to a roller-coaster ride. After the high of obtaining funding, the real work began. The initial call for members yielded over 50 students who attended an informational meeting and filled out registration forms. I found out that the majority of those interested were underclass students, so I began adjusting my preliminary book list. To advertise this venture, I took pictures of students as they delivered our first selection, Pelzer's *A Child Called It*. I had a couple of these pictures enlarged into poster size and taped them to the glass walls of the library. The pictures alone brought in a flood of curious potential members. Every month I added more. One mother came to school just to see her daughter's picture displayed on the library wall.

Once a month during the fifth block, which met daily, I grabbed a half hour for my book club members to meet in the library. During this time we talked briefly about the book we just read, did an activity that usually ended up on the glass wall, introduced and distributed the next book, and got a few pictures taken. Some of these activities were letter writing to book characters, drawings of main scenes, recommendations to future readers, and a reader's scavenger hunt. I had purchased a pack of bulletin borders from a teacher supply story that had a running book shelf of both contemporary and classic books usually offered at the high school level. I cut these strips into six-inch segments, distributed them to the members, and told them to find teachers who had read one of the books on their card and sign the back with the name of the books and their names. At the next meeting I gave out prizes to those who turned in the most names. This was a very fluid book club. Each month we added around a dozen new members and lost about a dozen members, depending on the book selection.

Teachers began asking me what I was doing with the books that had been read and returned. They wanted to use them. Although I seldom got back over half of the books from the students, I did have enough to give teachers class sets. One teacher who took Sharon Draper's *Forged by Fire* wrote up some of the best writing/research prompts I'd seen composed in the school.

One Book for the Whole Class Strategy

Besides finding benefactors to help out, there are other tricks to introducing interesting strategies and materials that are not necessarily tied to big price tags. One strategy is the "one book for the whole class" or the "I tear up books" method. For example, take a paperback such as *Gentle Hands* by Ben Carson and tear it up so that all the chapters are separated. (Pages that have the end of one chapter on the opposite side of the beginning of another need to be copied.) Each student gets a chapter to read, and then the class listens to the book being told student by student. A focused guide is distributed to each student to trace conflicts, interventions, choices, and resources that influenced the main character's life. For once, each student's reading assignment is important to the group and necessary for everyone's understanding of the book. This activity also demands oral summarizing and listening skills.

I've torn up fairy tale books and mythology books and used them for round-robin story telling as well as opportunities to teach point of view and diction. A wonderful book with examples of how one story can be told from different perspectives is *Once Upon a Fairy Tale* (Starbright Foundation, 2001). This charming book tells fairy tales chronologically while switching narrators throughout. Included with each book is a CD with readers such as Steven Spielberg, Barbra Streisand, Martha Stewart, Mike Myers, Kelsey Grammer, Robin Williams, Oprah Winfrey, and many more. Once we listen and look at how these stories are written, we take one of the torn-up fairy tales, read it, and rewrite it by mimicking the format used in *Once Upon a Fairy Tale.* Imagination, not money, is a teacher's best resource for filling his or her classroom with creativity.

Student Discussions Centering on Race and Poverty

When I do try to set up situations where the problems of poverty and inequity are to be discussed with the students, I find it easier to address this without linking the conversation to race or location. Sherman Alexie's accounts of life on and off the reservations make a powerful source of material for reading, writing, and discussing how others cope with situations similar to their own. One chapter of *The Lone Ranger and Tonto Fistfight in Heaven* (1993) titled "Indian Education" is a wonderful selection to use with inner-city students. It traces his school years from first grade through twelfth in short, single episodes. As we read each grade-level piece, we determine the theme. For example, first grade: bullies; third grade: censorship; and so on. After the reading, each student chooses one of the 12 to freewrite about, giving a personal experience that is similar in theme to Alexie's. Then we build a structure for our paper that begins with a global relationship to the chosen theme—how countries could bully smaller ones, for example. Next, students use the textual account of this theme, pulling and explaining quotes from Alexie's essay. Finally, they add their personal experiences with this topic, referring to their freewrites. The finished products are as well structured and thoughtful as any of their peers' in the suburban areas.

Teaching Poetry

Whether it's the influence of rap music and hip-hop or perhaps the fact that poems are shorter than prose pieces, I'm not sure, but nothing was easier than working with poetry in this school. I offered one teacher a group of poetry structures for her students to follow, poems to mimic for theme or format, and various ideas for products. My favorite publishing strategy is kite making. This was the first real success I had at introducing a full-blown hands-on activity with a couple of the teachers and their classes. After composing a series of original poems, students chose their favorite to present to the class and place on a kite to be suspended from the ceiling or against the walls. I precut rectangles of paper from a roll of butcher-block paper and used 18-inch balloon sticks from a local carnival supply company. The tails came from old rolls of thick yarn. Each student decorated his or her kite with markers, glitter, cut-out pictures, and, of course, a poem. With a ladder and large paper clips, I attached the kites to

(Continued)

(Continued)

the ceiling's metal strips or on the walls. As was my experience for years, the students loved reading others' kites and having theirs displayed as well.

Anyone who works with students in schools such as this can't help but be filled with the desire to give every ounce of expertise, energy, and creativity he or she can muster. The payback in internal satisfaction is tremendous, yet the knowledge that so much needs to be done can be equally overwhelming. I'm reminded of Anne Lamott's (1994) book title *Bird by Bird.* One at a time—we can only change things one child at a time, one school at a time, one teacher at a time. But that will eventually make all the difference. And Dickens with his "best of times, worst of times" can only remind us that ours is not a unique circumstance. We will continue to hold our "great expectations" like a flag before us as we return day after day, and we will make a difference. We will.

Reprinted with permission from Mary Kim Schreck.

Mary Kim says: "As literacy coaches we walk into an environment of the best and the worst with 'great expectations.'" In what ways does this statement mirror your experience as a coach?

_____

_____

_____

Mary Kim says that "body language is the first literacy." Do you agree or disagree? In what ways do you monitor your body language as you coach?

_____

_____

_____

Mary Kim describes several concrete strategies she uses to teach reading, writing, thinking, and speaking skills at the secondary level. Which strategies might you try?

_____

_____

_____

Which strategies in Mary Kim's piece could be used at the middle school level? At the elementary school level?

_____

_____

_____

You may contact Mary Kim at Marykim@aol.com to inquire about her poetry books (*The Red Desk, Pulse of the Seasons,* and *Crystal Doorknob*), her consulting work, and her keynote presentations.

NAN STARLING

This narrative describes a coach who travels from district to district across the country and supports teachers across the disciplines in several high schools. The following are professional development suggestions for using Nan's narrative:

- Coaches use the narrative as a basis for discussing definitions of coaching, strategies for nondirective coaching, issues of confidentiality, and ways to support teachers.
- Individual coaches use the final lists for checking needs for travel.
- Trainer of trainers use the narrative with new coaches to give an overview of the role of a coach.
- Coaches and teachers use the concrete strategies presented in Nan's narrative to improve classroom instruction.

Nan Starling taught full time for 35 years in high school classrooms and universities while also working as a team leader and part-time administrator in human resources. During her active retirement, Nan has coordinated character education contests for the Laws of Life in conjunction with Characterplus, in which over 12,000 students employed writing to affirm their values. In addition, Nan has worked as an independent professional development and coaching consultant for school districts. She is currently traveling across the United States as an instructional facilitator helping teachers and coaches raise student achievement through Talent Development High Schools, a program of Johns Hopkins University. An Emerson Excellence in Education recipient, Nan nurtures in others the enrichment that education has provided her. A published poet, essayist, and editor, Nan finds writing inseparable from her daily activities and communication.

The following is a Q&A session we shared. Nan's answers give us important insight into the roles and responsibilities of a coach.

How do you define your role as coach?
I've given quite a few answers because I play so many roles.

"Facilitator" is the main word that fits my role. In the spirit of "No Teacher Left Behind" (my term), I offer help to teachers and coaches of teachers and sometimes administrators to encourage and assist students in their desire to learn, their ability to learn, and the transference of their learning to patterns, skills, and concepts that they can apply to other learning situations, life skills, and job skills.

For example, in an urban school in Los Angeles with approximately 5,000 students, I work with a language arts teacher who successfully teaches classes of about 40 students. But he is overwhelmed with preparation for engaging students, grading papers, and record keeping. I am working with him to incorporate ways he can credit student work

(Continued)

(Continued)

without "grading" it, give students more responsibility for recording their work, spot-check students' completion, and grade students' best work according to their analyses. I wish I could reduce the size of his classes, but I cannot, so I can help him be as efficient as possible while he provides ways to give meaningful assessment.

"Trainer of trainers" is another term often used for my role. In some schools, I work with coaches who have frequent interactions with the teachers there. The coach and I reflect on his or her observations and activities between my visits. We evaluate areas of strength and concern and set goals for how we can support instruction during and after my visits. Recently we have been focusing on a few teachers during each visit and setting aside time for preconferences, modeling by the coach and me, joint planning and teaching, and debriefing with goal setting. We have selected teachers who show interest in change and will probably make a lasting impact on their students and share their successes with their colleagues.

For example, in Chicago I share the time during my visits with four coaches, usually focusing on two per visit. We then observe and discuss the progress and needs of the teachers in their schools to determine support to give during the visit (for example, helping teachers stay on pace with the district requirements or providing classroom management strategies for a teacher who needs help with students' behavior) and what plans to make for coaches' activities between my visits.

"Professional development presenter" is also a role I play. Either alone, with other presenters, or with on-site curriculum coaches, I present workshops that inform teachers about programs and curricula, introduce strategies to teachers, provide practice with strategies, and/or allow teachers time to collaborate.

Ultimately, I believe that my role is to assist teachers so that they can be as effective as possible. Because teachers have a variety of strengths and needs, I perform multiple roles. The most basic role I have undertaken involved finding and distributing classroom materials to teachers in a school that in November had not distributed teachers' manuals or textbooks to students although the school year had begun in September. This task was my first priority, since I could not support the course until the teachers had their supplies. In addition, I have helped teachers arrange classrooms, set up student seating charts, plan the scope and sequence of their curriculum, determine support for special needs students, and whatever else was needed.

Sometimes my role includes advocating to the administration about the needs of the teachers. Unfortunately, an outsider may be more influential than the school staff, so I selectively make requests for equipment, ask for meeting times, and make administrators aware of conditions that restrict or interfere with teachers' effectiveness. Essentially, I view myself as an advocate of the teachers, who can be a resource for their own understanding of what does and does not help them teach effectively and who can speak for them when they need support. Of course, not all requests can be fulfilled, but at least the teachers have someone to advocate for them. (Note: I do not attempt to advocate in matters that would involve the teachers' union.)

Another way to define this role is a "resource of resources." I encourage teachers to see their students as resources for checking for understanding/assessment. I encourage teachers to use their students for feedback about the progress and success of lessons. I ask teachers to incorporate strategies such as

- Having students repeat directions
- Showing thumbs up, thumbs down, or index cards with A, B, C, D, or Yes or No, white lap boards for writing and showing answers
- Think-Pair-Share, with the teacher listening to the sharing
- Choral answers
- Four corners
- Cooperative learning groups

Finally, because teachers are often isolated as well as so busy that they have little time for reflection, I play the role of questioner, listener, and counselor. I guard the confidentiality of our discussions and encourage teachers to reflect honestly on their strengths, weaknesses, and goals. I encourage endurance and commitment, keeping in mind that teachers are often exhausted by the number of students they are responsible for and the number of class preparations. Teachers can become discouraged when their schools and districts shift priorities and change reform models/programs before the staff has had time to learn how to implement them, much less see success. When teachers are supposed to jump from No Child Left Behind and state testing to literacy initiatives to improving passing rates and to preventing conflicts and to so many more initiatives, they rightfully feel overwhelmed. I see myself as someone who can empathize and help refocus.

In what ways have you included facilitation and/or "instruction" in your coaching, such as specific strategies and advice on lesson design?

As facilitator, I help teachers reflect on their teaching patterns and the impact on students. Through open-ended questioning and mostly listening, I offer the opportunity for teachers to process what they are doing in preparation, delivery, and follow-up of their lessons and their interaction with students. I offer confidentiality so that teachers are safe in sharing their doubts and failures. I offer strategies and theories from published experts and programs. I recount strategies I have observed other teachers use and share materials from them. And I suggest methods I have used in my teaching. Sometimes I model teaching and work directly with students. Sometimes I coplan and coteach lessons. Sometimes I observe teachers working alone. Whenever possible I have preconferences to set goals and identify areas of concentration. I always spend some time debriefing.

One of my functions near the end of a term is to stimulate analysis of the course materials and methods of delivery and to help teachers set goals and make revisions for the coming school year. For a school in California that is using a modified version of the course I support, I gave teachers a questionnaire that asked the following questions:

- What successes have you and your students experienced with the curricula?
- What lessons or units did you find were less successful?
- What issues are you concerned about in terms of course content, sequencing, pacing, student engagement, assessment, and so on?

(Continued)

(Continued)

- What changes/additions would you recommend?
- What advice would you give to teachers who begin using the curricula?
- What materials and/or strategies that you use would you like to share and explain or model for your colleagues who teach this course?
- What materials and/or strategies that other teachers in your school use would you like them to share and explain or model?
- What suggestions would you make so that the course skills can be reinforced and incorporated in other classes?

What are your strengths as a coach?

I am able to establish positive, helping relationships. I consciously strive to avoid judgments and openly admit that I have experienced most of the difficulties the teachers I work with are having, but I also admit that I think their jobs are quite difficult and that I don't have all the answers. I keep the focus on each teacher's needs and try not to linger too long on complaints or to prescribe universal solutions.

For example, when I encounter teachers who have "been there, done that" and don't want to try anything new, I state that I too have seen many reforms come and go and that no one program fits all. I don't pretend that I am an expert, but I do state that I have had much experience (there should be some benefit from aging and all those years of teaching) and success in my own teaching and have seen many other teachers who are successful. I am willing to share what has worked for me and for other teachers and help teachers adapt those ideas to their needs or look for other solutions. I try to focus on a practical strategy that the teacher can use immediately and see the benefit.

For teachers who say that they don't need help or don't need to change or don't like a new method or program—if the problem is measured by standardized tests or by lack of students' attention or by the number of students failing—I cite the facts and ask the teachers to attribute the causes and suggest solutions.

I base my coaching relationships on communication through sharing. I not only want to share what I know and think, but I also want to have the people I coach share what they know and think. Although the primary focus is the person receiving the coaching, I too want to learn. I want to respect the knowledge and experiences of those I coach, and I also want to keep myself fresh and current as I participate in the process of learning.

Through open-ended questioning, I seek to listen to the people I am coaching and look for direction through them. I believe I have the ability to see patterns and main issues that are not always apparent to others, and I can use supporting details to illustrate how these patterns emerge. When I make the overall situation clear to teachers, they often are able to analyze how they can repeat their successes and improve their weaknesses.

I ask for teachers to clarify the *what* in their teaching. I think it's essential that first they specify what they want their students to learn. The what is not only the facts of the content but the concepts the facts are based on. And of course the what needs to correlate with the school standards and requirements, which will then correlate with the state's.

Then I ask *why*—why students need to learn this information, this skill, this concept. If students don't know why they need to learn and remember the lesson, they won't. And if the teacher is not consciously aware of the need to help students see the why (usually both at the beginning of the lesson and at the end), then the students are not likely to see it.

After the what and why we can then determine the *how*, the way the lesson will help students experience the what. In coaching, I ask teachers to estimate the time required for the how, to break the lesson into parts lasting approximately 20 to 30 minutes, and to list the materials and preparation necessary for this lesson to run smoothly. I encourage teachers to brainstorm various methods of delivery and practice and to be realistic about the availability of materials and preparation time. I also encourage teachers to share preparation with their colleagues in order to expand their resources and to create collegiality.

In planning lessons, I ask teachers to end with *so what*. I suggest that, if only for a few minutes, students finish the lesson by processing what they have learned and how what they learned relates outside this class to other classes, to their feelings, to their interests, to ways of thinking, to ways the world operates through politics, economics, and so on (I suggest that either the teacher create a template for these topics that students may refer to as they answer "So what?" or that the teacher choose one or two topics for the students to relate to). I often suggest that teachers create a way for students to record and retain these applications (for example, in journals or on sentence strips posted in the classroom or in a class newsletter). I find that if teachers encourage students to review their so what's periodically (at the end of units or terms), students can see patterns in their learning and can transfer these patterns to other learnings.

For example, Mr. T. (Kansas City, Missouri), a 30-year veteran teacher from a rural high school who after retirement moved to an inner-city school to supplement his pension, was having difficulty in his new position. His teaching style of lecturing and assigning independent reading and worksheets, which had apparently worked in a school where classes of 20 to 25 students had been trained to be compliant, was not effective in the new school in classrooms of 30 to 35 urban students, so Mr. T.'s students were doing everything except what he wanted. They were not staying in their seats; they were blurting out comments and questions during his lecture and having conversations with their classmates, often across the room and over Mr. T.'s lectures. Mr. T. was stumped about how to make his students listen, complete assignments, and care about their grades.

Although our ultimate aim was to work on all components of the lessons, we began with improving student behavior. We stated specific times when simple procedures could help students recognize the purpose (why) and significance (so what) of the assignments. Based on a system I had used when my own students had not seen the value of completing assignments, Mr. T. established a procedure that helped students recognize the importance of completing assignments. When I found students unaware of the cumulative effects of their behavior, I determined procedures and time limits and created ways to break the class period into shorter activities and interactive lessons. For missing work, I had them record their grades as I returned papers, store their work in folders, and on Fridays tally and average their grades and list incomplete work so they could catch up. Mr. T. followed my model and fashioned a form on which

(Continued)

(Continued)

students wrote assignments, their value, and recorded their grades. He posted a master list, which students could reference. Along with other procedures that he instated, this recording of grades showed students how they were accountable for their grades and removed the mystery and perceived unfairness. Classroom behavior improved immediately as students took responsibility for themselves and even gave Mr. T. feedback on their ability to endure long lectures, and so on. Of course not all behavior, the students' or teacher's, changed at once, but both students and the teacher were more in charge of the classroom environment, and more learning took place.

Overall, my coaching mantra is "Say less; listen more." I'm sure I don't always practice this policy, but I continue to remind myself that whether the learner is a child, teen, or adult, lasting learning comes from within.

What are your challenges as a coach?

Resistance to change is strong. So many teachers have so many students and so little time that they don't feel they can add anything else. Most changes, at least at first, involve more time.

Blaming students is one attitude I have little patience with. When a teacher relinquishes his or her power and uses the fatalistic stance that the students will not behave and/or will not learn, I have to convince the teacher to recognize students' capabilities and to focus on students' interests and methods of learning.

Blaming administrators is another powerless stance that annoys me. I do know that conditions in many schools foster distrust and interfere with instruction, but I expect teachers to at least establish a learning environment in their own classrooms, and I have seen that happen. In the midst of chaos in some schools, I have seen some classes where students were excited about the lessons and where those classes created their own oasis of comfort and purpose.

The most frustrating challenge comes from teachers and administrators who do not want to invest their time and energy to improve or even to teach what they were hired to teach.

How important is the relationship between the coach and the educator he or she is coaching? How much time up front do you believe needs to be spent building relationships with those you will coach?

It is paramount that the coach and educator begin to establish trust immediately. First this trust needs to emerge from the coach's assurance that no specific information about the teacher will be used for evaluation or be shared with the administration unless the coach receives permission from the teacher. The coach must abide by this agreement and be aware that even the appearance of reporting evaluative comments to administrators can negate the trust between the coach and teacher. I try to hold my conversations with administrators in public areas so that it does not appear I am revealing confidential information. In addition, when administrators ask me to reveal confidential information, I state only generalities and ask administrators to observe teachers and make their own determination of the quality of teaching. Only if I saw a situation where students could be placed in danger would I report a teacher to an administrator without the teacher's permission. If I see an example of an excellent lesson, I may ask the teacher if I may report it to an administrator. Even then I am cautious that I do not, by omitting some teachers, imply a criticism of them.

The best way I have found to create a positive relationship is to be of use. If I can provide a resource or a strategy that improves instruction, I have set up the kind of relationship I seek. I consciously look for this opportunity and try to provide practical, immediately usable strategies as soon as possible.

Reprinted with permission from Nan Starling.

Coaching: Coplanning, Coteaching, Debriefing

By Nan Starling

The long-term goal of this model is that the coach and the teacher will establish a partnership that results in students achieving at high levels.

Getting to Know Your Teachers

- First, before acting, try to understand. Observe the classroom environment, routines, and teachers' styles.
- Learn each other's strengths and beliefs. Show your respect for each other's skills and individuality.
- Reach an agreement on working together, how you will work together, and how often.

Structure and Organization

- Have a schedule that both agree to and adhere to.
- Arrange time for pre- and postteaching conferences.
- Set limited goals in these conferences; focus on these goals but be flexible if other issues emerge.
- Emphasize strategies and procedures that increase students' learning.
- Spotlight student learning and classroom environment.

Preconference for Coplanning

- Together with the teacher, determine the objectives of the lesson and the focus of the reflection on it.
- Emphasize instructional strategies and classroom procedures that enhance student learning and classroom environment.
- Measure outcomes by assessment of student performance; be sure the two are directly related.

Coteaching the Lesson

- Determine who will present and/or lead which parts of the lesson.
- Decide who will be responsible for preparing which instructional materials and gathering supplies.
- Keep in mind that the teacher has daily responsibility for the students and needs to maintain authority.

(Continued)

(Continued)

Postlesson Debriefing

- Hold the conference ASAP while ideas and memories are fresh.
- Encourage the teacher to use self-reflection and to have most of the air time.
- Keep the focus on student learning.
- Examine student work for assessment.
- Use the lesson as a basis of goal-setting.

Coaching Conferences With Teachers

Prelesson Conference Questions for Coteaching

1. What issue, topic, or problem do you want to work on?

2. What lesson would you like to teach together? What are the goals/objectives in the lesson?

3. What prior knowledge do your students have on this lesson? What difficulties do you anticipate your students may have? Sensitivities? Reading skills? Cooperation?

4. Freshman seminar lesson plans are like a cookbook with recipes that you may alter to your taste. Which part(s) of this recipe (lesson) do you want to use? To delete? To add?

5. How will you assess what the students learn? How successful the lesson is?

6. What role do you want me (the coach) to take? If any student disrupts, how do you want me to handle the student?

7. What materials and supplies do we need for the lesson? Who will be responsible for what?

8. What else do we need to discuss?

Postlesson Conference Questions for Debriefing

1. How do you feel about how the lesson went?

2. What parts of the lesson design helped accomplish the lesson objectives?

3. What are some of the strategies and procedures that helped you achieve the lesson objectives?

4. Were students engaged in the lesson? How did you know?

5. What could be changed to improve the lesson? How might the change impact student responses?

6. How can I (the coach) support you in implementing these changes?

7. What areas do you want to work on for the future? On your own? With me?

Reprinted with permission from Nan Starling.

Nan says, "Whether the learner is a child, teen, or adult, lasting learning comes from within." If you agree, how does this statement influence your decisions as a coach?

_____

_____

_____

You read how Nan handles the issue of confidentiality. How do you handle this issue?

_____

_____

_____

What are some of Nan's nuggets of wisdom that you might use in your work?

_____

_____

_____

Nan offers you a number of practical suggestions and strategies. What ideas might work for you?

_____

_____

_____

You may contact Nan at nanstarling@charter.net to inquire about the Johns Hopkins program, her materials, and consulting work.

SUSIE MORICE

This narrative describes a coach who was hired by the district to work with a middle school staff to improve their instruction and, ultimately, student scores on state tests.

The following are professional development suggestions for using Susie's narrative:

- Coaches read and discuss how to coach a team of teachers.
- Administrators disseminate to middle school teachers to read and discuss what it means to meet and work as a team.
- Individuals read and reflect upon the role of the outside coach when working with a team of teachers preparing them to examine student work.

While a classroom teacher, Susie served in a variety of leadership positions from department chair to team leader to gifted education coordinator. Her early experiences as program director for the Gateway Writing Project, affiliate of the National Writing Project, have kept Susie firmly planted in both her own writing and in helping teachers with writing instruction. Thirty years in middle and high school classrooms allows Susie to call on that experience in her educational consulting work specializing in literacy coaching and middle school structures.

Looking at Student Work (and All the Work It Took to Get to That Point) in a Suburban Middle School

By Susie Morice

Coaching Teachers

At the core of coaching teachers in the field, is the work of building quality relationships. When that exists, everything else is easier. Just as in sports, magic happens when a coach and the athlete form a relationship, that is, when the athlete is "coachable" and the coach is knowledgeable and honest about reaching goals. We all have different degrees of readiness for learning, and the coaching task is often reciprocal. Successful teacher coaches take the time to know their teachers and recognize that they must learn where and how much to intervene. Then they construct learning opportunities that fit. All that takes time, time to build relationships.

As one of the local districts was initiating efforts to shift from a junior high to a middle school, the principal asked three colleagues and me to share some insights about what it meant to be a middle school teacher. A decade earlier I had made that transition myself in my home district. Middle school philosophy underscores the importance of meeting students' needs where they are. Kids in this whirling, hormonal time needed teachers who understood both the affective needs of 13-year-olds and the academic rigor needed to challenge them. I loved middle school—was downright passionate about it—and getting a chance to share some of my enthusiasm and wisdom with a neighboring district excited me.

This early contact with Big Suburban Middle School was just the beginning of what would become a longer relationship. It is, in fact, the relationship that makes all the difference in educational change. At first, I was merely a presenter, coming in on a professional development day to share some pointers on middle school transition. My success at that effort was, at best, planting some seeds of understanding. Even that was, perhaps, questionable. Three years later, however, I returned to this middle school to work for a school term with teacher teams in an ongoing endeavor to help teachers find more effective ways to use the middle school structures that their young principal was providing.

Each year for four years, the principal, the district, and the state standards were upping the ante. Teachers were implementing a new discipline referral and intervention system, scoring districtwide writing prompts, and sweating the annual AYP (Annual Yearly Progress) made so public with the state testing demands. Teachers wanted time to work together. They wanted common planning time. "We're overwhelmed" was a mantra.

Seeking to improve discipline in the building, to raise scores on the state test, and to acknowledge teachers' needs, the principal and his two assistants did some important structural changing. One of the most critical changes was finding common planning time so teachers could look at instruction. What happened initially, however, was what the principal called "admiring the problem." Teachers were not quite sure just what to do with this common planning time. Meetings seemed to engage in a repetitive pattern of looking at a problem or a problem student but taking little or no action to remedy the issue. Some meetings bogged down into fuss fests.

The principal asked me to spend time in his building as a sort of coach, working with teachers in their team meetings. "Help them get beyond this 'admiring the problem' kind of behavior," he asked, anxious to see team meetings become more productive. He stated this to his staff, yet he needed a coach to help teams achieve this change.

After a couple of conversations with the administrators, we arranged a meeting of the department chairs. What did they want from their team meetings? Why meet as a team? Department chairs wanted help with how to run a meeting and how to set up norms. They worried about using a 90-minute block effectively and time management strategies for their teachers. Because the leadership capacity in this group was already significant, it seemed a good place to start. After collecting input from the chairs, I felt it was time for me to sit in on team meetings to see just how they were functioning. They needed to get used to seeing my face, and I needed to get to know them in action.

The relationships were beginning. I was in the building often enough to be a familiar face. My goal was merely to help them gain time they could use in more productive ways.

It mattered to these teachers that I had been a 30-year veteran of the classroom. Most of my teaching career had been with middle school students, and I'd loved it. We shared that common ground.

Having an outside lens seemed nonthreatening to the teachers in the building. Not an evaluator, I was there to help teams reflect on their processes for communicating about important issues from curriculum to discipline. At each team meeting, I simply introduced myself and my goal of helping them use their team meetings as productively as possible, so they could finally get to the business of examining instruction. That first round of team visits, though, was merely to introduce myself and become acquainted with the structure of each team—who was who and what was what.

After I sat in on that first round of meetings, I recognized that these teachers needed to explore their own perceptions about team meetings.

(Continued)

(Continued)

Did they share a vision of what common team time could be? What were their hopes for team time? Squeezing some meeting time from their schedules, I rounded up the troops to explore their vision and set down some building goals for meetings.

First, I designated one teacher in the meeting to serve as a sort of special observer, a process observer, who would keep track of our ebb and flow in the meeting and then report back to us at the end of the meeting when we were on track, sidetracked, or off track. This would help us get a sense for the flow of our productivity in the meeting. I then set up norms for our conversation. I started with a couple of my own and asked them to add norms that they felt would make our time together productive and effective. The agenda I'd set for the meeting was written boldly on chart paper, keeping nuts-and-bolts logistics to a minimum and separate from the bigger issues, in this case establishing a shared vision for team meetings. We briefly reviewed the agenda. With norms for professional conversation set and an agenda before us, I posed the question "Why meet as a team?" After some clowning around that exposed the desire to "plan Friday night parties," we got serious. We brainstormed and then prioritized a list that would make any middle school proud:

- To be reflective on our role as teachers
- To collaborate on lesson ideas and curriculum
- To problem solve about student behavior and about student achievement
- To keep kids from falling through the cracks
- To share team-building ideas
- To listen and support fellow teachers and help them find solutions
- To integrate student activities and the community
- To take care of the nuts and bolts so kids get a consistent message
- To have a support network when parents are involved

These teachers had legitimate goals for team meetings, and my writing those down right in front of them gave them ownership of a new sense that team meetings really did need to be different. My role as a coach, at this point, was merely in facilitating conversation. Setting norms, following a prioritized agenda, asking a central question, and making visible their shared thinking were conscious strategies I was modeling in the hope of having the team begin to use some of these tools.

I was ready to sit in on team meetings as a process observer. I conveyed that I would monitor the meeting in an effort to help them gain valuable time they might in the future use for their team meeting goals such as collaborating on lesson ideas. I requested only to have a few minutes at the end of the meeting so that I might share my sense of the process flow.

For weeks I returned to the building to observe more team meetings. Little by little, teams began to show signs of positive change. Most teams began using agendas, and many very deliberately acknowledged norms for their conversations. When norms relaxed, it was evident: little progress was made on issues that could be settled readily. My coaching was light-handed: it was just a reminder that they shared a vision for meetings and they could, if they used clear agendas and norms, finally get to the business of looking at instruction. Yet this was slow to surface as a reality. As a coach, I might have pushed, but the momentum for more demonstrative change just wasn't there yet.

By second semester, the teams shared a vocabulary for meetings. As a coach, it didn't seem like rocket science. They needed to make agendas, be punctual, use norms, and prioritize topics. Early in the year, I was reminded of that frog in the boiling kettle—he doesn't notice he's cooking himself. These teachers only needed a nudge to remind them to hop out of the kettle so they could achieve a better environment for learning within the team. A coach who is somewhat subtle and who consistently reminds teachers of their goals can be a genuinely effective coach. Teachers are smart people. They don't appreciate a coach who comes into the building to "fix" them. My goal was simply to provide another lens on their process, helping them reflect on their own effectiveness.

In February, the Building Leadership Team was scheduled to meet. This group of teachers represented the various teams in the building. Typically, this group used their meetings to hash through logistical items, often bogging down before they ever reached for those big idea types of issues, such as instruction. I presented to the leadership team my feedback from having observed teams across the building over the course of several months and suggested that we all revisit our purpose for team meetings. I stepped forward, at this point, as a facilitator.

First, I posed the same question I'd asked them at the start of the term: "Why meet as a team?" Quickly, the group brainstormed a list quite similar to the one they'd drafted in the fall. This time, however, they were much more serious about examining what really mattered to them. It was a healthy reminder of their shared goals. As we prioritized their list, examining student work rose quickly to the top of the list. They weren't quite sure how to do that and asked to learn the protocols for looking at student work. I suggested the Harvard Project Zero protocols, as they are easy to use and the professional dialogue that emerges is rich.

The coach sets up opportunities for teachers to reflect, to see themselves honestly so they can shape their learning in a direction that makes sense to them. Recognizing where the team stands and anticipating readiness, the coach can know what skill to introduce next. These educators were poised for learning protocols for looking at student work. With careful guidance, the coach can bring new expectations forward with the group and help the whole school community raise the bar. The team leaders at Big Suburban Middle School had gained valuable time by streamlining their shared planning time and could finally begin to look at student work and the instruction that guided that work.

At the March meeting, we met after school for two hours. Critical here is that the coach didn't step up and say, "Today I'm here to show you how to look at student work." Instead, the request came from the teachers. They wanted to learn the protocols and pushed for that learning experience because they were ready.

Effective teacher coaching is a delicate dance. Had I sashayed into the scene in the fall, dictating that these teachers needed to be using their team meetings for examining instruction and looking at student work born of that instruction, the teachers would likely have recognized the heavy foot of an outsider coming in to fix them. Instead, we built a relationship of camaraderie and trust. They knew I was there to help, not to dictate. I needed to learn who they were and where they were on their learning curve before we could two-step our way to change.

(Continued)

(Continued)

> What did I learn about coaching teachers?
>
> - Take the time to build honest relationships with the teachers.
> - Listen carefully.
> - Learn where your teachers are in their pedagogy and share resources that move them forward in their learning.
> - Find the point of intersection between what the administrator has hired you to come in and do and what the teachers are ready to change.
> - Help teachers see themselves as learners.
> - Set goals together, helping teachers to recognize they own their goals.
> - Consistently, yet gently, remind the teachers of the goals they set.
> - Be present in the building as often as possible; make your face a familiar smile.
> - Model what you want your teachers to do.
> - Facilitate rather than dictate, allowing your intelligent new colleagues to surface their own mental models.
> - Coach where your background skills fit; your inherent enthusiasm for a particular venue matters. If you are passionate about writer's workshop, for example, then coach toward that workshop approach—your passion is contagious, and the teachers you coach deserve that.
>
> Reprinted with permission from Susan Morice.

Susie says, "Effective teacher coaching is a delicate dance." What does this statement mean to you?

_____

_____

_____

Susie is an expert at asking questions that elicit thoughtful responses. What questions might you use to move teachers to improve instruction?

_____

_____

_____

As you reflect on Susie's experience, what additional suggestions or strategies might you use in your coaching practice?

_____

_____

_____

You may contact Susie at susiemorice@charter.net to inquire about her consulting work.

LOLA MAPES

This narrative describes an elementary classroom teacher facilitating the investigation of literacy at the K–6 level. The following are professional development suggestions for using Lola's narrative:

> - Coaches read and discuss how to share professional literature with teachers.
> - Elementary principal disseminates to the staff to discuss ways to investigate learning for teachers.
> - Literacy coaches read and discuss current literacy resources to use with teachers.

During her 31 years of teaching at Clive Elementary in the West Des Moines, Iowa, schools, Lola was actively involved as the language arts chairperson in the study of literacy learning. She worked with Dr. Linda Henke in creating the Beyond-the-Basal (B-T-B) literacy program, and during this time, Donald Graves recorded a session in her classroom helping fourth graders talk and think through their ideas in developing a piece of fiction. As the recipient of the Christa McAuliffe Award, Lola spent the year's sabbatical sharing her "literacy learning" with colleagues in the Midwest. She documented her experiences in two Iowa Writing Project publications: Two Weeks in May, *coauthored with Dr. Henke, and* Eighty-Seven Questions and a Few Tentative Answers. *Lola served as a facilitator in both the Iowa and Clayton, Missouri, Writing Projects. Since her retirement in 1994, she has worked as a staff development facilitator and consultant in the Clayton and Maplewood-Richmond Heights, Missouri, schools. Presently, she is a supervisor for Iowa State University student teachers. Lola currently is a great-grandmother who is truly retired and plays the trombone in weekly concerts in her home city.*

By Lola Mapes

Several years ago, before coaching was viewed beyond the sports arena—and as a way for teachers to learn together—our school's staff development structure was organized around four subject areas: reading/language arts, math, social studies, and science. As the building chairperson for the reading/language arts in our K–6 elementary school, I was expected to work with five to seven teachers in our school to facilitate study of a particular area in which the group was interested. Teachers chose in which area they wished to be involved. The groups met once a week before school for approximately 45 minutes, and the time allotment for a particular study was flexible—sometimes a semester, sometimes a year.

When our district adopted the B-T-B literacy program, the seven teachers on the reading/language arts group felt a compelling need for time to read and discuss professional literacy relevant to the new program. The teachers in this group represented all grade levels except kindergarten and third and the guidance counselor.

(Continued)

(Continued)

The teachers in this group knew very well what they needed, as they were apprehensive about the "new" approach to teaching reading and writing, so they decided to spend the first month of the year reading *Writing: Teachers and Children at Work* by Donald Graves (2003), *When Writers Read* by Jane Hansen (2001), *The Art of Teaching Writing* by Lucy Calkins (1986), and *The Journal Book* edited by Toby Fulwiler (1987). There were no "assignments" each week; rather, each teacher read in one or more of the four books as well as articles in National Council of Teachers of English (NCTE) publications. When the group met on Thursday, each shared both general information they had gleaned as well as specific strategies they had used with their students. There were often aha moments and occasionally some "Oh-No-Help!" moments.

After the group became a bit more comfortable with the B-T-B program, our group meetings focused on the use of the journal/learning log/daybook/ notebook. (We never did agree on what to call it!)

From the beginning we subscribed to Thoreau's view of the journal as "a record of growth and experience, not a preserve of things well done or well said" (cited by Stapleton, 1960, p. 135). That seemed to free our thinking so that our prompts would go far beyond "it's time to journal" and instead push students' thinking beyond their academic world. "After all," commented one of the teachers, "they're only here six hours a day, and, just as we do, so do kids have a life outside of school." Then he added, "Sometimes we forget that, I think." The group also adopted Toby Fulwiler's (1987) challenge: "Every time you ask students to write in class, do something active and deliberate with what they have written" (p. 7).

Each week the teachers brought a copy of the prompts they had issued as well as some of the students' responses. They shared many ways they had used the journals' content "actively and deliberately." There was lively talk, some chuckles, and occasionally a reaction to a response that seemed to be crying for help. Throughout our study, we accumulated the prompts, then shared them with the teachers on the other subject-area committees. And suddenly there was a "journal talk" in the teachers' lounge. Each subject area group began exploring ways the journal could be used in social studies, science, and math.

As the chairperson, I was one of the group. Again, there wasn't a need for assignments; rather, each session was focused on what each person believed to be "for the good of the group."

Reprinted with permission from Lola R. Mapes.

As you think about Lola's narrative, how might you share professional literature with the teachers with whom you work?

_____

_____

_____

_____

_____

After reading the diverse portraits of coaching found in this chapter, what are some similarities and differences you discovered?

_____

_____

_____

_____

_____

As you read the narratives, what appears to be the most difficult aspects of coaching?

_____

_____

_____

_____

_____

What additional information would your narrative of coaching include that you did not find in these narratives?

_____

_____

_____

_____

Now that you have read and reflected on the diverse narratives of these coaches, consider the importance of having a collegial group of coaches with whom you can discuss, ruminate, argue, and clarify the issues you face when coaching. Why is it important?

_____

_____

_____

_____

How might you create a collegial group of coaches?

_____

_____

_____

_____

_____

SUMMARY

In this chapter, several coaches shared their narratives. These narratives demonstrate the diversity of experiences coaches find in the work. Each of these coaches is actively involved in the act of writing. Mary Kim has published three books of poetry, Nan has published several poems and articles, Susie has written a biography, and Lola has published several articles. These ladies did not initially see themselves as writers but as teachers of writing. Now they are writers and coaches of writing, as well as coaches of reading, thinking, and speaking—all the things that comprise literacy. And they coach teachers who don't think like them, pushing them to examine their practices of literacy in order to improve their classroom instruction for all students.

❖ ❖ ❖

Chapter 5 describes where and how we found time to coach in a variety of settings with a variety of teachers.

Scheduling Time
for Coaching

This time, like all times, is a very good one, if we but know what to do with it.

—Ralph Waldo Emerson

This chapter describes five of the time structures we use to deliver coaching. This is a chapter about the "process" or how-to of coaching, not the content. These time structures were developed through collaboration with administrators and staff developers to deliver the coaching process. In scheduling your time for coaching, you may or may not have control over the time structures you use; however, learning how others have scheduled time may inform your thinking and future planning.

Over the past several years, we have used variations of five different time structures for coaching.

1. Team-time structure

2. Release-time professional development

3. District or school professional development days for coaching

4. Before-school coaching

5. Walk/talk coaching

In this chapter, you will find a concise description of each structure and suggestions for its use. The remainder of the book gives you examples of coaches using these structures in urban, suburban, and rural settings.

A note about data before we address structure: the coaching work described in this book resulted from the districts' looking at their data and implementing coaches to support the needed work based on the data. The data informed the coaching. Therefore, the coaches were not involved in the data analysis. However, if you need to learn about data and data analysis, the following books may be helpful:

- *Using Data to Close the Achievement Gap: How to Measure Equity in Our Schools* by R. Johnson (2002). Thousand Oaks, CA: Corwin Press.
- *Results: The Key to Continuous School Improvement* by M. Schmoker (1999). Alexandria, VA: Association of Supervision and Curriculum Development.
- *The Leader's Guide to Standards: A Blueprint for Educational Equity and Excellence* by D. B. Reeves (2002). San Francisco: Jossey-Bass.
- *The Learning Leader: How to Focus School Improvement for Better Results* by D. B. Reeves (2006). Alexandria, VA: Association of Supervision and Curriculum Development.

For an overview of what needs to be done to improve teaching and learning, read Mike Schmoker's (2006) *Results Now: How We Can Achieve Unprecedented Improvements in Teaching and Learning.*

TEAM-TIME STRUCTURE

The Team-Time Structure is based on collaboration. Research on collaboration shows it improves academic achievement. Teachers change their practices more quickly and systemically when they work in collaboration (Hall & Hord, 2001). This structure works best in middle schools and elementary schools where the staff is divided into teams of teachers. When teachers function on a team, they usually have team planning time and the coach works with the team during their planning time. Collaboration arises organically as teachers learn new strategies from the coach, practice them in their classrooms, and receive feedback from the coaches who observe them. When the teams discuss the strategies and their effectiveness as well as examine student work generated from the implementation of the strategies, teachers collaborate as they discuss, examine, and refine their practice.

The coach begins by building relationships with the teachers, then presenting the new material to the teams. Susie Morice's educational narrative of her work (see Chapter 4) describes the efficacy and benefits of the Team-Time Structure. In Chapter 7 you will find a description of the Team-Time Structure used in two middle schools for a period of two years, with improvement in test scores for seventh-grade communication arts.

The advantage of using teacher planning time is that teachers do not have to stay beyond their normal day for the training. In addition, this usually saves district funds, because teachers are not paid extra for attending the sessions. The cost only entails the coach's fee. In addition, coaches usually find this model advantageous in building relationships, due to the smaller numbers in each group.

The disadvantage is that teachers lose some of their planning time and may resent the intrusion of professional development during this time (see Dorcas's comments in Chapter 3). If teachers do not function as a team, professional development could still be offered throughout the day and during individual teacher planning time. The professional development would then reach only the teachers who were free each period that the coach presented the material.

Advantages:

- Teachers spend no required time outside the school day.
- This structure requires no additional funds (except for coach's fee if using an outside consultant).
- Teachers are usually more focused during team time rather than during afterschool time.
- Coaching during team time supports team relationships and builds community between the teachers and the coach.

Disadvantages:

- Teachers lose some of their planning time.
- Teachers may resent the intrusion of coaching during team time.
- Teachers may resent the addition of an "outsider" during team time.
- Teachers may be required to participate involuntarily.

RELEASE-TIME PROFESSIONAL DEVELOPMENT

Release-Time Professional Development provides an opportunity for staff to leave their buildings to attend professional development offered by local universities, service centers, or educational groups. If the coaches provide the professional development as described in this book, the success of the professional development partially depends upon the strengths of the coach's presenting skills to a large group.

In Chapter 8 you will find a detailed description of coaches using Release-Time Professional Development to work with teams of teachers from different districts over a period of 10 years. The coaches meet with the teams of teachers four times a year in two overnight retreats and two full-day workshops.

With this model, the coach often assumes the role of "presenter" in addition to coach; this can work to the coach's advantage or disadvantage, depending upon his or her presentation skills. The coach may search for professional development opportunities in the area that will strengthen the work the coach is doing in the school. As coaches, we alert our teachers to workshops on literacy practices being offered in the area.

Advantages:

- Teachers usually work free from school distractions.
- Teachers can network with professionals from other districts, thus expanding their perspectives.
- Teachers have the opportunity to learn from the experts in the field.
- Teachers may voluntarily participate in the work.

Disadvantages:

- District must provide substitutes for teachers.
- Teachers may lose the collaboration of working with their school team.
- Students lose instructional time with teachers.

DISTRICT OR SCHOOL PROFESSIONAL DEVELOPMENT DAYS

You are probably familiar with this model; districts allot so many professional development days per year and usually bring in outside speakers to fill them. If you are coaching in a district, you might consider requesting the use of these days. You can use them for full-scale presentations to staff or to break up staff into smaller teams for collaboration.

This model works well to introduce a new coach to the entire staff of the school and to get everyone on the same page. Even if you are not working with the entire staff (for example, in Chapter 8, the coach worked only with sixth- and seventh-grade teams), it is wise to present to the entire staff so that everyone in the building is familiar with why we are there.

Advantages:

- The coach meets the entire staff with an opportunity to build the relationship between the staff and the coach.
- The coach demonstrates strategies to the entire staff for classroom implementation.
- The entire staff works and learns together with the coach.

Disadvantages:

- If the coach does not present well to large groups, it could diminish the coach's overall effectiveness.
- The coach must present material that is meaningful across content areas.
- The coach may find it impossible to follow up with all the participants.
- There is involuntary participation.

BEFORE-SCHOOL COACHING

Model A: The coach used time before school to meet with staff members who voluntarily arrived early. These meetings were large group meetings designed to address professional development issues. In Chapter 7 you will read about the collaboration among staff members who regularly attended early morning gatherings at two middle schools.

One middle school wanted to meet monthly about school discipline throughout the school year. The coach used Becky Bailey's book (2000) *Conscious Discipline* to guide the discussions (the principal paid for the cost of the books out of his school budget). The other middle school chose to focus on different topics each session.

This was also a time for staff to tell about favorite educational books they read and report on workshops or conferences they had attended. The coach also recommended books and resources. It was a popular, motivating opportunity to create collaboration and collegiality within the school culture. The school continues this practice today.

Advantages:

- There are no additional costs unless breakfast is served. (We found that coffee and rolls made us happier. The principals provided these from a separate budget).
- There is voluntary participation.
- The group is usually energetic and eager to discuss.
- Teachers may take ideas directly from the meeting into their classrooms.
- The same teachers attend each month, which builds community within this group.

Disadvantages:

- The same teachers attend each month, so the information never directly reaches those who don't attend.
- It creates an "us/them" mentality, with the attending teachers feeling that the absent teachers are the ones who really need the information.

Model B: Once a week before school, teachers who volunteered met in the library of their high school with a coach who volunteered her time. This was a small group of high school teachers who were examining their classroom practices and looking for answers to specific issues, such as classroom management, homework completion, cultural proficiency, and so on. Together they decided on an agenda for the semester and addressed one issue weekly to find strategies to use in their classrooms. This collaboration was cost-free and built community within the group as they collaborated to find the most successful strategies to address each issue of concern. Appendix F contains the list of their selected topics and the ideas they generated as a result of these early morning collaborations.

Advantages:

- This is a no-cost model.
- This builds almost instant rapport and community because of its voluntary nature and the interest of those who participate.
- There is a collaboration of teachers across content areas who may not have collaborated in the past.
- Attitudes improve as teachers share meaningful and useful information.
- This is completely voluntary, so motivation is high.

Disadvantage:

- Information reaches only those in attendance (however, the group presented to the entire faculty at the end of the year about what they researched, discussed, implemented, and learned).

WALK/TALK MODEL

The Walk/Talk Model is simply a framework for collegial conversation that satisfies the need to talk and exercise. When my colleague Susie Morice (whose educational narrative is found in Chapter 4) and I were scheduled to meet each Friday, we decided to take it outside—literally—and walk and talk at the same time. Immediately after lunch on Fridays, we took to the sidewalks surrounding the middle school where we worked. During our 30-minute walk, we brainstormed ideas and solved the challenges we faced in the classroom. If you are a coach who prefers moving to sitting, and the teacher with whom you are working prefers the same, why not suggest a Walk/Talk to process instruction? You both should feel better and think more clearly when you are finished walking and talking.

Advantages:

- This is a no-cost structure.
- This oxygenates the brain and exercises the body.
- This builds close relationships.
- This gives mental breaks to the participants.
- This provides privacy for conversations.

Disadvantages:

- Some staff don't enjoy walking and/or being outside.
- Some schools are not situated in spaces where this is possible (Susie and I walked around the gym if weather did not permit outside walking).

These time frame models of coaching can be found throughout the remainder of this book, both in the educational narratives and in the informational chapters. Feel free to modify these time frame models in any way that better fits your needs.

What coaching structures might work in your coaching situations?

_____

_____

_____

_____

How might you modify any of the structures listed above to fit your needs?

_____

_____

_____

_____

QUESTIONS FOR COACHES TO USE WITH TEACHERS

When you work with teachers, no matter what structure you are using, consider using the questions listed below to elicit discussion about what needs to happen in their classrooms.

Overarching Questions

What do you want to occur in your classroom?

_____

_____

_____

Is what you are currently doing getting you what you want?

_____

_____

_____

What are students learning?

_____

_____

_____

How will I and they know how they are learning?

_____

_____

_____

What evidence do I have to show that they are/are not learning?

_____

_____

_____

What will be done to help students begin to learn the new content?

_____

_____

_____

What will we do to help students continue to learn the new content?

_____

_____

_____

SUMMARY

This chapter offered you several time structures for coaching used successfully over the past decade. Please modify them to fit your coaching needs.

In this chapter you examined

1. Time structures for coaching
   - Team-Time Structure
   - Release-Time Professional Development
   - District or School Professional Development Days for Coaching
   - Before-School Coaching
   - Walk/Talk Coaching

2. Questions for coaches to use with teachers

❖   ❖   ❖

In Chapter 6, you will find three coaching scenarios to read and reflect upon how a coach might mediate the challenges they present as coaches work with teachers who don't think like them.

6

Analyzing Coaching Scenarios

As ironic as it may sound, we're far more inspiring to others when we're willing to listen than when we're giving them advice.

—Wayne Dyer

Coaching scenarios offer you an opportunity to reflect upon and discuss the work of others. This chapter is about the how-to or process of coaching teachers who do not think like you. How well do the coaches handle the process of coaching in the following three scenarios? You can read these and decide individually, or you can use these in a group. The three scenarios described below represent diverse grade levels and diverse situations:

- The first is a report from an outside, independent consultant sent to an administrator at the conclusion of several days in the school as a literacy coach.
- The second is the description of a discipline issue one middle school staff wanted the coach to mediate.
- The third is a classroom observation of a teacher who asked for help in classroom management.

These coaching scenarios may be useful if you are training coaches. During professional development sessions, they could be used for group discussion.

SCENARIO ONE: A FOLLOW-UP LETTER TO AN ADMINISTRATOR

The letter below is based on work at an inner-city high school where the student body was 99.9% African American and the teaching staff was split between African American teachers and Caucasian teachers. In this letter, the coach, an outside consultant hired by the district, attempted to convey with tact and integrity what she had witnessed during her literacy coaching experience.

Date: May 24, 2006
To: Dr. John L. Martin
From: You, the Coach
Re: Work at A. High School

Dr. Martin, thank you for the opportunity to work at A. High School. The following summarizes my observations and suggestions. These reflect my opinion only, based on 15 days of interaction with staff and students.

Observations:

1. A. High School is an extremely well-run high school with strong leadership and with teachers who connect well to students. The students are given clear expectations for behavior, and during the 15 days I spent at A., I experienced students who were polite, positive, and eager to learn. Not one student acted inappropriately toward me, and, in fact, students were far more welcoming and eager to learn than I had been led to expect.

2. Team I consists of a group of teachers who willingly gave up a majority of their conference period for seven days in order to examine the research on writing pedagogy, look at student work, and share examples of successful lesson design. They eagerly discussed possibilities for improved academic achievement and methods to incorporate increased student writing across the curriculum. Some team members are interested in meeting informally this summer to discuss designing an interdisciplinary unit that they might implement next year. The enthusiasm and belief in student ability was obvious among the educators on this team. Several of them borrowed books from me to read on their own time, and they shared willingly and openly among themselves.

3. The Read 180 Program appears to be an opportunity to move students to reading at grade level. The commitment of the department/administration to select strong, committed teachers for this work is a must for the program to work at optimal levels, according to the research.

4. My observations of the junior and senior students with whom I worked in classes and in the guidance office are that the students are capable and willing. What they need to understand and practice are the steps in the writing and reading process. Below are some suggestions to address this observation.

5. Ms. B., Ms. C., and Mr. D. were helpful, supportive, and encouraging. A. High School is fortunate in having committed staff in the area of literacy who believe that all children can learn at high levels.

Suggestions:

1. English teachers begin their instructional blocks with a journal response. This would provide consistency of instruction, practice in writing, brain-compatible

time for the mind/body to prepare for the day's lesson, and an opportunity for students to share their writing. Ms. E. of Team I has a wealth of journal prompts that she has used this semester. What sets hers above the ordinary is that she writes one prompt on the board each day, followed by two to three additional questions to extend student thinking and expand their writing. This is critical (and seldom done) for students who have not been in a writer's workshop model in previous years. This past semester, her student writing has increased from a few sentences to two or three paragraphs in length. In addition, she said her students come into the room wanting to write.

2. Teachers might benefit from a workshop on understanding the difference between teaching and assigning, since "assigning" work is not "teaching." Teachers might benefit from learning concrete instructional strategies (scaffolding) that motivate and support students as they work on "assignments."

3. If a piece of literature, short story, novel, play, poem, and so on is to be used in a whole class assignment, teachers should insist that excerpts are read aloud in class. Then students will hear the language, see the language, and interact with the language before they are just "assigned" to answer the questions at the end of the piece in their literature books. This also is appropriate across the curriculum. In working with students, I found them often attempting to answer the questions without having interacted with the text. A way to eliminate this challenge would be to have the text read aloud during the first part of the lesson. Teachers should read aloud to students and have volunteer students read aloud to classmates.

4. Obtain "A" papers from area schools, such as "High Achieving" High School and "Outstanding" High School (two proximate high schools with scores at the top in state testing) to use as models and share them with staff and discuss how A. High School students can achieve at the same levels (*because they can!*) if they have the instruction, scaffolding, writing time in class with a teacher/coach, access to computers, and teachers who believe that they can.

5. Expose staff to current research on the teaching of writing and offer them concrete strategies to improve instruction. This would include a paradigm shift from believing that good writing is "correct" writing to understanding that good writing begins with student fluency as students develop ideas and, after multiple drafts, evolves into grammatically correct papers. It does not begin with correctness that never fully develops into higher order, sophisticated writing. This entails throwing out the red pens, letting students write without censure as they develop their ideas, and then demanding that the final product for publication be a perfect copy of which they (and their teachers and parents) can be proud.

6. Students then need opportunities for publication such as sharing their writing in class, essay contests, poetry slams, writer's workshops, and so on (the students with whom I worked had amazing ideas, could write extended metaphors, had far better listening skills than I possess, and were eager to write and share their ideas with their peers).

7. Continue and expand the poetry slam that Ms. E. and others directed. Literacy events such as this one build on student strengths and showcase for students and staff the incredible wealth of student intelligence that lies within the walls of A. High School.

Reflect upon this report.

What are the strengths of the teaching staff?

_____

_____

_____

What are the perceived weaknesses of the staff/school?

_____

_____

_____

What additional suggestions might you offer to mediate this coaching situation?

_____

_____

_____

If you were the next coach to come into this school to work with teachers, what actions would you take to create a positive coaching experience for yourself and a productive one for the teachers?

_____

_____

_____

SCENARIO TWO: STUDENT BEHAVIOR AT SCHOOL A

Student behavior is a huge issue in schools. If the staff perceives there is a discipline problem in the school, as a coach you may need to address the issue. Read the scenario below and reflect upon what you might do to help staff address this issue.

School A is in a middle-class outer suburban school district, one that was largely rural but now is growing due to people moving from the large city and suburban areas nearby to this district. Although there has always been some diversity, the diversity is growing, and teachers face cultural issues they have not faced before. Some teachers responded enthusiastically at the prospect of working with diverse students; however, others, unfamiliar with the new cultures, responded with blame.

Their answer to what they perceived as the growing discipline issues was to impose stricter discipline and zero tolerance punishments. A catch-22 resulted. A student with no former infraction on his or her record could now be handcuffed and led from the building by police for shoving another student on the bus (even if the other student shoved first). As administrators attempted to mediate the situation, some teachers felt administrators were not being consistent or stringent enough with their punishment, and this produced a feeling of a lack of control on the part of some teachers. Kids acted out, teachers sent them to the office, and then the decision was out of their hands.

Some teachers blamed the kids for what they perceived as "out of control" conditions in the school. However, to the coaches, who have worked in a variety of other settings, the behavior of the students might appear near "exemplary" in contrast to other schools. This resulted in a "what you don't know you don't know" situation. Having been used to a highly authoritarian "do not question" type of adult control, some teachers felt out of control and angry when they were faced with students who did question or even talk back. Rather than attempting to understand the root cause of the student behavior, they wanted more control, both in the classroom, from the administration, and throughout the school. The sense of tighter control continued to alienate the students rather than build relationships.

Assuming the teachers want well-behaved students, what are they currently doing (or not doing) to get what they want?

_____

_____

_____

If you were asked to address the above situation, how might you respond?

_____

_____

_____

What steps might you consider to alleviate teacher stress?

_____

_____

_____

How might you support teachers to assume responsibility for classroom management?

_____

_____

_____

Below are some suggestions to mediate the student behavior issue:

1. Read Ruby Payne's (2001) _A Framework for Understanding Poverty._ Discuss why the new students, many from backgrounds of generational poverty, use physical force to confront and control their altercations. Decide as a staff what strategies you might implement to ensure a safe environment where students can learn to mediate their differences without physical confrontation.

2. Literacy implementation: When students are sent to the office, the administrator has the students write what happened. He then gives them a problem-solving sheet on which they write what they intend to do the next time when confronted with a similar situation. He talks over with them what they wrote and helps them set goals for their future behaviors.

3. There are many good goal-setting structures available. Ruby Payne's work includes goal-setting cognitive structures. A powerful goal-setting book for upper elementary, middle, and high school students is _Goal Setting for Students_ by John Bishop (2003).

4. Read Becky Bailey's (2000) _Conscious Discipline: 7 Basic Skills for Brain Smart Classroom Management_ as a staff. Discuss one chapter per month at a faculty meeting.

The above actions may help the students, but what does a coach do to support the teachers as they struggle with learned helplessness?

Teachers need to find one thing that works in their classroom, experience the success of the strategy, and then continue to implement it. One strategy that worked extremely well in a school such as the one described above was movement. We suggested that teachers incorporate some kind of movement every six to eight minutes or so. We demonstrated the lesson and showed teachers how they could write in their margins the movement they intended to incorporate. For example, if teachers were presenting an eight-minute minilesson on punctuation, after the presentation they would ask the students to please "stand up" and "sit down." This is an example of movement that is not connected to the lesson but revives the body and brain.

If teachers want to incorporate movement that is directly connected to the lesson, they may want to teach students hand signals for marks of punctuation and have students use them throughout the minilesson. This not only keeps students alert and engaged but allows the brain to process the information through more than one channel, now using kinesthetic movement in addition to the auditory and visual channels in which the minilesson is presented.

Just as we use movement throughout our professional development presentations, we show teachers how the implementation of this simple strategy can transform their classrooms. Teachers commented that they were shocked at the difference in behaviors once they incorporated movement into their classroom presentations. Students calmed down and were less fidgety and more engaged with the material. Jensen's book (1998) *Teaching With the Brain in Mind* is a wonderful resource of strategies and information to improve instruction in the classroom and during professional development workshops.

SCENARIO THREE: THE TEACHER OBSERVATION

According to research, the optimal teacher observation includes three stages (Costa & Garmston, 2002; Marczely, 2001). These include the preconference with the teacher, the actual observation, and the postconference.

During the preconference for this lesson, this teacher shares with the coach why she wants to be observed; in this case, the teacher wants feedback on her classroom management. During the observation, the coach used the coaching sheet (provided in Appendix C) and scripted the lesson. Scripting occurs when the coach writes down everything the teacher says. Realistically, the coach will not capture each word but attempt to write as much as possible. Scripting is a powerful tool because it allows the coach to use the teacher's own words when meeting in the follow-up conference. Some teachers do not want to be videotaped, and scripting may be the next best thing. When teachers see and hear their own words repeated back to them, they are more likely to face the truth.

The following is a portion of the lesson included in the follow-up e-mail to the teacher. In it, you can "observe" the issue of classroom behaviors. The e-mail was sent the same day as the observation. A follow-up conference was scheduled for the next available time.

This teacher was using a board game to teach vocabulary.

The following is the script of the teacher's words during the lesson, unless indicated as class actions (in brackets).

Rachel's class: Board games are passed out, and each student has one.
1:06 p.m.

Class, let's get started.
I'm sorry, Carl, you're right. Let me repeat that one.
Yes. Yes. Yes. Wait. Yes. Yes. Very good. Ah, don't move. Don't move yet. Okay. You may clear your boards for the last game. Mike, detention? Do you want another detention? Excuse me. Are you ready? This is our last game. All right, here we go. Eyes up here.
Detention? Because I've asked you three times.
You know, if I told you that there are only seven different cards . . .
Shhhh.
Daryl, sit down.
Daryl, sit down.
Excellent.
Excellent.

(Continued)

(Continued)

> All right, now I'm going to give you some instructions . . . Did you hear what I said?
> Game chips are coming down this way . . . Please put . . . Excuse me, excuse me.
> Would you please pass . . . ?
> Josh, Josh!
> Shhhh.
> Now, pass your cards thataway.
> You know, I got mixed reviews on this game. Some of you like it. I can't help it.
> Thank you.
> Shhhh.
> Let's go . . .
> Heather?
> Lindsey?
> Shhhh.
> Shhhh.
> Shhhh.
> 1 2 3 4 [students quiet]
> Everyone should have . . .
> Next one's a detention.
> Lacey, I'm sorry, Lacey. Aaaahhhh. Raise arms. Shhhh. Shhhh.
> Shhh. Shhh. All right, ladies and gentlemen,
> Shhhh. [Waiting for students to be quiet] All right. Look at your vocabulary. You're
> supposed to be listening.
> Shhhh. Shhhh.
>
> End of class.

What are your perceptions from reading the script?

_____

_____

_____

The above is a small section of the scripted lesson, but it contains enough to illustrate the lack of classroom management. However, the script alone cannot reveal the entire situation, for the students were playing the game in the midst of the classroom "chaos." The script is one piece of the observation.

Rachel received the entire scripting of the lesson, which was several pages in length. This scripting was typed, since the coach types faster than she writes, so she takes a laptop with her and scripts directly onto the computer.

The coach e-mailed Rachel after the observation. E-mail has both advantages and disadvantages. One advantage is the quick response a coach can provide a teacher; however, e-mails can be misinterpreted, since the reader must rely on the printed word without the benefit of body language cues, opportunities for dialogue, and differences in written communication styles. Ideally, the coach meets with the observed teacher in person, but if the coach is an outside coach who cannot remain at the school for a postconference, e-mail is one way to quickly facilitate communication between the coach and the teacher.

E-mail to Rachel following the observation by the coach:

Dear Rachel,

Thanks for asking me to observe your class. I scripted your words, although I didn't write down the content but concentrated on the pedagogical comments. The entire scripted lesson is attached to this e-mail.

How do you think the lesson went? What would you have done differently? What would you have done the same?

As I said yesterday, most students were on task. You used several modalities and built in kinesthetic activities. The students appeared to enjoy the lesson.

Read through what you said and reflect on how your language supports learning and if there are times when it continues the interruption. In Becky Bailey's book *Conscious Discipline,* she gives phrases to use when class is interrupted.

Think about the tone of your voice. Are you using the adult voice? Did you use a parent voice or a placating child's voice during this lesson? Out of the three voices—the adult, the child, and the parent—the goal is to stay in the adult voice.

In Ruby Payne's book *A Framework for Understanding Poverty,* there is a section on the three voices. Please review that section. Children who are at risk might become confrontive if the teacher uses the parent voice.

Please look at your schedule and let me know asap when we can meet.

What do you notice about the e-mail? Do you find it too direct?

_____

_____

_____

How might you respond differently to Rachel?

_____

_____

_____

There were clearly issues of classroom control in this teacher's classroom; however, there were positive things occurring too. She was using a game to reinforce vocabulary attainment as suggested in Marzano and Pickering's (2005) *Building Academic Vocabulary: Teacher's Manual,* and the students appeared to like her. Research on tone and passive language would be a powerful resource for this teacher. She fits the description of passive women teachers who use passive language, then resort to aggressive language, rather than using assertive language in their instruction.

These scenarios offer you an opportunity to assess your coaching skills in three different situations.

What have you learned from reading the scenarios?

_____

_____

_____

How will you incorporate what you've learned into your coaching practice?

_____

_____

_____

SUMMARY

In this chapter, you read three scenarios where coaches are called upon to use diverse skills. These include writing a report of one's work and suggestions for the building administrator, mediating teachers' concerns over student behavior, and scripting a teacher's lesson followed by feedback via e-mail. These scenarios offer opportunities for reflection, discussion, and future planning.

❖   ❖   ❖

In Chapter 7 you will find a model lesson using several literacy strategies you might use when you coach. In addition, there are several suggestions for professional development workshops to reach teachers who don't think like you.

7

Using Classroom Demonstrations and Professional Development Workshops as Coaching Tools

Education is our passport to the future, for tomorrow belongs to the people who prepare for it today.

—Malcolm X, author, civil rights activist

Coaching takes many forms, and as coaches, we are often asked to do demonstration lessons as well as present workshops for teachers. This chapter includes three coaching workshops we have used successfully. Each of these coaching experiences includes both the how-to and the what-if of coaching. They demonstrate the process and the content of coaching. Each includes writing as an integral piece. These workshops support teachers to become teachers of writing and writers themselves, a necessary component that leads to improved student achievement (Schmoker, 2006; Smith, 1983). The following professional development experiences illustrate the power of coaching when it is used to

> - Demonstrate the power of writing with students or teachers
> - Differentiate a professional development workshop
> - Present a "writing to learn" workshop in the content areas

As you think about the importance of writing in the workshops you present, ask the following questions:

Do you have teachers write when you meet with them? If so, what kinds of writing do you have teachers do when you meet with them?

_____

_____

_____

If not, then how might you do that?

_____

_____

_____

You can use writing prompts with teachers just as teachers use them with students. Using a writing prompt and having participants write to the prompt for two or three minutes is a powerful way to begin your team meetings. For example, you might ask teachers to write what they have observed in their classrooms since the last time you met with them. You can keep these writings short; nevertheless, they are powerful vehicles to evoke background knowledge and set the stage for conversation.

You can find suggestions on how to build a school culture of readers and writers in *How to Teach Students Who Don't Look Like You* (Davis, 2006). Chapter 12 outlines how to inspire learners to love reading and writing (including teachers), and Chapter 14 outlines how to build a balanced literacy classroom using a reading and writing workshop approach. You can share the following guidelines for writing in a balanced literacy classroom with those you coach:

- Student choice of topics
- Personal conferences
- The teacher writing with students
- Peer response
- Specific, positive feedback
- Publication of student writing
- Student choice in reading
- Shared discussions about reading and writing
- Journal writing and sharing (p. 124)

When you model these with those whom you coach during your time together, you walk the talk and build collegiality in literacy. I write when I give a prompt to others (often on the overhead in sight of others), and I share. Nothing speaks louder than our actions.

Even though the guidelines above apply to English classes, many apply to other disciplines. Writing to learn in the content areas is a powerful way to introduce teachers to writing strategies that work across the disciplines.

If you are asked to demonstrate the power of using writing with either students or teachers, consider the following.

DEMONSTRATING THE POWER OF WRITING WITH STUDENTS OR TEACHERS (ELEMENTARY, SECONDARY, ADULT LEVELS)

Do you want a literacy lesson that works every time? The following lesson has been used with elementary school students, middle school students, high school students, university students, men in prison, adolescents in a runaway shelter, women in a homeless shelter, and teachers in a variety of settings.

If you need to model a lesson for staff at a school, this is an excellent one to try. This was modeled with students and adults the coaches had not met before they walked into their classrooms. It works well for presenting to an unknown audience.

Preparation for the Demonstration

1. Find some writing that connects with the audience you will be teaching. This may be the most important piece of the lesson. Suggestions for finding provocative writing that will motivate your audience to produce stunning writing in a matter of minutes is an exciting task. Consider keeping a folder of essays as you spot them in newspapers, your favorite magazines, student publications, and so on. Some that have connected to audiences are the following:

   - Collections of essays and stories written by adolescents
   - Sandra Cisneros's book, *A House on Mango Street* (1989)
   - Poems that reflect the cultures of the students in the class, such as *Cool Salsa: Bilingual Poems on Growing Up Latino in the United States* (Carlson, 1994)

   Find pieces that touched you to the heart when you first read them, so you can share that emotion with your group.

2. Find someone in the class who will read these to the group. Don't read them yourself unless absolutely necessary. The peer group in the class will become more engaged if the pieces are read by their peers. Look for someone who mirrors the author of the writing. For example, if the piece is written by a young Black male, look for an adolescent male of color to read the piece.

3. Consider allowing a student to choose a poem. In one class a Latina girl chose a far more sophisticated poem from *Cool Salsa* to share with the class than the teacher had planned. The girl engaged her peers immediately.

4. Choose a variety of works to present. Not too many—two or three short pieces are enough. An exception to this is if you are a storyteller and want to present a longer piece yourself. Search for diversity in presentation, including gender and ethnicity. Since students are usually exposed more to White people talking at them (on the TV news, teachers, etc.), this is a powerful opportunity to ask students of color to share the writings with the class. This strategy works to engage the students of color because you have honored them with a position of power in the lesson.

5. Give the pieces of writing to the readers ahead of time. Have one copy for them and another for you and one for the teacher or group for whom you are modeling. This allows the reader to practice and become more comfortable. It works better if the audience does *not* have a copy of the material being read to them because it forces them to listen and then connect the story to their own lives rather than dwelling too much on the model writing.

Building Community Before the Lesson

Spend some time getting to know your audience and establishing their comfort zone with you. Tell them exactly what you will be doing and why.

For example:

"Thank you for allowing me to be here today and taking up your time. I really appreciate your generosity. Today I am modeling a lesson on writing for your teacher. The purpose of this lesson is twofold: first, it shows you the writing genius inside of you and reveals your writing voice; second, it demonstrates for your teacher how simply we can reveal the genius within each one of you.

"How many of you like music? [You raise your hand really high and usually all students raise their hands.] Think of one of your favorite musicians ["one of" rather than your "favorite" allows the students to quickly make a choice]. Does everybody have someone in mind? How many notes does it take for you to recognize a song by your favorite musician? Raise your hands. One? Some raise hands [keep your hands up]; two, more raise; three, more; four—[everybody's hand is up].

"That is the musician's unique sound. You too have a unique sound. When you write, we call your unique sound your writing voice. Voice is one of the most exciting aspects of writing, if not the most. It's what sets your writing apart from every other person alive. What we're going to do today will demonstrate your writing voice to yourself, and to others, if you wish to share."

When you are coaching teachers, explain to them all the subtleties you have incorporated into your model. For example, in the previous sequence, which takes a couple of minutes, you can find the following:

- Honoring the students by thanking them
- Honoring the students by telling them exactly what you will be doing
- Honoring the students by telling them why you will be modeling the lesson
- Connecting to student interest by telling them you will be revealing their inner genius
- Connecting to students by using music as your analogy
- Using brain-friendly strategies by asking the questions in such a way that all students will be involved. No one will remain invisible.
- Using brain-friendly strategies by using physical movement where each student will raise his or her hand during the questions

It is important to point out these intentional strategies to those you are coaching. You know you are incorporating them, but your teachers may not see them or understand why you are doing something unless you make it explicit.

Suggest that teachers go through their written lesson plans and embed physical movement every few minutes. Use a colored pen to denote movement. If you embed movement every 6–8 minutes, you will keep students' bodies more relaxed and connected to the lessons.

The following presents a more complete outline of this lesson. Grade-appropriate literature was selected. As stated before, this lesson can be modified to fit any age level, depending upon the writings you choose as models. If children are too young to write or cannot write in English, they might illustrate their stories that have not been transcribed.

Demonstrating the power of writing with students or teachers

Below is the demonstration lesson. You are reading both the strategy, why it is used, and what the teacher says. If it were possible, there would be a voiceover explaining the strategies the teacher uses as she conducts the lesson; instead, the strategies are written in bold face in boxes. Notice how many strategies are used. While the coach demonstrates the lesson, she asks the teacher to observe and write down the strategies she observes the coach using.

Greet/meet/share

The teacher greets and meets the students. He or she can stand at the door and welcome students as they enter, making eye contact and saying hello.

Building community; I Care strategies

The teacher tells the students exactly why and what he or she plans to do, explaining goals and telling them the state standards that will be addressed in the lesson.

The daily check-in; see Senge, 2000

The teacher uses a building community strategy such as the daily check-in. Using this activity, the teacher asks a question, then gives an option to students to answer or say "pass." For example, the teacher might ask, "What is something you enjoy doing on Saturdays?" One student begins, then students answer in turn or choose to say "pass." This activity gives all students an opportunity to speak, every voice is valued, there are no wrong answers, the teacher and the class learn things about each other, and it allows students to switch their focus from outside to the inside of the classroom. The norms are listed below.

Norms

1. Answer in one word or phrase loudly enough for all to hear.

2. You may choose to say "Pass."

Reflection—higher-level thinking

The students process the activity with the teacher.

Process/Reflect: The teacher asks the students to reflect on the check-in, then poses a similar question: "What kinds of things happened when we did the check-in?"

Following this, she tells students to "take a minute and either think to yourself or talk to someone sitting near you."

Then students share their reflections, citing that the activity offers

- No wrong answers
- Humor
- Everyone's voice in the air
- Community building
- Commonalities with peers

Even though this sounds time-intensive, it can all be done in fewer than five minutes, including the processing.

The teacher continues the lesson, introducing metaphor and movement.

Metaphor

"We did the activity for all the reasons you stated, and today we're going to focus on one special reason—your unique voice. What is your voice? Come up with a metaphor that describes your unique voice." The class shares their metaphors.

The teacher continues.

Visualization

"Think back to your favorite musicians.

"Just like your favorite musician's unique sound, you also have that unique sound when you write. Your teacher, after a few weeks, can probably recognize who wrote which paper without a name on it, even when it's typed."

I Care strategies—telling students what they're going to do in class today

"Today we're going to access your unique writing voice, and the reason we're doing this is because it is important for you to cultivate your unique voice and learn how and when to use it both in writing and speaking. We're going to begin by using some examples of others' unique voices. All of these poems and writings share things in common, so let's hear them."

I Care strategies—including students in delivery of content and choosing a variety of students

"Will the students who agreed to read the poems please come forward?"

Suggested writing for fifth grade:

- Read Mary Kim's poem about a favorite piece of clothing.
- Read Gary Soto's poem about his favorite shoes.
- Read Langston Hughes's poem about friendship.

Suggested writing for twelfth grade:

- Read Kevin's essay from *The Laws of Life* (Veljkovic & Schwartz, 2001).
- Read "Prison Life" and "My Son" from prison anthology created in the prison class (Davis, 1990).
- Ask if anyone reads Spanish and would like to read the Spanish poems from *Cool Salsa*.
- Ask students to differentiate between the voices of the authors.

Note: Choose literature appropriate for the participants in your group. The following is used with students in fifth through ninth grades. You may adjust the topic according to your age group, depending upon the literature you choose.

| Group work/modalities and movement/state change |

"Okay, your teacher says you work in groups, so please find your group, and when you're settled in your group, raise your left hand like this."

| Brainstorm to access background knowledge |

"In your group, decide who will take notes in your group: note taker, raise your hand. Now quickly, we're only going to take a short time—brainstorm all the words that you can think of that have to do with friendship. These words could have been in the poems or they didn't have to. Go! Stop. Okay. Let's hear some of these. Note taker, please read three words from your list."

| I Care strategies—include some from all groups |

"Next group, please share three but none that we've heard. Now you've heard lots of words. Thank your group members and return to your seat."

| Individual class work—modalities |

"You have heard four poems that talk about favorite clothes and how a piece of favorite clothing is like a good friend and a beautiful poem just about friendship, so it's time to tap your inner voice and write something of your own."

| Setting norms and boundaries, lowering stress and threat |

"Before you do, please know a couple of things. First, you do not have to share what you wrote in class unless you want to. Second, this is very special private time, so protect your writing time. Don't be distracted by anyone or anything. Protect yourself. If you can't think of anything to write, just put your pen to paper and write 'I can't think of anything to write' over and over until something pops into your head."

| Goal setting |

"We're going to set a goal to write a personal piece using your unique voice during the next few minutes. This is just a rough, rough, rough, rough draft; it is not a perfectly finished product. And remember, I said you don't have to share unless you want to."

| Brain research: giving choices—prompts range from recall thinking level to higher-level metaphorical thinking |

"Your writing prompt is 'Think about what friendship means to you. Do you have a special friend you would like to write about? Do you have a special piece of clothing you would like to compare to one of your friends or to friendship in general?' Finally, if there is another topic you feel like writing on, go ahead. Any comments or questions (opportunity to ask questions—lower stress and threat)?

"All right, then for the next several minutes, you have private, quiet writing time. Usually, I would write too, but since I have not worked with you before, I'm going to quietly walk around the room to see if I can support you in any way.

"We're ready to begin. Let's have our bodies tell our minds we're ready."

Brain research—movement

(Everyone stretch high into the air and take a deep breath)

"Now turn your brain on. Like this. Begin."

7–10 minutes writing time

I Care strategies

With seconds left, the teacher says,

"Finish that thought" (this allows writers to finish their thought rather than stopping in mid-thought).

Movement—state change

"Shake out your hands.

"Take a minute, read what you wrote, and circle any parts you really like."

Put back into groups—if time.

Count off in groups. Decide who will be a timekeeper.

"Begin with #1. You each have one minute to share. You may read your piece to the group or you may choose not to read it; however, if you don't read it, you still have one minute and the group sits quietly for the time to pass.

"Now, who would like to read to the class or nominate someone to read to the class?"

Brain research—norms for reading to class

- Good listening skills
- 100% snap or clap when finished
- Jot down words or phrases you like
- "I wonder"

A detailed explanation of the response model is found in Chapter 11.

Have two to three students read, depending upon time.

Final processing: exit questions

"Please write out the answers to these questions on a half sheet of paper to hand in to me as you leave.

- What did we do in class today?
- Why did we do it?
- How does it connect to your life?"

Teacher summarizes class work

"Today, we set goals—wrote—listened to poetry and prose—heard each student's voice in the room—engaged the whole brain—shared work."

The teacher collects the exit questions from each student, saying good-bye and making eye contact.

The teacher collapses into a chair (just kidding—perhaps).

SUGGESTIONS FOR USING THIS ACTIVITY IN OTHER DISCIPLINES

1. Select a good article in the discipline in which you teach.

2. Read it together in class.

3. Build background knowledge and vocabulary knowledge as needed to ensure all students understand the article.

4. Give students a choice:
   a. Students can write themselves into the article as a scientist, a historian, a spy, and so on.
   b. Students can become an inanimate object in the article by personifying the object and write from a first-person point of view. For example, if the article is about the proposed moon landing, the student might become the nose cone of the rocket and tell the story from that point of view.
   c. Using a historical article, students can write themselves in as a character.
   d. Have students write from both points of view as they read and discuss a controversial topic. Have them take the opposite view in an article that argues from one side. They also can write from the opposite gender, a different age, ethnicity, and so on. Some of the best writing for this assignment came from the men in a college writing prison class when they wrote from the persona of the woman who was in their life when their trial took place.

How might you use this lesson with the teachers and students with whom you work?

_____

_____

_____

Writing activities such as the one described above build community and create a space where every voice is heard. As coaches who care passionately about the future of our children, we are the educators who must prepare for it today through our coaching.

The next example shows how you can differentiate a presentation so that it honors the background knowledge and learning styles of the participants.

DIFFERENTIATING A PROFESSIONAL DEVELOPMENT WORKSHOP: HONORING ADULT LITERACY SKILLS AND CHOICE

Have you ever been asked to do a literacy workshop for staff? Few people understand how much work goes into planning a workshop. Perhaps some of the following will support your work.

Three years ago, Sue McAdamis, president of National Staff Development Council (NSDC) and professional development director of the award-winning Rockwood School District of the St. Louis area, suggested that I "differentiate" the three-day workshop I do for their teachers. I had presented the workshop the previous summers in a nondifferentiated format, offering the same material to the entire group throughout the three days. Taking her suggestion, I differentiated the workshop, and what a difference it made. By differentiating, we offered participants the option of choosing their own method of delivery throughout the three-day workshop, thus honoring their learning style and their background knowledge of the material.

For example, examine the outline below. To differentiate a workshop, do the following:

1. Set up three rooms and several conversation pits, if available (don't forget about outside for the folks who prefer to be outside). One room is for the large group presentation. This room holds your handouts, your overhead, computer, coffee, goodies, and all the things you need for your central presentation.

2. Video room: The second room can be a small room or private place for participants to watch videos.

3. Book room: This is a room filled with as many books as you can find to use as resources for your workshop. Over the years, I have collected books related to literacy, and in this room I lay out the books for participants.

4. Conversation area: This can be an area outside the presentation room where two or more folks can sit and carry on a conversation about the work. Especially appreciated is a picnic table outside for the participants who process better in the open air.

After an initial introduction, you as the presenter offer participants a "differentiated" experience. They may choose to stay with the large group for any or all of the time slots in the presentation, or they may choose to use one or more of the sites listed above.

This truly honors educators. You are saying to them that you trust them to choose what they need to learn best throughout the entire scope of the workshop. How do teachers respond? They love it. Most of the teachers will stay with the large group; however, those who learn best individually might leave and go to the book room. Those who learn best through processing out loud with others may choose the conversation pit. Those who desire the visual input of a video may choose to view and learn in the video room.

Will an educator ever abuse these options? Not often. However, it may occur occasionally. Instead of getting angry, realize that this person would probably have gotten off task had he or she been in the large group with you, too. I remember workshops where I did work other than what was presented in the workshop, and I did it under the presenter's nose. But this only happened when a presenter did not engage my brain and provide the input, processing time, and physical movement to keep me engaged. As long as you provide brain-compatible presentations (see Marcia Tate's 2003 book, *Workshops Don't Grow Dendrites*), you can count on those educators staying engaged, and if they don't, they would not have engaged, no matter how much freedom and differentiation you allow.

Differentiating workshops may not be an option in every district where you work. It treats teachers as professionals and takes someone such as Sue to believe and trust that her teachers will choose wisely. If you are working in a "hierarchically" based district, you may find the administrators less than willing to believe that teachers will make good choices.

What steps can you take to differentiate the presentations/workshops you do as a coach?

LITERACY WORKSHOP: WRITING TO LEARN IN THE CONTENT AREAS

Below is an outline of a two-day writing in the content area workshop. This is a differentiated learning experience that offers educators an opportunity to choose what they believe will most benefit their instruction. After instruction in Robert Marzano's strategies for building background knowledge through the acquisition of vocabulary, teachers choose the strategies to implement in their lessons. They can choose from the resources offered during the workshop and from Janet Allen's (2004) *Tools for Teaching Content Literacy.* Below is a sample agenda; you can build it to fit your own needs. This can also be offered in a three-day workshop format.

WRITING TO LEARN IN THE CONTENT AREAS

Textbooks

1. *Building Academic Vocabulary: Teacher's Manual* by Robert J. Marzano and Debra J. Pickering (2005).
2. *Tools for Teaching Content Literacy* by Janet Allen (2004).

Dates: Thursday, June 8, and Friday, June 9
Time: 8:00–3:30
Webster University credit: 1 hour available
Presenter/Instructor: Bonnie Davis
Level: K–12

This workshop is for all levels, since it is differentiated to meet your individual needs.

"Writing to Learn in the Content Areas" is a course designed to provide teachers with the research, strategies, tools, and resources to create writing-rich lessons in their content areas. Teachers will study the vocabulary research of Marzano and Pickering (2005) in their book *Building Academic Vocabulary* to build background knowledge in their content areas for their students. In addition, they will compose lessons using Janet Allen's (2004) *Tools for Teaching Content Literacy.* The three days will be spent in reading and digesting the research and in creating personalized lessons for content subject matter. Teachers will share their lessons with the class members, and a district coordinator will visit their classes to observe their teaching the lessons they designed during this course.

Day 1: How to Build Background Knowledge in Your Content Area by Improving the Vocabulary of All of Your Students

8:00	Introductions; participants discuss why they took the workshop
8:15	Rationale: research and reasons for "writing to learn" in the content area
8:30	Building academic vocabulary
10:00	Break
10:15	Work time for participants; participants now differentiate their instruction, choosing to work with the strategies that most appeal to their teaching style and student population
11:00	Discussion; sharing
11:30	Lunch
1:00	"Writing to learn" strategies—Janet Allen's (2004) *Tools for Teaching Content Literacy*
2:00	Work time—participant choice
3:00	Sharing with colleagues
3:30	Adjourn

(Continued)

(Continued)

Day 2: Writing in Your Content Areas—Ideas, Lessons, Projects (you choose what works for you and your students and create a lesson packet in your content area)

8:00	"For the Good of the Group"
8:15	Janet Allen's (2004) *Tools for Teaching Content Literacy*—continued
10:00	Break
10:15	Work time—participant choice
11:30	Lunch
1:00	Strategies/tools for writing to learn
2:00	Work time—participant choice
3:00	Final sharing
3:30	Adjourn

Completed assignment for credit: Teachers must complete a lesson packet, using "writing to learn" as the central vehicle for student learning in their content area. Teachers will share the lesson packet with the class and turn it in to the instructor to be graded.

Differentiating presentations and workshops causes us to walk the talk. For years we have encouraged teachers to differentiate their instruction while we asked them to sit and passively learn in our workshops. Differentiating our workshops has created a powerful learning environment for all involved.

How important is choice in this workshop?

_____

_____

_____

How might you add more differentiation and choice in your presentations?

_____

_____

_____

SUMMARY

This chapter outlined three coaching experiences:

1. The classroom demonstration

2. Differentiating a workshop presentation

3. The writing to learn workshop

These three workshops—the demonstration using writing, the differentiating of content and process for a three-day workshop, and the writing to learn workshop—offer tools for coaches to use while honoring both students and the teachers who teach them. You can pick and choose what pieces of each might work for you as you build your coaching repertoire.

❖   ❖   ❖

In Chapter 8 you will find how these and other literacy experiences fit into a year-long professional development plan to increase student achievement.

8

Using Literacy Strategies Across Content Areas to Improve Student Achievement

To be a teacher in the right sense is to be a learner. I am not a teacher, only a fellow student.

—Søren Kierkegaard

This chapter, based on real work in a real district, is an example of the process, the content, and the results of literacy coaching. Even though this coaching was done at the middle school level (Grades 6 through 8), the process and content are applicable elsewhere. The areas of concern, written below, are found at the elementary level and the high school level as well. As you read the chapter, consider how you can use the information to inform your coaching work, no matter what level you coach. How might you transfer this work to your district or school coaching? The following are suggestions:

- Find how this district's schools compare to yours
- Examine the plan used to decide if it fits your coaching work
- Use the sample letters and workshop outlines as models for your work
- Review Marzano's research to find what matches your needs
- Show teachers the description of the work and ask them if it would match their needs
- Use the chapter in a workshop for coaches as a centerpiece for discussion
- Use the section on scripting to introduce scripting to coaches
- Use the questions for examining student work with teacher teams
- Read the part on classroom management with a staff to determine their classroom management needs
- Show the teacher pieces to a staff and have them discuss them
- Use the administrators' writing with administrators and have them reflect on the work done in their schools
- Use the entire chapter as a case study with a university class, faculty, professional developers, or administrators

Spelled out is the road map we used to engage the staff in the process of examining their instruction, improving their instruction, and, ultimately, improving student achievement. Just as Kierkegaard said that "to be a teacher in the right sense is to be a learner," we learned that "to be a coach in the right sense is to be a learner." We coached, and we learned as we coached. Perhaps our learning will save you time and mistakes. One good coaching resource is the School Improvement Network's (2005) DVD set, *Instructional Coaching: School-Based Staff Development for Improved Teacher and Student Learning.* In these, Joellen Killion, Jim Knight, and Stephen Barkley provide expert advice on coaching. This DVD program allows the viewer to see coaches working in real schools as they meet, train, encourage, and motivate teachers.

The work described in this chapter began a few years ago when Dr. Cheryl Compton, assistant superintendent in charge of curriculum/instruction, contacted me about coaching work. She was concerned that the staff had worked hard the year before to improve instruction but had not seen the results they had hoped to see.

After a year of implementing coaching, Dr. Compton had this to say about the coaching process:

Coaching is such a key component of any plan to raise achievement. We often talk about embedding professional development into our daily work. It is difficult for teachers to implement new ideas and strategies without collegial conversation. Growth comes through observation and inquiry. It is so important for teachers to have that outside coach, someone who serves in a nonevaluation role, to provide ongoing support in the classroom and through follow-up conversation. The coach models, coteaches, observes, and inquires to invite deeper levels of thinking by the teacher. The coach invites participation by developing a trusting relationship with

> *the teachers. Teachers want to learn and grow. They want to help students achieve at high levels. They also want to be sure they are taking risks and trying new ideas and strategies in a safe and supportive environment. Our work with Bonnie achieved all of these objectives. The results: year one scores improved by 10% to 12%! This work does make a difference!*
>
> Reprinted with permission from Cheryl Compton, PhD, superintendent of the Ritenour School District, St. Louis, Missouri

In the meantime, they had disaggregated data and examined the state tests to find their areas of weakness. She identified their areas of concern, and she believed a literacy coach could coach teachers to improve their instruction in those areas of need. The areas of concern are the following:

- Students' lack of proficiency in differentiating between comparison and contrast
- Students' lack of proficiency in transferring writing skills learned during classroom instruction to standardized tests
- Students' lack of proficiency at completing academic tasks

Too often students misread the questions on the tests, used poor writing skills to answer the questions, and left items on the standardized tests incomplete. Knowing we had a finite number of weeks, the administrator had chosen three strategies she wanted to emphasize. These used cognitive structures to improve instruction and taught students goal-setting skills to improve their task completion. With these areas of concern in mind, we chose to use the Venn diagram, the Frayer model, nonlinguistic representations, and goal-setting models. Using Marzano, Pickering, and Pollock's (2001) *Classroom Instruction That Works: Research-Based Strategies for Increasing Student Achievement* as a guide, we set out to coach teams of teachers on instructional strategies to mediate their areas of concern.

However, we knew just "telling" teachers these things would change nothing and certainly was not "coaching." We also knew we would be working with many teachers who did not think like us—teachers who taught different content and viewed the world through different lenses. We had to find ways to connect with the teachers and build collegiality in order for the teachers to share their work. We needed to provide teams of teachers with the opportunity to come together to share lessons and the student work generated as a result of their instruction. They had to discuss and evaluate the results of the implementation of the strategies in order to help increasing numbers of students improve their academic achievement. Yet, "mere collegiality" wouldn't "cut it," in the words of Mike Schmoker (2006, p. 179). We needed more.

Judith Warren Little found that when collaboration or collegiality lacks a focus on achievement results, there may be little change in the quality of teaching (cited in Schmoker, 2006, pp. 177–178). On the other hand, according to the research of Fullan, Darling-Hammond, and Little (p. 178), when teachers focus on student achievement results, their collaboration generates "higher quality solutions to instructional problems, increased teacher confidence, and, not surprisingly, remarkable gains in achievement" (cited in Schmoker, 2006, p. 178). This focus on student achievement results became our goal. We believed by focusing on strategies to support improved instruction in the areas of need, we could improve student achievement.

We implemented a coaching model whose intent was "to grow intellectually, to learn more about learning, and to mutually increase their [teachers'] capacity for self-improvement" (Costa & Garmston, 2002, p. 112). This would not be a deficit model, one that relied on "fixing bad teachers," but rather one where we coaches worked "at the coaching process as hard as the teacher is working at the teaching process" (p. 112). We coaches knew we would be learning as much as, if not more than, those we coached. Even though we would be introducing strategies to improve teachers' instruction, we wouldn't be telling teachers what to do; we would be modeling and working alongside them as they designed how they would implement and teach the material.

THE TARGETED GROUP

We agreed that the coaches would meet with the sixth-grade and seventh-grade English/history teachers at the district's two middle schools. Teachers in charge of special education would also attend the meetings. At the meetings, held during teachers' planning time, we would introduce a strategy compatible with the targeted areas of concern. Then teachers would implement the strategy, be observed, receive individual feedback, and meet in teams to share student work. Each of these steps is an important one. Teachers need to learn the new strategies, and they need observation of their implementation of that strategy. Giving them individual feedback sets the stage for growth. In fact, Costa and Garmston (2002) state that "processing the instructional experience allows the teacher to facilitate construction of new meanings and insights" (p. 155). Finally, teachers need to meet in groups to examine student work.

What ideas from the passage above might work in your coaching situation?

_____

_____

_____

_____

INTRODUCTORY WORKSHOP

To honor the knowledge of the entire staff, we held an introductory workshop that explained the role of the coach, what was to be implemented, and why. We explained why a limited number of staff was targeted (resources and time) and how the implementation would occur. Staff had an opportunity to ask questions and reflect upon the work. We introduced this framework during the workshop:

- Coach presents research-based instructional strategy at team meeting.
- Teachers design lessons and implement the strategy in their classroom instruction.
- Coaches observe the teachers and give nonevaluative feedback to a question posed by the teacher relating to the implemented strategy.
- Teachers look at student work to assess the impact of lessons and strategies.

Some staff members who were not going to take part in the coaching model were apathetic about the information, and the staff who would be involved expressed concerns ranging from lack of time to excitement about trying something new to improve instruction.

FOLLOW-UP LETTER

We wrote the following letter to the staff to further explain our role in the building.

Dear Teachers,

Thank you for your participation in our workshop last week! We look forward to working with you this year.

We will begin our work next week. During our first meeting, we will examine Marzano's research on similarities and differences. Using his suggested cognitive structure, the Venn diagram, we will examine ways to use it during the following week within an already existing lesson. On Nov. 11 or 12, we will look at student work generated as a result of your using the Venn diagram with your students.

Please bring the following to our first and second meetings:

Meeting 1: The handout from last week and specific times when you would like to be observed for nonevaluative feedback on the question you pose to us.

Meeting 2: *Three examples of student work* using the Venn diagram. Bring what you consider a poor example, a typical example, and a good example. We will examine your student work during our second meeting.

Our strategy during our work together is the following:

- Learn, do, show
- Examine the model
- Teach/use it with students
- Share and examine student work

We will do observations during the weeks we work together and give you specific, nonevaluative feedback.

We will focus on these three areas:

- Comparison/contrast
- Nonlinguistic representations
- Goal setting

We look forward to seeing you next week.

THE FRAMEWORK FOR TEAM MEETINGS

The team meetings were held approximately every two weeks. During this time, we introduced the strategies.

Our team meetings followed this time frame:

Greetings and statement of purpose: 5 minutes

Introduction of strategy: 15 minutes

Logistics (planning for observations and conferences): 5 minutes

Strategy 1: *Comparison/Contrast*
First two meetings, spaced two weeks apart: On the day of the second meeting with staff, coach observes teachers implementing the strategy.
Third meeting: Teachers bring examples of student work. On the day of the third meeting, coach observes additional teachers implementing strategy.
Publication of student work

Strategy 2: *Nonlinguistic Representation*
First meeting: Coach demonstrates application of nonlinguistic representation and ties it to comparison/contrast.
Second meeting: Teachers bring student work and discuss observations.
Third meeting: Same as second

Strategy 3: *Goal Setting*
First meeting: Coach demonstrates goal setting.
Second meeting: Teachers share stories of using goal setting.
Third meeting: Teachers process the year.

PROCESSING THE TEAM MEETINGS

We agreed to keep our portion of the meeting to 25–30 minutes so that teachers still had time during their planning time to take care of their own business.

We began these meetings in November and continued them until the week before the state exams in April. This is a framework that can be implemented quickly with few materials. Below are some of the advantages and disadvantages of using a model such as this one.

Advantages:

- Staff hears implementation strategy with peers and can discuss it during the meeting.
- Coach is available for Q&A and for observations and feedback.
- Coach is not a staff member, so does not bring school "baggage" to the meetings.

- Coach does not know staff members, so negative assumptions are limited.
- Sessions occur during planning periods, so no additional time is required of teachers.
- Three concrete areas of strategies have been identified that are compatible with the data found on standardized tests.
- The three areas of strategies can be applied across disciplines.

Disadvantages:

- Time is too short and teachers lose planning time.
- Teachers have other things on their minds. Some teachers later in the year need to be at special meetings and miss meetings.
- Coach does not know the teachers, so needs to spend time building relationships.
- Coach does not have information about teachers and staff that might be pertinent to the learning.
- Administrators can't be present at each meeting.

Once again, these strategies work; however, as Schmoker (2006) states, "'Identifying similarities and differences' is a powerful teaching strategy—at the top of Marzano's list. But it won't have much impact until a team finds a good situation in which to apply it, until we adapt and adjust this strategy on the basis of assessment results in actual lessons" (p. 117). The proof is in the student work. As we continued to examine student work and labored to improve student achievement, we found the following:

UNEXPECTED OCCURRENCES

Meetings were voluntary at one school and mandatory at the other. One English teacher often skipped team meetings, therefore creating a single-classroom teacher on that team at the meetings. One school had common planning periods for both sixth-grade teams and seventh-grade teams, therefore allowing for better conversation and dialogue. At the school where the team consisted of only one history/English teacher, less diversity in thought occurred.

One unintended and positive result was that other staff members wanted to attend the meetings, so during some planning periods, the coach would be met by the entire team consisting of the English teacher, history teacher, science teacher, math teacher, and special education teachers. This created the richest avenue for change, since the entire team was present and engaged with the work.

As the year progressed, more and more teachers wanted to join the meetings. The principal at one school designed a before-school meeting for anyone interested in talking about classroom instruction and school issues. He provided breakfast, and we met for 30–45 minutes. This was entirely voluntary and resulted in 10+ staff members at each meeting. These meetings provided an outlet for discussion, introduction of new ideas, and a forum to frame and discuss school issues. It may not be significant, but the gender balance at these meetings consisted of the principal and assistant principal, who were both males, and one male teacher. The remainder of the attendees were female staff and support staff.

During Year 1, I served as the sole literacy coach; however, during Year 2, a colleague of mine came on board because she lived in the area and I had moved from Missouri to California. I recommended Susie because I knew her well and she had been coaching literacy for several years in a variety of schools. In the 1990s, Susie and I had taught together at a middle school in one of the highest achieving districts in the state. We had served on the same seventh-grade team, and Susie was the literacy coordinator for the school. We met weekly with our teams, and she and I met each Friday, when we "walked and talked" for a planning period to discuss our curriculum. We had an excellent relationship for three years, and she mentored me in areas of content and relating to middle school students.

With two of us working together, we found once again advantages and disadvantages of working with an additional coach:

Advantages:

- We could process and plan together.
- We complemented each other's strengths.
- Some teachers bond better with one coach than the other.

Disadvantages:

- Each of us spent less time with the staff, thereby potentially lessening the overall effect the relationship might have in bringing about change.
- The time between meetings was longer, so I found myself meeting with staff every four to six weeks, rather than every other week.
- Some teachers bond better with one coach than the other (this is both an advantage and a disadvantage).

After Year 1, Susie and I focused on teacher instruction and student work, rather than on introducing more strategies from Marzano, Pickering, and Pollock's (2001) *Classroom Instruction That Works*. We believed there was a need for teachers to use some of the strategies they already practiced but with more rigorous content. We were supporting teachers to understand what quality work at the secondary level consisted of and to insist that their students engage in that work. Too often, student expectations were mired in preconceptions about students' abilities based on race, class, and former achievement.

TEACHER OBSERVATIONS

We observed the teachers on the teams largely based on a question each teacher gave us. After reflecting on their practice and deciding what they wanted observed, teachers invited us in to give them feedback directly related to their concerns.

Appendix C gives you a sample of a guide sheet we used when observing teachers. We also made this guide sheet available to them. However, the actual observation was based on the question(s) posed by the teacher. Ideally, we would supplement the observation with videotape, so that during the postconference, the teacher can see herself or himself as you discuss the lesson.

The following is an example of part of a scripted lesson in which the teacher asked us to observe (1) how much time up front should I spend to build community before I begin teaching content? and (2) how well do I keep students on task?

SCRIPTING

Joan

Sixth-Grade Social Studies

11:13 a.m.

I have things to share with you but I need you to be ready to hear them.

Rubric. Here's what I want you to do.

Everybody, eyes up here.

One rubric per story. Kleenex box on desk.

Start staplers around.

Okay. All right, folks. Okay. I understand, but it's supposed to be ready to go. Okay, listen up. I'll tell you when we're quiet.

You never start learning, do you? The brain is a muscle, you've got to flex it.

Here's what I'd like for you to do.

Would you collect from this row, Andrea? And Tom?

All right. Thank you, sir. Thanks for catching that, Alex.

I'm troubled by that. It's a safety concern.

Okay, time to shift gears, guys. Time to shift gears.

What did you do that for? That's silly.

All right. Here's what we're going to do now. First of all, we're going to go to our notebook. . . . So see how fast you can get your notebook out and everything put away.

Okay. Right? Recycling, we're still third to last, but we're closing in on third period.

Can I finish? Okay.

(Continued)

(Continued)

> All right, we've got to get going. We've got to get going. Q/A with students.
>
> That's our bad.
>
> Okay, are you guys ready?
>
> Okay. Okay. We're proud of you and we need to continue. Okay.
>
> Can someone explain . . . ?
>
> Wait a minute. I believe we can't hear when we all talk at the same time.
>
> 11:25 [Begin class focus on content]
>
> I'm going to teach you a big word today that is going to make you feel really smart.
>
> Hold on, as soon as it's quiet, I'll tell you what I need you to write down. Hold on, hold on, let me get a word in edgewise.
>
> Socioeconomic impact—it only looks scary. You guys know what that means. I want you to think while you're writing and give other people time to think. Now, does anyone have a good guess . . .

The lesson went on, but by this time, there was feedback available concerning her two questions. In a follow-up e-mail, this was suggested:

> Dear Joan,
>
> Thank you for asking me to observe your class. I scripted what I could capture, focusing on your directions and pedagogy, not on content. Marzano suggests asking yourself these questions after an observation:
>
> What do I think went well?
> What did not go well?
> What will I do differently in the future?
>
> You asked for observations on how much time you should spend on building community before you begin teaching content and how well you keep students on task.
> As you read over the scripting, what conclusions do you reach?
> Please let me know when we can meet to discuss your observation.
> Thanks!
> Bonnie

What do you observe? Does this teacher build community before she begins her lesson?

_____

_____

_____

Are there indications in the scripting as to whether students are on or off task? If so, what are they?

_____

_____

_____

FOLLOW-UP CONFERENCE

Notice that the e-mail includes neither praise nor criticism. The nondirective feedback is objective observation with questions to stimulate and guide the dialogue between us in our follow-up conference. These questions preceded the follow-up conference in which she and I talked about her concerns. We brainstormed activities that would build community while focusing on the content.

For example, since the teacher wanted to better utilize class time and connect with the concept she planned to teach, she could have used a writing prompt that ties to the content to place students immediately within the context of the concepts to be taught that day. When students walk in, they respond to the writing prompt posted on the board. After students write to the prompt, she would ask for volunteers to share their responses. As the community builds in the classroom, more students begin to share. She can then segue to the concepts from the material shared from the writing prompts.

She could have also used a "check-in" question (Senge, 2000) that relates to the content. For example, she might ask, "How much money would make you feel rich?" Then she would go around the class, giving each student an opportunity to answer or say "pass." When finished, she might tie this to the content with a statement such as, "Today we're going to talk about the socioeconomic impact of the South on . . ."

The follow-up conference is a rich opportunity to connect with teachers and support their reflection on their instruction. When approached in a nonthreatening, nonevaluative manner, teachers respond in kind. This teacher used the above suggestions to establish a writing ritual to use to begin her class. This focused the students and set the stage for her content lesson.

LOOKING AT STUDENT WORK

Looking at student work focuses teachers on the question of what is proficient student work. Student work might reflect that it does not represent what students at a certain grade level are capable of doing. Douglas Reeves (cited in Sausner, 2005) remarks that you can ask five different grade-level teachers for samples of student "proficient" work and receive "five radically different qualities of work" (p. 32). This appears to be a major issue. Susie and I found that student work sometimes fell below the grade-level expectations that we saw in more academically achieving schools while still above that of some we found in poor achieving schools where we also coached. More than once, teachers whose son or daughter attended a prestigious private school in the area would comment on the level of work their child was doing, which was far above what was expected of the students in their classes, but did not see the disconnect. We attempted to get teachers out to observe in these schools; however, if they were too far removed from the school culture in which the private school teachers worked, they tended to miss the connection to what their students were capable of with similar instruction.

I experienced this firsthand when I left one school district after 24 years for another district. In the first district, a good solid district where students scored above the median on the state tests, I had learned to expect one level of student achievement. However, because "I didn't know what I didn't know" about student potential, I undersold my students' abilities. When I moved to the high-achieving school district and changed from teaching twelfth-grade students to seventh-grade students, I found that some of my seventh-grade students could do the work my former twelfth-grade students had been doing. I had to readjust my expectations. I found this out from my team members such as Susie. In 1991, we had daily team meetings and were looking at student work. We were not familiar with the term "professional learning communities," but we functioned as a collegial, reflective team who examined student work and modified our lessons to meet the needs of our students. This certainly contributed to the achievement of our students and to the success of this middle school that to this day consistently ranks among the highest in the state.

At the middle schools in the district where we were coaching, we found student work displayed in the hallways that reflected the level of work that students in high-achieving elementary schools were doing. It was once again a matter of what staff didn't know they didn't know—not a matter of laziness. They literally in some cases didn't know what "good expectations" were at that level.

Looking at student work gave us the opportunity to examine growth over time as well as teacher and team expectations.

Advantages for looking at student work include the following:

- Teachers collaborate with team members.
- Teachers understand the alignment between standards, instruction, and assessments.
- Teachers improve pedagogical skills.
- Teachers focus on extended student learning and outcomes.
- Teachers have the opportunity to share reflections and metacognition.

When teachers engage in looking at student work, they usually experience some level of cognitive dissonance in which "their beliefs and practices are dramatically challenged as they study their teaching and student learning" (Langer, Colton, & Goff, 2003, p. 27). This kind of cognitive dissonance seldom occurs during the teacher's day (Tompson & Zeuli, 1999), so teachers need an intervention over time that provides an analysis of student work (Goff, Colton, & Langer, 2000; Putnam & Borko, 2000) in order to grow as reflective practitioners and change classroom practice.

We ask teachers to bring student work along with their assignment and the rubrics they use when grading the assignment. When we meet with teachers to look at student work, after connecting with the teachers, we pose questions. For example, we may ask

- What does the work tell us about John's ability to use a comparison and contrast cognitive structure effectively?
- What is working for John?
- What still isn't working for John?
- Have I given John enough instruction and practice in using the Venn diagram or other cognitive structures used in the lesson?
- What should I do next?

In the above example, teachers examined student work resulting from the use of cognitive structures to reinforce learning, such as the Venn diagram; however, when teachers think about their entire assignment, we want them to question the appropriateness of the assignment and the amount of instruction and practice inherent in the assignment. As we proceed, we engage the teachers in dialogue to "expose their own thinking effectively and make that thinking open to the influence of others" (Senge, 2000, p. 9). The more we model this, the more teachers are willing to expose their vulnerabilities so that we can all learn from the process.

As we examine the entire assignment, we want teachers to reflect upon the kinds of teaching strategies that would most effectively teach the concept. For example, with these teachers, we would discuss the Marzano strategy we had tried that would now best teach the concepts of their lessons, or if one of the ones we had practiced, in fact, actually fit into their new assignments. And if they felt it was a fit, then we want to know why. "Why?" is a question we often found lacking, both in teacher reflection and in teacher instruction. What and when were more prevalent than why and what-if. These kinds of questions force both the teacher and the students to think at higher levels. The important point is that teachers look at their assignments, examine the student work, and reflect upon what they were doing, then ask themselves how they might teach this lesson differently the next time. Cathy A. Toll poses another important question in *The Literacy Coach's Desk Reference* (2005), when she asks teachers the following: "When you think about the kind of readers and writers you want your students to be, the kind of teaching you want to do, and the kind of classroom you want to have, what gets in the way?" (p. 173).

Other questions teachers might ask are the following:

- What are students learning?
- How will they and I know how they are learning the material?
- What will be done to help students begin to learn the new content?
- What will we do to help students continue to learn the new content?
- What will be done to help students be effective learners?

The importance of looking at student work over time is critical, because the evolving of the student work can help break teachers' preconceived ideas about ability in their students. If a teacher approaches the student work believing that John can only do so well and will never do as well as Mary, then this is an issue. In many schools, this is a huge issue. Teachers often refer to certain students as smart and others as not so. Our system of honors classes reinforces this paradigm. Looking at student work over time gives us an opportunity to chip away at these deep-seated ideas about ability in students. Teachers are redirected to their own instruction as a means for students achieving success, rather than blaming it on students' lack of ability.

How do you find exemplary work to share with the teachers you coach?

You can serve as a conduit to show teachers what student work can look like. But there are issues here. If Susie and I had just brought in samples of student work from the high-achieving district where we had formerly taught, it may have impressed some teachers and caused them to raise their expectations. However, for some staff, this would have antagonized them and made them more resistant to our suggestions. It is far better if we can support the teachers in obtaining excellent student work from their own students and then creating a set of models they can use in the future that arose from their student population.

In the meantime, how does one support the school in highlighting student works that serve as models of excellence? One must ensure that the principals are on board and recognize the problem and then work with them to improve the situation. Some simple guidelines improve the levels of student work.

When I taught seventh grade, I required that all writing to be graded or "published" had to be typed, with the exception of class journals. This eliminated so many headaches on my part and on the students' part. Immediately, however, an equity issue of access to computers can arise if the teacher does not build in writing time in the classroom for all students. Luckily, I was able to adapt Nancie Atwell's (1998) reading and writing workshop model to my classroom, and that eliminated the problem of access to technology for typed papers. During the writing workshop, students were always working on drafts or in the process of typing. Some students enjoyed drafting on the computer, and they worked at home, brought discs in, and so on. I was flexible with time and allowed students to be writing, keyboarding, reading, writing in their journals, and so on during workshop time. This way there were always several students in the room working on different areas of literacy. Some students might go to the computer room during class time; some might have laptops or computers available in the classroom; others might be working on another aspect of the writing/reading workshop. But, bottom line: all essays and stories were typed for the final draft and for publication. Now when student papers and projects were displayed in the hallways, everything was in print, not handwritten, easily making the work look more professional.

Another suggestion would be to have a parent or a graphic artist visit your class and show students how to improve the look of their papers and projects. Just a simple lesson in design can improve the visual aspect of any project. It definitely will improve the visual aspects of a published work.

As a coach, if you are looking for exemplary student work, one suggestion is to check out what the best private schools in your area are teaching in literature courses in the eighth, ninth, and tenth grades. In the eighth grade, you may find *To Kill a Mockingbird, Romeo and Juliet,* and Greek and Roman mythology. In the ninth grade, you may find *Lord of the Flies, The Catcher in the Rye,* more Shakespeare, the *Iliad,* the *Odyssey,* the *Aeneid.* The written expectation is usually a research paper and several five-paragraph essays emphasizing the persuasive essay and other argumentative forms.

Now check out lower-achieving public schools. Do they offer students the same rigor and hold the same expectations? Oftentimes no. They may expect students to write a paragraph, not an essay, by ninth grade, and they may be reading Hinton's *The Outsiders* in ninth grade. There is nothing wrong with *The Outsiders;* however, when you have students in private schools or high-achieving public schools reading rigorous texts, they are going to continue to outscore other students on state tests, SATs and ACT, and so on. This does raise a conundrum. What about student interest? Good teachers must create interest in their students as they tackle rigorous texts. Coaching is one avenue for supporting teachers to find methods to do just that.

SCHOOL DISCIPLINE AND CLASSROOM MANAGEMENT

In this era of high-stakes testing, school discipline and classroom management can become the scapegoat for teachers who feel out of control. This happened to me when I transferred from twelfth grade to seventh grade. Discipline in my college composition course consisting of twelfth graders was not an issue: the students were engaged, motivated, and academically successful. Yet when I began to teach seventh graders after having taught seniors and adults for the previous 12 years, I experienced discipline problems. Students were confrontational and off-task. First I blamed it on the students. But eventually, with the help of my more experienced team members (who served as coaches, but we didn't give them that title in the early 1990s), I began to realize that I was the one who had to change, and mostly, I had to change my instructional delivery. Luckily, I was able to institute Nancie Atwell's reading and writing workshop model, and that solved my discipline challenges. Students became so engaged in reading books of their choice and writing their own stories, and I was able to build relationships with them and build a community of learners.

Rather than confronting issues of instruction or cultural proficiency, teachers may see discipline as a major issue. We encounter this issue in our coaching. At the schools discussed here, Susie and I held a different perspective about the schools' discipline than the teachers teaching in them. Coming from a school district that used a nonhierarchical system of discipline and encouraged students to question the status quo, Susie and I were used to high-spirited students who confronted us and the lessons we taught on a daily basis. Therefore, we found the students in these middle schools to be docile and respectful. In fact, we found it difficult to get students to question authority and the status quo. At the same time, we were working in a variety of schools, from the very wealthy to the very poor, and found that discipline depended upon the school culture, the expectations of the staff and administration, and the individual classroom.

In order to support staff in examining the issue of discipline in their classrooms and schools, we suggest the following:

- *Observations in Other Schools.* Have teachers observe in a variety of schools. Teachers need to see that there are inner-city schools with terrific discipline and there are schools out of control in inner-city, suburban, and outer-suburb schools. Not only is there a school culture that determines the discipline, but there is a hierarchical and nonhierarchical system. Schools that foster belief systems and programs that build responsibility often find their nonhierarchical system builds a community of learners. After staff observes at several schools, have a faculty discussion of what was observed.
- *Changes in Instructional Delivery.* Sometimes students acting out in class is due to a lack of variety in the delivery of instruction. When teachers vary their instruction and embed movement and brain-compatible activities (see Eric Jensen, 1998), teachers see a difference in student engagement.
- *Brain-Compatible Instruction.* Once again, using *Teaching With the Brain in Mind* (Jensen, 1998) or other sound brain-compatible teaching books offers a sound basis for pedagogy.
- *Good Directions.* We used Rich Allen's (2002) *Impact Teaching* as a guide for giving powerful directions.
- *A Time-Out Area in the Classroom.* Use a time-out area in your classroom for students to choose when they feel out of control.
- *The Family School House.* Promote the buy-in that every staff member is responsible for every child. When staff sees the student population as one family, student behavior improves.
- *Positive Commands.* Use only positive statements for behavior commands. For example, "Walk!" instead of "Don't run!"

TEACHER EXAMPLES

The following teachers share how they partnered with us to improve their instruction:

- **John Hefflinger**—Middle school math teacher who also teaches English and reading
- **Erin Groff**—Middle school art teacher
- **Julie Pallardy**—Middle school special education teacher

John Hefflinger

John is a sixth-grade math teacher who teaches one period of English per day, as do the other teachers on his team. When we met him, he was close to burnout, having taught 17 years and transferred from one middle school to the other. He opened his heart and his practice to the professional development the coaches offered, and his engagement with his classroom practice skyrocketed.

In John's words:

I am entering my 19th year as a teacher, all but 4 years of it in middle school. As I begin this new year, I do so with enthusiasm and eagerness. This was not always the case. Somewhere in the middle of my career I lost my drive due to a series of unfortunate events. My career began again when I met Dr. Kevin Carl, Dr. Gerry Kettenbach, and Dr. Bonnie Davis. These three individuals believed in me and saw my potential as an educator. Dr. Carl brought me into a new environment. Dr. Kettenbach reintroduced me to the world of professional development and let me know it was OK to think out of the box. Dr. Davis taught me to look at teaching through a different lens. With her lead and encouragement, a new world has opened up. Everything from the way I set up my room to interaction with colleagues has changed. I have a new perspective on teaching and learning. As each student enters my class, I see a fresh lump of clay ready to be molded into a lifelong learner. Each lump is different; some are lighter than others, some are more refined than others, and some are easier to work with than others. Nevertheless, I see an opportunity for me to have an influence on the future, which is why I became an educator in the first place. As a result of Dr. Kettenbach's direction and encouragement and Dr. Davis's instruction and insight, I was selected as the 2005/2006 Outstanding Middle School Teacher of the Year.

Reprinted with permission from John Hefflinger.

John's Description of His Classroom

What follows are some of my classroom practices, many of which I learned from our literacy coaches and their workshops. They have been the catalyst for my professional development and have caused me to rethink my approach to teaching. They have reignited a dwindling flame, resuscitated a love for learning and teaching.

Wednesday Ramble (Reading or Language Arts): Every Wednesday students put away their books and write. They are given 10 minutes to write about anything they want. They must write for the entire 10 minutes. When the timer goes off, they must stop, even if in mid-sentence. Then students gather for sharing time. During this sharing time, students are encouraged to read, but no one is forced. On the rare occasion when a student suffers from writers' block, affectionately called "brain constipation," I will give the student a writing prompt. The Wednesday Ramble writings are kept in a folder to allow students the opportunity to look back at previous weeks. This activity is greatly anticipated, and when I forget or the schedule doesn't permit us to have Wednesday Ramble, I hear about it from the kids.

Exit Cards (All Classes): I use exit cards in several different ways. The feedback from the students is invaluable. I might ask them to tell me what they learned that they didn't already know, to write about what confused them about today's lesson, to write about what they now know they don't know, or to just write about anything, anything at all. My usual practice is to read each exit card and use the information to help me in planning or modifying the next lesson. When I do this, I make a point of telling the students that I am

(Continued)

(Continued)

going to revisit the previous lesson and modify it, or a certain skill taught in the lesson, based on the information I received from their exit cards. I have often found it necessary to respond in writing to a few comments made on the exit cards. This was always a thrill for the kids to receive a note from the teacher, and it also encourages students to take the activity seriously because they knew it was meaningful. I use exit cards two or three times a week.

Word Problems (Math): The Achilles' heel of math is the dreaded word problem. I have tried many different techniques to teach how to solve word problems: make a list, look for a pattern, make a table, guess and check, work backward, draw a picture, to name a few. Just this year I came up with a new technique. I wrote a word problem on a sheet of poster board. Then I cut out each word, placing a magnet on the back. I then reassembled the problem on the dry erase board. When the kids came into the room, we discussed how "garbage" words get in the way of solving word problems. Students are then placed in groups and each group is given a copy of the problem and a pair of scissors. The groups are instructed to identify words they consider to be garbage words. Next they are told to cut out each word in the problem and separate, or pull out, the garbage words. The next step can happen in different ways. I may have groups come to the board and, using my model, show the class what their cleaned-up problem looks like and then open up for discussion. Sometimes I will have each group write the cleaned-up problem on a large sheet of paper and hang it on the board or wall and then have our discussions. Students seem to enjoy this activity.

Seat Changes (Any Class): Much to the disappointment of my subs, I have no seating charts. Students in my room don't sit in one seat for very long. On occasion, when I have a struggling student working well with another student, I will keep them together. The kids never know how I will mix them. I may tell the youngest or oldest child at each table to stand and trade places with each other. Sometimes I do seat changes at the beginning of class, sometimes at the end, and sometimes, not often, in the middle of class. I tell my kids that the world is full of friends they haven't met yet. Seat changes give kids an opportunity to possibly meet a new friend or at least work with someone they wouldn't have chosen on their own.

Vocabulary (Math Class): On the next page is a copy of the vocabulary sheet I use in my math classes, modified to fit the page. Students are given 26 sheets at the beginning of the year. These are placed in their binders to be used throughout the year. I keep a Master Vocabulary Binder in the front of the room that is updated as the kids update theirs. When we begin a new unit, I will display the vocabulary words and have students write the word and then make a guess as to its meaning. Sometimes I will let the students work in their table groups, but most of the time this is an individual activity. After we go through the list, we will discuss student guesses, and then I will give them the definition we will use in class. I tell the students to avoid using the dictionary, as it will often use adult language, and we want to use our language. As we progress through the unit, students are encouraged to list the steps and/or write examples in the box provided. Students soon catch on that this is a valuable tool when I tell them they may use this on certain assessments such as state tests. This also encourages them to become "a student," as they now have something to take home and "study."

WORD Abundant number	Steps involved and/or examples
MY GUESS	
MEANING When the sum of a number's proper factors equal more than that number	

WORD Algebraic expression	Steps involved and/or examples
MY GUESS	
MEANING An expression that contains at least one variable	

I Know What I Don't Know (All Classes): As I mentioned earlier, I have had students tell me in exit cards what they now know that they don't know. I will also have them write it out and take it home to their parents with the hope that Mom and/or Dad will be a part of the student's learning and help the student discover what he or she doesn't know. I need to add here that during the first week of school, I inform the kids there are two types of people in my classroom: students (those who study) and seat occupiers. I let them know it is my quest to have them all be students before they move on to the next grade. During the course of the year, many kids will come up and ask if they have become a "student" yet. This gives us an opportunity to conference. That being said, the I-know-what-I-don't-know activity encourages the students to discover away from the classroom. Sometimes I will stop whatever activity is going on at the time and have the students write I-know-what-I-don't-know statements and then get together in small groups or with a partner to see if they can help each other. This activity must be closely monitored to keeps kids on task. I supply any resource material I can to assist students in this time of peer helping peer.

I do my best to be the "guide on the side, not the sage on the stage" during this time.

Communicating With Parents (All Classes): I have found that establishing communication with parents is crucial to educating children. When the child knows that Mom, Dad, and teacher are a team and we communicate, that child becomes less of a problem. My goal is to convince

(Continued)

(Continued)

the parents we are indeed a team. The first week of school I e-mail each parent a copy of my grading scheme. Each parent is e-mailed our team's homework daily. Those who don't have access to e-mail can pick up the assignments by calling the school's homework hotline. The form below is something I e-mail parents. I will use this form as a way of communicating positive notes. This form can be printed and sent home with the child or sent via snail mail for those parents who don't have access to e-mail. Also, this school year I will hold town hall–type meetings with my parents. These meetings will be held once or twice a quarter. The purpose will be to create a sense of being on a team. I believe it is important for the parents to view me as a teammate working with them for their child. At these meetings we will discuss how they, the parents, are dealing with the transition to middle school. Parents will be encouraged to share strategies they have used to help their child become better organized, one of the most difficult skills for a middle schooler to master. The range of issues that can be discussed are endless. My goal is to have these discussions parent-driven. I will serve only as a moderator and the catalyst. One of the difficulties will be to avoid getting involved in a parent conference, where one parent wants to talk only about his or her child and only with the teacher.

MATH NOTES

PARENT BULLETIN

Date: March 29, 2006

Subject: Math quiz

Dear Mr. Anderson,

John needs to take a math quiz that he missed this week.

I am making myself available Thursday morning at 8 a.m. so your child can take the quiz. If coming in the morning is not an option, then your child can stay after school Thursday and take the quiz in Mrs. Montgomery's room.

Please call me at (636) 443-4468 or return this note with your signature.

Class Meetings (All Classes): Last year I started having class meetings. I would greet the students at the door telling them they needed no books or supplies for that day. My tables and desk were moved aside and the chairs were arranged in a circle. After attendance, the students and I would discuss class or school issues. I tried to get the discussion rolling and then sit back and listen as the kids led the way. Only on a few occasions would I have to change the direction the kids were going. The kids really liked these informal discussions, and I was able to learn volumes about what was going on in the hallways and byways of our school.

> **No D's or F's Allowed (All Classes):** I believe any child placed in my room is capable of earning at least a 70% for a quarter grade. If at any time during the quarter a child's quarter grade drops below 70%, he or she is invited to stay after school with me until we bring that grade back up to 70%. If I am unable to stay after school with the child, I will send necessary work to the Study Club supervisor, where the child can work to bring up the grade. This no-failure policy has been a big success with parents, and I have received cooperation from them.
>
> Reprinted with permission from John Hefflinger.

Read about John's writing club experience in Appendix G.

Erin Groff

Erin Groff is a middle school art teacher. She was a second-year teacher when we met her, and she too soaked up everything we offered. She writes:

> *Many of the strategies I learned from our coaches increased participation in my classes and helped me to connect with students. The changes I made were simple. For example, I gave each student a handshake when they entered the room and a high five when they left. These actions sent the message to all learners that they were welcome in my room. Eventually, some students even started giving me high fives when they saw me in the hallway. This is a far cry from the days when my students looked the other way when they saw me coming!*
>
> *Bonnie and Susie demonstrated ways to connect with students when distributing supplies that is another simple, effective change. Instead of passing out papers myself or calling on the same volunteers repeatedly, I followed their lead and chose helpers by saying, "Which person at your table has the most pets?" or "Who was born the farthest away from Missouri?" This strategy was fun, and it helped us learn about each other while increasing student participation.*
>
> *Bonnie encouraged us to let the students move around the classroom to break the ice and give their brains a break. She suggested the "ABC's of stretching" taken from Becky Bailey's book* Conscious Discipline, *which I incorporated into the beginning of my classes. For example, N stood for neck rolls and D represented dance. It was fun to think of an activity for every letter, and the students reminded me of the ritual if I ever forgot! This encouraged many students to break out of their comfort zones and become an active part of the class community.*
>
> *These are just a few of the effective strategies I've tried since I began working with Bonnie. They were fun to develop and easy to incorporate. Most important, they improved my rapport with students and helped me reach students who otherwise might have been overlooked in my lessons.*
>
> Reprinted with permission from Erin Groff.

Julie Pallardy

Julie is a special education teacher with 29 years of experience who has worked with special needs students from early childhood through twelfth grade.

She currently teaches special needs middle school students in a contained classroom. Her professional duties include being the department head in charge of development and implementation of service delivery models that facilitate maximum regular classroom instruction for special needs students. She is also the special education summer school coordinator. She currently participates in Teachers' Academy (described in Chapter 10).

A Big Solution: Teaching Students How to Understand and Manipulate the Terms Used to Give Directions on Standardized Tests

Goal. Students learn and use in a meaningful way the terms used to give directions on standardized tests.

Philosophy. Most students can learn vocabulary and transfer this knowledge to new situations with new content. However, for some students, especially those with special needs, the new content and vocabulary can be confusing. The students described here need an intense lesson where the content does not interfere but complements the vocabulary. The theme of these lessons has been elephants, but this type of instruction may be adapted to any theme.

The students watched a video on the elephants and took notes. Any graphic organizer may be used as the teacher sees fit. The information in the video provided them with background knowledge to use in learning the vocabulary.

Describe. The students were told the story of the blind men meeting an elephant and how each man described the elephant differently, based on the part of the elephant he touched. Some students may benefit from acting out the story. A graphic organizer that includes the five senses works well with this activity. They then complete a writing activity to describe an elephant.

Contrast and Compare. Students research the Asian and African elephants. They take notes and then complete a Venn diagram to contrast and compare the elephants. Then they complete a written activity to contrast and compare the two kinds of elephants.

Infer. This lesson requires more instruction on the word "infer." Lots of discussion needs to take place on making good guesses (inferences) and bad guesses. The students need to practice making good and bad guesses using clues. They then read an article about elephant trunks so that they have information and clues to use in making an inference. The students were to infer the answer to the question "What would happen to an elephant if the trunk was severely injured?"

Trace. Any story with a sequence can be used to trace a sequence of steps. The students watched *Horton Hatches an Egg* and traced the steps that Horton took to hatch the egg. The students used a graphic organizer with sequencing steps. Picture notes can be used instead of word notes to trace the sequence.

Formulate. The students discussed the term "formulate" and the different kinds of plans they may formulate. They need to be reminded that a plan has many parts. The students were asked to formulate a plan for a fundraiser to feed an elephant. The students need to research the cost of feeding an elephant. There are many graphic organizers that can be used for this. Then a writing activity can be finished. They can produce posters and flyers for the fundraiser and actually put on the fundraiser if it is feasible.

Predict. The students will research the daily feeding, cleaning, exercise, and waste production of an elephant. They need to identify these as the variables used in predicting what would happen if an elephant lived in their backyard.

Analyze. Students research information on the declining elephant population. Using a graphic organizer, have the students separate the different factors that are contributing to the declining elephant population.

Explain. The elephant is considered a cornerstone animal in the environment. After researching this, have the students explain why the elephant is a cornerstone animal.

Summarize. The students read or act out the story of "How the Elephant Got His Trunk." They are then to summarize the main points of the story.

Support. By now the students have an extensive knowledge of elephants. They can use their previous notes and writings in this activity. The most important part of the elephant is its foot, trunk, size, or ear. Support your answer with information from your elephant book.

Evaluate. The students will research the use of elephants in the circus. They can use a graphic organizer to take notes. They then need to list good and bad points of having elephants in the circus. They then need to make a final judgment regarding the use of elephants in the circus and support it with facts.

Students create notebooks of their learning. Because of all the activities in which they engage during this unit, they learn the material. One observer was so impressed with their learning that she had no idea they were special needs students. Students enjoy using the elephant as the vehicle for learning the terms; however, they could replace the elephant with many other animals, objects, or persons and do the same activities. This is just one example of creating concrete activities from the lessons that must be taught. This adds fun and variety to the daily grind of vocabulary study.

Reprinted with permission from Julie Pallardy.

PRINCIPALS' REFLECTIONS

At the end of year two, the principals of the middle schools reflected upon the coaching work that had occurred in their schools.

Principal of Middle School A

Anyone who's been in any line of work for a period of time has attended numerous workshops, seen the light, and come back ready to change the world. One week later, 99.9% of us are doing the same old thing in the same old way, and our investment of registration fees and time might as well have been flushed down the drain. I suppose the minimal change hypothesis may apply, and microchanges may occur in how we do business that magnify over time, but I don't think that they justify the expenditure of resources.

The one single thing that makes a difference in folks actually applying what they've learned and been so inspired by is the support they find back at work for implementing those changes. They need support from their supervisor *and* from their colleagues. What, you say, we're not supposed to suck it up and do it all on our own? No, I say, you're not, and you're pretty much a fool if you think you can consistently do so—or you should tackle the problem of world hunger if you're that successful all on your own.

The support supervisors give can take many forms. They need to validate the new learning and, it often seems, give permission to try new things. A couple of years ago I supported a couple of teachers attending Marilyn Burn's Math Solution workshops. They came back very inspired and ready to implement. I encouraged them and purchased a few materials they needed. A few weeks into the school year, one of them talked to me about how she felt she was muddling through and wasn't sure she was doing it right. I shared that when I did similar work, I experienced the same thing, and that it would start forming a groove and that, while progress seemed slow at first, the groundwork laid would allow faster work and deeper understanding later. With this permission, she continued to work with the concepts and has improved her teaching. Uncertainty is part of new learning and implementation, and supervisors need to validate the experience and encourage folks to work through it.

Another kind of support that supervisors can provide is time. Teachers implementing new things often need to observe and dialogue with others who are engaging in the same kind of work, either in their own school or another school. Ideally, more than one person from a school attends the same training, not just to have someone to talk to about it, but to have implementation partners. For them to implement together, they need to have time to observe each other and talk. If they share a plan period, they can talk but can't observe each other. If they don't share a plan time, they can observe each other but may not have time to talk. In either instance, the principal may need to provide subs or cover classes himself or herself to allow the collaboration to happen—not just once, but on an ongoing basis.

Similar support can be provided through the use of instructional coaches or teacher leaders. In either model, the support provided is *not* supervisory or evaluative in nature—it is supportive and challenging. The use of teacher leaders generally requires the school/district to assign a teaching position to coaching colleagues—an ongoing commitment on the part of the organization. An alternative is the use of instructional coaches that are contracted during the implementation of a new teaching strategy or curriculum. Jefferson began this process five years ago with a one-time training for the whole faculty in Ruby Payne's Frameworks for Understanding Poverty. We then contracted the same consultant to train the faculty in some instructional strategies for closing the achievement gap between the general population and select subgroups. This led to a districtwide middle school initiative to train communication arts and social studies teachers in various strategies to improve student thinking and achievement. To ensure that implementation occurred, the consultant met regularly with these teachers and their instructional teams to reinforce the techniques and introduce new techniques. She also regularly did brief observations with feedback to each teacher on how that teacher was implementing the strategies and the observable impact on students.

This made all the difference in our implementation of these strategies over other implementations that I've seen schools attempt. Too often, once the door closes—despite best intentions—folks return to the comfortable and the known. Having an instructional coach keeps people honest to the commitments they've made to themselves. While the initial implementation was mandatory for the communication arts and social studies teachers, participation became voluntary over time. The consultant remained just as involved and with a varying group of teachers. To facilitate extended involvement, we've featured breakfast meetings for anyone wishing to participate each morning the consultant is in the building, and this has proven, in itself, to be a support in its own right.

The step in which we're currently engaged is teachers taking ownership of the coaching through a peer coaching model. The consultant is not as available as she was in prior years, and this has been an ideal means to segue into a peer support model. While only in our fourth month of implementation, we've made a significant discovery—classrooms are a lot like purses. It sounds good and generous to say, "Drop in any time and give me some feedback on my teaching," but it seems to be the cultural equivalent of saying, "Go ahead and rifle through my purse and let me know what you find." Yeah, right—like that's going to happen. While unwritten, we've all learned from our mothers, sisters, and daughters—stay out of the purse. Similarly, as teachers, we've all pretty much learned that, while we tolerate administrators observing us and will work with a special education teacher in our room, we don't expect any other adults to be there—even having parents drop in can feel invasive, threatening, and sometimes downright creepy! So now I'm suggesting that we observe each other and provide feedback—yeah, right.

Time is a factor, sure, but our model asks only 10 minutes a week—we all waste at least that much time. The real factor seems to be the unwillingness to "violate" someone else's classroom. Several teachers who initially signed on have dropped out of the implementation but seem welcome to being observed—they just don't want to observe anyone else. Who'da thought? Just this morning we discovered that a simple paradigm shift may make all the difference—we're not observing each others' teaching, we're observing the impact on student engagement. Maybe we can convince folks to observe each others' students, and this will allow us all to focus more clearly on our own students—only time will tell.

In conclusion, I'd encourage principals and superintendents to make two major commitments. The first is to support any training with support

(Continued)

(Continued)

> during implementation—both through release time and through the use of instructional coaches and teacher leaders. The second is handing that process off, over time, to teachers so that peer coaching is the norm. Doing so will result in substantial and enduring change in how teachers think about teaching and, more important, learning.
>
> —Gerry Kettenbach, PhD
> Principal

Reprinted with permission from Gerry Kettenbach, PhD.

Principal of Middle School B

The coaching that Bonnie and Susie have been doing for the past couple of years has had a positive effect on my staff. They have become more open with discussing their needs with each other, and I feel that the growth gained through the difficult conversations with one another has been fantastic. Both the new teachers and the veteran teachers have gained so much for the meetings with the coaches by sharing techniques that have worked in other districts.

As an administrator I have grown so much by participating in the coaching activities that Bonnie and Susie have provided my staff. It has helped me to help reinforce the strategies taught in the classroom as well as strengthened my leadership within my building.

—Mike Ebert
Principal

Reprinted with permission from Michael Ebert.

SUMMARY

This chapter described the work that two coaches did in two middle schools over a two-year period. After Year 1, state test scores rose 10% in the highest category and decreased 10% in the lowest. Even though we know that many factors can cause test scores, in one year, to change by 10%, we were encouraged by the improvement, and more important, the teachers were encouraged by the improvement. The improvement in state test scores set the stage for the second year and supported the work by the coaches. Dr. Compton's, Dr. Kettenbach's, and Mr. Ebert's comments on coaching eloquently summarize the work of the past few years as the teachers in these schools moved from isolation to professional learning communities.

❖   ❖   ❖

Chapter 9 describes a coaching model used with teams of teachers to improve instruction. You will find strategies to build community among large groups of teachers as well as formats for workshops and teacher retreats. Included are multiple suggestions for coaching teachers throughout the school year.

Coaching Teams of Teachers to Improve Instruction

Say less; listen more.

—Nan Starling

This chapter focuses on how to coach *teams* of teachers to improve instruction. These teams are comprised of teachers who teach in inner-city, suburban, and rural districts, teachers who don't think like you, and teachers who do. We bring them all together with the goal of improving instruction to improve student achievement. This chapter is truly a blend of the how-to and the what-if of coaching. You can use the how-to information for the following kinds of professional development:

- Coaching teams of teachers within your building
- Coaching teams of teachers from different schools within your district
- Coaching teams of teachers from different districts within your state/region
- Coaching teams of teachers from diverse areas
- Coaching or working with educators in a presentation format

The what-if or content portion of this chapter includes the following:

- Samples of reflective writings by teachers
- Samples of lesson plans with state standards by a teacher

- Research paper assignment and reflection
- Suggestions for books to use for content with teachers
- Examples of a letter to administrators
- Examples of a syllabus for a university course
- Questions for you to use for your coaching and with teachers
- Profiles of students written by teachers
- Topics to use for writing with high school students
- Student writing

Not all of the chapter will apply to your coaching experience; however, the principles we apply here undergird quality professional development.

In this endeavor, we engage teachers in a community of learners who experience long-term professional development that begins with collegiality and ends in publication of their work. For 10 years, we have been working with teams of teachers throughout the state.

We have a rigorous evaluation piece built into this work. Contact information for this evaluation is included at the end of this chapter. We have data that show improvement in student achievement. However, since this is but one of the teachers' professional development experiences throughout the year, we are unable to isolate this effort as the sole reason when students improve on standardized tests. But we are able to document improvement in teacher instruction through the published narratives of the teachers as well as our observations of classroom instruction.

WHY IT WORKS

This project includes the best in professional development: collegiality, long-term professional development, nonevaluative feedback, teachers as writers and readers, and publication. This coaching has served to improve teacher instruction on many levels, and listed below are some reasons why it works:

- Relationships are key, and we emphasize building relationships throughout the year.
- We have learned to "say less, listen more."
- Adult learning styles are honored.
- Amenities are first rate and top quality.
- New content is presented in brain-compatible ways.
- Choice is always an option.
- Outstanding consultants present the material.
- Opportunities for physical movement and exercise are built into the workshops.
- Teachers know they will be sharing their work, so accountability is inherent in the project.
- Teachers do action research throughout the year and publish their findings at the end of each year.
- Teachers begin and end the year with models of student achievement.
- Feedback is always welcome, and there is a lengthy evaluation piece of the project by an outside evaluator.

HOW IT WORKS

The coaching work that we have collaborated on for the past decade is called the Missouri Humanities Program, or what we lovingly call MOHum. MOHum is a team-centered approach to learning where teams of teachers come together throughout an entire school year to focus on their instruction and improve their teaching. This model of professional development positively influences student learning (DuFour, Eaker, & DuFour, 2005; Elmore, 2002; Murphy, 1992; Showers, Joyce, & Bennett, 1987). The MOHum Project is funded through a grant from the Department of Elementary and Secondary Education (DESE) in the state of Missouri.

When we began the program in 1997, we were unaware of labels such as "professional learning communities" and "professional learning teams." Now we find that our model is an example of both of these terms as we function as literacy coaches for the teams. The MOHum Project addresses student achievement through exemplary, ongoing, long-term professional development designed to improve teacher instruction and raise student achievement. We provide collegiality and collaboration through the team model, present the theory, and model the instructional practice. Finally, through the extensive evaluation and accountability instrument, we continue to evolve the project through the shared decision making of both the administrators of the project and the scores of professional teachers participating in the project, year after year.

The Fall Retreat—The First PD of the Year

We begin the ongoing professional development each year in the fall with an overnight outing. Each year we include new teams and returning teams. Once teachers take part, they beg to be included. Their inclusion depends upon whether the administrators in their buildings approve their participation, since it does require that they miss four days of instruction during the school year and districts must cover the cost of substitutes.

For the first meeting of the year, MOHum teams meet at a rural retreat 50 miles from the urban area in which most of them teach. At first we met on Sundays and Mondays, but for the past few years we have met on Thursday afternoon through Friday, due to preferences by the participants.

Sue Heggarty, a professional developer with the Cooperating School Districts, and I have codirected this project for the past decade. One of Sue's areas of expertise is action research, and in Chapter 10, there is a description of her work with teacher reflections based on an action research model. We prepare for our roles as literacy coaches throughout the summer. We read voraciously to find the best books for the teachers, and we develop relationships with the administrators from the participating schools. We work hard to ensure that the experience is enriching and productive. Because of this, the evaluations by participants of the project have been outstanding for a decade, and the DESE has refunded this grant each year.

When our 40–60 or so participants (in teams of 4–6) arrive, we warmly greet them—hugs often for returning teachers, warm handshakes and eye contact for the new ones. Each participant receives a notebook with information for the year and two books. At the retreat, we spend our time doing team building, sharing teaching anecdotes, and setting the stage for a year of professional development centering on literacy.

PD Content for the Retreat

In 2004–2005, for example, we focused on improving literacy instruction in middle and high schools, and teachers participating in MOHum received Janet Allen's (2004) book *Tools for Teaching Content Literacy*. Using this book, we examined cognitive structures that support student learning with the teachers. Then teachers chose one cognitive structure to try with their students and reported back their progress at the October workshop.

Since the teachers in the MOHum Project teach a variety of disciplines such as English, history, art, science, and math, the literacy strategies are multidisciplinary and interdisciplinary strategies. In today's classrooms, teaching literacy is every teacher's job. We firmly believe that the more tools teachers have, the more knowledge of their content, and the more confidence that what they know can work in their classrooms, the better their students will achieve.

In addition to the presentations we do, we choose outstanding literacy coaches to work with our teachers. In 2004, Mary Kim Schreck, consultant and author, presented at the September retreat. She worked with teachers, giving them numerous rubrics and examples of student work. Together, teachers created rubrics and discussed the necessity of using them when they teach literacy. They left with a rubric they had created for their own classroom instruction as well as knowledge about the cognitive structure they planned to implement before we next met.

In addition to a book of pedagogy, we provide teachers with a novel or nonfiction book around which we center discussions throughout the year. Teachers often have little time to find new texts that motivate students, yet we see students respond enthusiastically to a piece of literature that grabs them; therefore, we believe that it is part of our responsibility to find new materials as well as new pedagogy to help teachers in the MOHum Project.

In 2005, literacy expert Willy Wood worked with our teachers. Willy was the former director of communication arts for the State of Missouri and influential in the development of the state assessments. He knows what the teachers need to be teaching the students, and he delivers literacy content using brain-compatible instruction. This year he focused on teaching vocabulary, and the teachers received Marzano and Pickering's (2005) *Building Academic Vocabulary* to use throughout the year.

Book choice is always a crucial decision for literacy coaches. Sue and I are both White women, and we interact in this project with 40% or more African American teachers. We attempt to honor the cultures of our participants in our book choices, activities choices, menus, and so on, and this is one way we do that. We also firmly believe that all students should encounter texts from a variety of cultures.

One year we chose *Betsey Brown*, since author Shange's (1985) book was set in St. Louis and appealed to the participants. Another year teachers received a copy of *Mississippi Solo* by Eddy Harris (1998). Eddy Harris is from the

St. Louis area and is often available to meet with teachers. After giving teachers the book, Sue demonstrated "close reading" strategies with passages from the book and offered lesson ideas and additional strategies for using the nonfiction book in the classroom. Once again, teachers were asked to find a piece of *Mississippi Solo* that they could incorporate into their instruction, whether they taught science or English. We offered the caveat that they could accompany us to a state or national conference and present their work as well as student work that centered on using this book and strategies from Janet Allen's book.

The Fall Workshop Day

Teachers return for a workshop day in the fall. One year we designed a workshop, modeling the tenets of differentiated instruction, to demonstrate to teachers how they enjoy choosing the work in which they plan to engage, just as students need choice. They chose workshops that best fit their interests and disciplines. Four choices were offered: an art and history interdisciplinary lesson, using art posters produced by the Missouri Arts Council; a participatory lesson on rubrics, using *Mississippi Solo*; a video field trip, described in Robert Marzano's (2004) book *Building Background Knowledge for Academic Achievement*; and a lesson on concept attainment, using the Janet Allen book. Once again, evaluations were glowing because teachers participated in the professional development that best met their needs.

The Winter Workshop Day

In the winter, we have another full-day workshop, and for the past several years we have held it at the Missouri History Museum, a wonderful museum in a large urban park. The museum houses outstanding artifacts of African American history that we tie to the books we use in the project. After a morning of workshops, teachers are able to view, discuss, and digest the displays at the museum.

The Spring Retreat

The spring retreat shifts our focus to the writing that teachers will do to integrate their year-long study into the repertoire of their instruction. As literacy coaches, supporting teacher writing is one of our favorite parts of the project. Teachers conduct action research (see Chapter 10) in their classrooms, focusing on a strategy or a single student, then write up the results for stipends and publication. For the retreat, teachers bring student work, or the "proof" that they have implemented the strategies and that they work. Teachers do a "gallery walk" of displayed student work and have time to talk with each other about the improvement they have seen in student work and achievement. This gallery walk serves as a prewriting strategy as teachers talk and process their action research projects.

Next we create a writing workshop with our teachers to draft their action research into articles that we publish during the summer. For the past four years, we have offered a stipend for teachers to do the writing about their teaching and their own students' work. Yet, even with the stipend, sometimes it has been a struggle to get teachers to write about their work, even though the research tells us that if we expect our students to write and read, we need to be writers and readers ourselves. Creating the writing workshop format for the final retreat has given teachers the time to begin their drafts and to share them with their colleagues, causing more teachers to hand in articles for stipends and publication. We find that the time we spent creating a rapport with and among these teachers to build a writing community helps teachers share their writing with each other. We use the strategies from the Gateway Writing Project and the writing project described in Chapter 11 to introduce teachers to the writing process. This lowers stress and threat and paves the way for teachers to write and publish or to share with an audience—the last step of the writing process.

Sharing Racial Histories to Build Community for Shared Writing

To create a comfort level for writing, we do writing experiences to warm up the teachers' writing muscles and stimulate their brains. This past year we used Chapter 5, "Exploring Our Racial Identity," and Chapter 6, "A Day in the Life," from *How to Teach Students Who Don't Look Like You: Culturally Relevant Teaching Strategies* (Davis, 2006) to jumpstart the writing process. We asked teachers to write their racial histories and then share them with other participants. The results astounded even us. As teachers shared the narratives of their lives, there were few dry eyes in the room. This activity bonded our teachers more than any others we implemented during the past decade. As White teachers listened to the experiences that Black teachers had in common, White teachers gasped at what they didn't know they didn't know. They begged for more. We could have spent the entire day (or more) sharing and learning from each other. Consider these chapters to bond the group and build respect for each other's culture.

Professional Presentation by Teachers

As literacy coaches, we also encourage teachers to reflect upon their professional careers and write and present at conferences. Teachers in the MOHum Project have presented at the National Council of Teachers of English (NCTE) convention each year for several years. In 2004, when they presented MOHum, in addition to receiving outstanding reviews, they were asked to write up ideas presented for publication. Teachers also present with us at National Staff Development Council (NSDC). In addition, they present at two state conferences offered yearly in Missouri: the Write to Learn Conference and the Show-Me Professional Development Conference. One year, the teachers presented the teaching ideas they created using *Mississippi Solo* and additional strategies on how to use nonfiction in the classroom.

Most popular in these presentations is always the student work. Just as teachers share student work and do a gallery walk at the final retreat, wider audiences at conferences are able to examine the student work, the real proof of the success of this program.

Teachers' Writings

In June, we read the teachers' writings submitted by the teachers and publish the writings in a booklet that is handed out in the fall as models for the upcoming year. Teachers, in a community of learners, experience long-term professional development that begins with collegiality and ends in publication of their work. What a powerful design!

Letter to Administrators

At the end of the school year, we send the following letter to the administrators of our teachers, knowing that in order to work with the teams of teachers, we must have the buy-in of the administrators.

Example of Letter Sent to Administrators

Date:

Dear (put each administrator's name in separately for each MOHum team):

We want to thank you for supporting your team of teachers who participated in IEC/CSD's **Missouri Humanities Project (MOHum)** funded by the Department of Elementary and Secondary Education (DESE). The teachers worked together in a collegial fashion with 12 other teams consisting of 60 educators from districts throughout the metropolitan area. This was the largest MOHum group in its 10-year history. Together we formed one large **professional learning community** that focused on literacy and how to weave reading and writing instruction throughout the disciplines.

At this time, the teachers are writing reflections about the action research they completed with their students and how the MOHum experience supported, expanded, and enriched their instructional practices. We will read these and give team members feedback as well as a stipend of $250 for each completed reflection.

Next year, should we be funded, we plan to use Robert Marzano's (2004) latest book, *Building Background Knowledge for Academic Achievement,* and spend the year focusing on instructional strategies to build background knowledge. This is especially important for at-risk students and your AYP students. This should be an important and exciting year for MOHum. Because of the demand for inclusion in the MOHum Project, we are asking that you complete the enclosed form to reserve a place for your team to continue the important work in which they are currently involved. If you have any questions, please e-mail or call us.

GRADUATE CREDIT OFFERED

An additional incentive for teachers is that they may receive graduate credit for participating in the MOHum Project. The following is the syllabus we used for the 2005–2006 school year.

Syllabus

Special Topics: EDU 594

Independent Study: 2005–2006 Missouri Humanities Project: Direct Instruction of Vocabulary Across the Curriculum

Instructors: Dr. Bonnie M. Davis and Ms. Sue Heggarty
Cooperating School Districts
8225 Florissant Road
St. Louis, MO 63121
314.692.9702

Textbook: *Building Background Knowledge for Academic Achievement* **by Robert J. Marzano (2004)**

Credit Hours: 3

Assignments: Participants will complete an Action Research Project (AR Project) using the strategies learned during the Missouri Humanities Project (MOHum) retreats and workshops. The MOHum AR Project will be formally written up and presented for inclusion in a published journal that will be submitted to the Missouri Department of Elementary and Secondary Education (DESE). The Action Research will also be shared with the 10 teams of teachers throughout the area who participated in the project.

Attendance: Mandatory at all sessions.

Standards: Missouri state standards are the basis for materials used in all workshops throughout the MOHum Project.

Sessions:

Fall Retreat (October 6 and 7, 2005)
Students will participate in a two-day retreat with other MOHum participants. Mr. Willy Wood will present on vocabulary instruction, using Robert J. Marzano's (2004) research and strategies as found in the text *Building Background Knowledge for Academic Achievement.*

Fall Workshop (November 9, 2005)
Teachers meet for a full-day workshop focusing on building background knowledge through direct instruction of vocabulary. They initiate their design for the AR Project.

Winter Workshop (January 27, 2006)
Teachers meet at the Missouri History Museum to continue work on building background knowledge through direct instruction of vocabulary. They discuss their progress on their AR Project.

Spring Retreat (March 30–31, 2006)
Teachers meet for a two-day retreat with Mr. Willy Wood to complete their study of building background knowledge through direct instruction of vocabulary. They share their AR Project with others.

Action Research Project Due Date (June 1, 2006)
Teachers hand in their AR Project for feedback from instructors. Modifications are made, and the AR Project is included in the document to be sent to DESE in July 2006.

DESE Report (July 2006)
AR Projects will be sent to DESE for compliance with the grant report on the MOHum Project, 2005–2006.

Questions for Reflection:

As you read about this professional development experience, what aspects of the professional development work do you find appealing?

_____

_____

_____

Describe the variety of roles the coaches take on in this professional development experience.

_____

_____

_____

Even though this is a specific professional development project, what can you take from this to use in your coaching?

_____

_____

_____

MOHUM TEACHER WORK

The following three teachers provide evidence of their classroom instruction in these writings:

- **Derek Rowley**, High School English Teacher
- **Stephanie Hughes**, Sixth-Grade English Teacher
- **Gloria Brazell**, Middle School Art Teacher

Derek Rowley

Derek Rowley is a high school English teacher who is also a professional musician. After teaching several years in a high-achieving private school, Derek entered the world of public education, teaching in a high-poverty school where he is determined to make a difference. He is a fiction writer and the author of a serial story in the Hatteras Island publication, Ocean _magazine. He can be reached at d.rowley@mrhsd.k12.mo.us._

Analysis of an Assignment: The "Dreaded" Research Paper

By Derek Rowley

Just recently I read through the issue of _English Journal_ (Vol. 95, No. 4) devoted entirely to research writing, and when I saw phrases like

(Continued)

(Continued)

"teaching the dreaded research paper" and "injecting some life back into research writing," it made me think, not for the first time, that some teachers may have lost perspective about the point of research writing or at least what this sort of writing really can be.

I teach writing primarily through genre; in a workshop format, juniors in English III focus on poetry, personal narrative, short story, and on different types of essays, one at a time, and the longer I do this, the more I realize how much crossover there is between genres. Good short stories often involve the poetic use of language. Poems often tell stories, or parts of stories. The essays most interesting to me usually involve a narrative component. And research writing, in the real world, that is, the world of people who make a living writing and those who read that writing, involves more genres, or elements of genres, than the traditional research paper with internal citations and a works cited page.

Teachers who use a workshop format—students in the same class pursuing different writing projects on a variety of topics and genres simultaneously—know that for students to learn, they must be engaged in the subject, and one way to provide that opportunity is to allow students to choose their own topic to write about.

This year, when it was time to teach research writing, I called it simply that: research writing—not strictly a research paper and not necessarily an essay. Instead I offered five choices: argumentative essay, report, profile, narrative fiction, and multigenre paper. The idea was to have students identify not only a topic of interest to them, as they had been doing all year, but also to identify the most effective genre in which to pursue that topic and to find ways in which research and writing could broaden and deepen one's own knowledge and understanding of the topic. And, in addition to exploring topic and genre as areas of study in themselves, I asked students to present some type of primary source material as well—a personal interview with an expert in the area, reading primary documents, or other ways of learning about one's topic that did not involve reading someone else's digested account of the topic on a Web site or in a book.

Students submitted a wide range of responses to the assignment. Jessica (I'll use only first names here) embraced the assignment fully; ever since I first taught her as a freshman, Jessica had been reading books on Henry VIII, so she immediately chose him as a topic—specifically, his marriages and resulting children.

For years we have taught students to document sources where they find information. "Parenthetical citations," we say. "Then, put all the info in your works cited page." But what if students write about something that they really know a lot about? What if a lot of the information in the paper is not exactly common knowledge but also without an obvious source, having been subsumed into the student's own body of knowledge about the topic? Bravo, I said to Jessica; you're officially an expert on Henry VIII, and you've only begun. So I asked her the same question I had presented to the whole class when I had first introduced the assignment: "How can additional research help support, deepen, and broaden your knowledge of this topic?" I told her to keep reading about the topic and to make an effort to record the sources of any information that she had learned recently. I asked her to write down every title of everything she could think of that she had read about Henry VIII in the last few years and to put that in her works cited page, even if there weren't actual citations in her paper specifically referring to it.

What emerged was a lengthy, interesting, and informative paper about the human side of Henry VIII—deep, specific, and thorough—but a bit short on internal citations. Her works cited list had traditional nonfiction texts, including some Web sites, but also some historical fiction. Part of Jessica's task was to separate fact from fiction when presenting a nonfiction account of Henry VIII, but would she be in danger of inadvertently presenting some fiction as fact? Might she accidentally present some undocumented information as her own that came, more or less, from a single source? Possibly. Did she learn a ton about Henry VIII, how to integrate information from another source into her own writing, and how to document these sources? Absolutely. She also learned about the realistically fuzzy line between knowledge that is "ours" and that which is "borrowed."

The truth is that "real" writers document sources in a variety of ways. In a scholarly paper, they use APA or MLA style parenthetical citations and have a formal list of sources at the end. But most magazines just don't present writing this way, probably because most casual readers don't really want to read information in that format.

In order to see more typical examples of giving credit to sources, I gave students a chunk from a recent *New York Times Magazine* article on child abuse and had them underline the places that the author gave credit to the source of the facts she presented. Rather than parenthetical citations, she introduced facts with clauses such as "Experts like Alfred Kinsey minimized the dangers of sexual abuse" and "In 1998, Bruce Rind, Robert Bauserman and Philip Tromovitch published an article in *Psychological Bulletin,* a journal of the American Psychological Association, analyzing 59 studies of the long-term effects of sexual abuse and adult-child sexual contact on college students" before quoting her source. We looked at what the writer said about the source as she presented it; in the latter instance, we know exactly what the source is and are able to evaluate its degree of reliability and make inferences about any bias present, and the thread of the *New York Times Magazine* writer's narrative is unbroken. Students worked to use those kinds of techniques in their writing as well as the more formal ones.

In reviewing the stack of papers I received in response to this assignment, it's clear that most students learned something about the topic they picked. Some papers still look like a patchwork of info cut and pasted, albeit appropriately documented, from other sources and feel rather lifeless and automatic. Most of these papers demonstrate scrupulous attention to MLA format documentation, and students clearly learned how to do this, if they didn't already know how. But the most interesting papers were the ones that didn't fit a ready-made structure. One student wrote about small recording studios in St. Louis; her brother owns one, and she researched others. She worked her citations into her sentences, and the piece flows naturally and reads like a feature article in a newspaper or magazine. Another student interviewed his Mexican relatives about Cinco de Mayo and integrated their misconceptions about the origin of the holiday into his otherwise traditional, factual account based primarily on standard sources. His use of these primary sources—his relatives—made the piece very personal and engaging and also demonstrated firsthand that most Americans, including Chicanos themselves, don't know the origin of this holiday.

(Continued)

(Continued)

> In the end, student writing seems most sincere and engaging when they use models from so-called real life.
>
> Reprinted with permission from Derek Rowley.

If you were coaching Derek, what feedback might you give him?

_____

_____

_____

In this second piece of writing, Derek writes a profile of his student in a reflection that will guide his future instructional decisions.

Profile of a Student

When I gave the annual research writing assignment this year, I encouraged students to choose a topic they were genuinely interested in and to find ways in which research could support, deepen, and broaden their knowledge of this topic.

Brittany wrote about teen pregnancy because she had firsthand knowledge of the topic and she believed it was important and worth writing about. Her opening sentence is "I, Brittany, have been pregnant." She wrote with feeling about how, after becoming pregnant, she decided to have the baby but was convinced by her parents to have an abortion. "When I made that mistake, my mother tried to make it right," she wrote. "But people look down on you more for getting the abortion." She says that she lost a good friend who did not approve of her decision. She says also, "My point is that it can happen to anybody. Teen girls are getting pregnant more and more these days. And they try to make things better by getting abortions, but people don't always look at that as the right thing to do."

Then she goes on to present facts about teen pregnancy rates in specific states and abortion statistics. In my final assessment of the piece, I told Brittany that her research was not thorough enough, and there was still a clear need for more editing even in the final draft, but that the personal element she presented in the paper made it an extremely memorable piece. In the final paragraph, she wrote, "When I got pregnant, it really was an accident. But when it came down to it, I wanted to keep my baby because I wanted somebody to always love me because I really wasn't getting it at home. But I realize that there [are] people out there that really do love me and I didn't have to go that route."

Brittany struggled to maintain a passing grade in this class this year, but when I read about her experiences in her writing, it became clear that there were probably good reasons for her to be distracted. It also became clear how writing at its best can be a source of self-discovery, even at its most unpolished.

Whether Brittany's choices have been the best for her or not, she'll never know, but it seems likely that from now on she'll base her decisions on what she thinks is best and will be less likely to do things to try to please others, having learned that no matter what we do, there's always someone who won't approve.

Reprinted with permission from Derek Rowley.

How do you think Derek's personal reflection about his student might inform his future decisions about instruction?

_____

_____

_____

Documents

- Research Writing Assignment
- Suggestion Topics

Research Writing Assignment

Name_____

English III   Mr. Rowley

Directions

The most common mistake people make when doing any sort of research writing is starting to write before they really know enough about the subject. Your assignment is to spend second and third quarter reading about your topic and learning a lot about it before drafting. Choose one of the genres listed below. The topics are up to you. If you're doing a historical topic, stick to the 20th or 21st century.

First Quarter

Choose a topic—something you're interested in.

Second and Third Quarters

- Read about your topic.
- Be sure you have the right topic—it should be interesting to you.
- Be sure your focus is not too broad or too narrow.
- Confer with me about your topic; tell me what you're learning.
- Keep a list of sources you consult; use MLA format.
- Type up a list of all the sources you read—drafts of this list due at end of second and third quarters.

Fourth Quarter

- Start drafting the piece.
- Have writing conferences (at least two), revise, consult scoring guide.
- Submit the final draft at the end of fourth quarter.

Other Requirements

- Include information cited from a variety of sources; there is no minimum or maximum number of sources.

(*Continued*)

(Continued)

- Work with some primary source material—interview an expert in the field, read a primary document, or read another source that does not contain someone else's take on your topic.
- If you are not able to find a wide variety of sources on your topic, shift your focus or change your topic.
- If you are writing an informational text, cite your sources in the body of your paper; if you are writing a narrative text (a story), include only a works cited page with a few comments about what elements in your story came from which sources.
- Submit your works cited page with every draft you turn in.
- The final draft must be long enough to demonstrate knowledge of the topic in depth; however, there is no maximum or minimum page length.
- The final draft of your paper should be both interesting and informative. If you're bored with your writing or your topic, your reader probably will be too.
- Be sure that by the end of second quarter, you have a topic that is interesting to you and also manageable in terms of length.

Choose One of These Genres

- **Argumentative Essay.** State an argument about something and defend it. Include facts from a variety of resources to back up your claims. For example, "Coronary bypass surgery is performed in the United States more often than it should be." Research might be cited from newspapers, medical journals, health care insurance companies' annual reports, online sites directed toward patients and their families, and interviews with doctors or others working in the health field.
- **Report.** Also known as an article or informational essay. Sum up the state of affairs on a current event or feature. For example, you could describe what choices 18-year-olds have today—how many go to college, where they go and why, and what jobs people are getting right out of high school. Research might come from newspaper articles, magazines directed toward 18-year-olds, college journals, interviews with college counselors, interviews with people who regularly hire 18-year-olds. This genre frequently involves narrative elements; sometimes telling one or more stories is a great way to provide information or make a point.
- **Short Story.** Author Philip Roth recently published a novel in which Charles Lindbergh is elected president of the United States in 1940. In order to write this book, Roth needed to have an in-depth knowledge of the United States, of World War II, and of other historical events and people from that period. Choose a topic, read a lot about it, and use that information in a piece of fiction. For example, Robin Cook and Michael Palmer each write medical thriller novels that are rich with details about medical procedures and the health field. Michael Crichton's *Prey,* a recent best-selling thriller novel, has a bibliography in the back with all the sources he consulted for information about nanotechnology, the subject of the book.
- **Profile.** A short biography of a person, sometimes including an interview. For instance, you might research, interview, and write up the story of Joe Edwards, the owner of Blueberry Hill in the Delmar Loop and the man responsible for the development and nurturing of this historic neighborhood in St. Louis for the past 30 years. This profile would also include some St. Louis history.
- **Multigenre Paper.** Take a single topic and explore it in a variety of genres. See the example of the dinosaur multigenre paper from Tom Romano's book and see also Sharon Draper's *Tears of a Tiger.*

Suggested Research Topics

Name_____

English III   Mr. Rowley

   You will need to adjust some of these topics so that they are not too broad or too narrow. Be sure to keep in mind the guidelines for the assignment when you choose a topic. Be prepared to broaden, narrow, or shift your focus as you read about your topic second quarter. The topics listed here are suggestions only; you are *not* required to choose something off this list. Historical topics should focus on the 20th or 21st century.

- A short story told from the point of view of a soldier during World War I or World War II
- A short story told from the point of view of a woman who goes to work for the first time while her husband is away fighting in World War II
- The history of American education
- A short story about a child labor victim
- The history of child labor laws
- Immigration
- The war in Iraq—how the United States ended up there and what we're doing now
- The history of St. Louis, of Maplewood, and/or Richmond Heights
- The history of MRH High School
- A comparison of Brentwood (or any other high school) and MRH High Schools
- Why learning to speak Spanish is important
- The history, production, and popularity of diesel trucks
- A specific holiday—how it began and why it is (or is not) significant today
- Guns and their place in U.S. society
- The history of baseball (or another sport) and its impact on American society
- Intelligent Design and the Discovery Institute
- How society seems to view women athletes
- The *St. Louis Post-Dispatch*—its origins, important events in the history of the life of the newspaper, and its role in St. Louisians' lives today
- The role of alcohol in people's lives
- The evolution of the guitar
- North Korea and how it came to be a current nuclear threat
- The story of Joe Edwards, the owner of Blueberry Hill in the Delmar Loop and the man responsible for the development and nurturing of this historic neighborhood in St. Louis for the past 30 years
- A history of rap and/or hip-hop music
- Women's suffrage
- The New Deal—who benefited, who didn't
- The cold war
- Civil rights movement
- Vietnam
- The history of the stock market
- The stock market crashes of 1929, 1980s, and 2000
- The most important fashion designers today
- The decline of network television

Stephanie Hughes, Middle School Teacher

Stephanie Hughes is a second-year teacher at an urban middle school and has been a member of MOHum for two years. She writes her reflection of her summer teaching experience in the form of a prose poem. In it she profiles the students in her class, focusing on one student.

"People who shut their eyes to reality simply invite their own destruction, and anyone who insists on remaining in a state of innocence long after innocence is dead turns himself into a monster."

—James Baldwin

Reflection: Prose Poem

Michael has a shoebox full of writing.

"Michael is lazy."—advice given me on the first day of school

I taught summer school this year, six weeks with a deadly daily schedule. Classes are two and a half hours long; I teach two classes each day, no break, no recess. When I have to use the bathroom, I send a note down to the principal's office and someone comes to relieve me for those few minutes. I don't know how the kids do it.

Kids are in summer school for two reasons. Either they have low skills and need extra instruction before they move up, or they have behavior problems. The kids with behavior problems are generally bright, so now you have two groups of kids in a room, and only one scripted curriculum with which to serve them. Luckily, I don't teach from scripts.

For the first two weeks, Michael was indeed part of a group of boys reluctant to work, quick to swear, eager to play dice, and certain to prove they were bored and hard. The first week was the hardest for all of us.

(I was shocked to hear their language, their use of vulgar words, and even more shocked when they were surprised that I threw them out of class.) I went over my rules: "No 'f-word,' no inappropriate language, and when I put you out, you go silently and gracefully and wait for me to come speak to you."

The kids were shocked. They'd use the f-word, I'd throw them out, they'd stare at me in disbelief. Once, during lunch, I heard one of my students say to an administrator, "F— this s—!" I was certain the administrator would take her out of the cafeteria. Imagine my shock: the administrator said, "Oh, you play too much." No wonder it took a week for my kids to understand my rules.

I am tired of defending the students I teach. I am weary of hearing: "Oh, those poor teachers. I hear those kids are terrible."

Please. I just came out of a hard six weeks teaching a group of tough kids, many with parole officers, and I still insist they are brilliant and willing.

Consider: what boundaries and norms for school are kids thirteen-years-old supposed to perceive and internalize if cursing at an administrator is normal?

Slowly, for unknown reasons, Michael began to warm up to me. One day, many kids were absent, including his usual cadre. He scooched his desk up right next to mine, between my desk and the window. He began pointing out interesting cars to me, quietly.

"Check out those rims, Miss Hughes."
He was supposed to be working, but I was curious about him, and wanted to get to know him. I put Langston Hughes (the stuffed doll we always have in my room) on his desk. Michael started talking about his dad working shift work, never being home, ignoring him. I say, yeah, shift work is hard, and when your parent comes home he's tired and sleeps. Michael says his dad doesn't know anything about him.

"How do you know he's ignoring you?" I ask.

Michael says his dad grounds him all the time, puts him in his room, doesn't want him on the streets. I know Michael has a brother returning from prison, and another who's been shot eight times. I say,

"Maybe your dad wants to keep you safe, after your brothers . . ."

Michael doesn't believe this.

"What do you do in your room?" I ask.

Michael says, "I read the same six books. I've got those book memorized."

"Do you ever write while you're in there? I mean, I know it might sound boring, like school, but you could be writing. You might get some good stuff," I say.

Michael grins slyly: "I write."

"Really? I would love to see some of that."

"Some of it's too violent for you."

"Okay. Well, if you ever get anything that's not too violent, I'd love to see it."

"I've got shoe boxes."

(Continued)

(Continued)

This is exciting. I know my eyes are shining, and I'm trying not to smile too hard.
"Shoe boxes?"

"I keep all my writing in shoe boxes. I keep it away."

"Michael. I would give anything to see one of those shoe boxes."

"Okay, Miss Hughes. I'll bring you one on Monday."

Tell me Michael doesn't deserve a rigorous day filled with order and stimulation. Instead, my school district has given him a boxed, scripted curriculum and warned me not to deviate from it. I really have no other option, though, do I?

These are smart, gentle, funny kids. Once, I accidentally set the globe down on top of Langston Hughes. It looked like he was sprawled out beneath the whole earth. Marcus said, "Look!"

I looked and said to him, "Whoa. That's a little intense. It's like Mr. Hughes is bearing the weight of the world."

Marcus murmured (murmured!), "He really did."

Look who I'm responsible for! Who are these children, with me, sentenced to my room for a summer? I am supposed to goad Marcus and Michael into making letter cards and then spelling out words by rote, and then orally spelling them with the whole class. The curriculum calls for no writing at all, no analytical, no comprehensive, no creative. The kids respond orally to my commands, in unison. I time them for reading fluency with a stopwatch, and hopefully they read more words per minute at Week 6 than at Week 1.

Week 5, I brought in Poetry Workshop. It was long overdue.

I struggle with the growing anger inside of me. I am tired of being told, "Curb your enthusiasm, Miss Hughes."
I am tired of being "mentored" by veteran teachers who make suggestions like the following: "I've learned to cultivate bad breath because it keeps the kids away from me."

I am tired of being told to lie on attendance reports, to not even try to call parents, to keep the kids quiet and in their seats, and to never deviate from the script.

I find myself thinking, "If this were my child . . ."

I want you to think the same. I want you to imagine that the child you love is somehow transported to this district by the river, not too far from your suburban home. The security guard picks a fight with him on his way into school, the cafeteria is out of food so there is no breakfast, there is no working copier so he spends four hours copying his own worksheets from the board, he has no recess, the bathroom doors are locked, and his teachers have been discouraged from using his name, because the script doesn't call for it.

Wouldn't you do anything, wouldn't you lie down in front of traffic, take a day from work, spend your time and capital and resources to save a kid from a day of that?

Mark me: I am not choosing the worst examples of schooling in my school for the sake of my argument. I am showing you a normal experience for my kids. Our kids.

Michael has been schooled for seven years. He has shoe boxes full of writing, and has never brought them to school. He has, however, been allowed to use foul language, and has heard it from his teachers.

(Last week, I again heard the holler of a teacher down the hall from me,
"Sit your asses down!"
It no longer surprises me. My kids watch my face. I let it show what I'm feeling. Disappointment, sadness, fury. I try to make my eyes say to them:

"I don't care what you hear. Words matter, and that is not okay."

Eventually, my kids believe me.)

When I started writing these dispatches, I committed to telling you the most hopeful, living parts of my experience. I felt there were enough negative stories about city schools, I didn't want to laundry-list the worst parts for you. Now, after two years, I believe there is a place for anger, and I want you to come to that place with me. My kids are as smart as you were once, and as willing as you are now, and as deserving as we all ever will be.

School will begin again here in a month or so. I fear the distances between the schools where education takes place and those where education matters less than control, silence, and compulsion grows greater.

(Continued)

(Continued)

Answer me this: how do we insist that public education mean the same for all? Do we believe public schools remain incubators of great possibility? Are we certain that it is the responsibility and honor of our nation to provide education? What does schooling mean?

I have many suggestions for you, if you ask, "What should I do?"
Let me begin with one. This year, visit a city school. Take three hours, come downtown, and visit a school. Choose your favorite grade, the grade your own child is in, your favorite subject . . . it doesn't matter. If you want me to find a class and teacher for you, ask me. I believe our schools need your presence. The children and teachers and administrators need to be seen, and need to understand that the stakes are high enough to warrant your presence, and eyes. Look at the bulletin boards, watch the children, and pay attention to the teachers and facilities you see.

Why? Because perspective, presence, and relationship matter. We need to engage with these schools, that the growing apartheid I am witnessing doesn't continue unnoticed. Later, when you see news about our schools, or hear stories, or need to write a letter to your congressmen, you will better feel the small share of responsibility that is already ours.

Reprinted with permission from Stephanie Hughes.

Stephanie's prose poem paints a portrait from her perspective of the education her students are or are not receiving. How do you respond to her reflection?

_____

_____

_____

What positive instructional strategies is Stephanie using in her classroom instruction?

_____

_____

_____

Where in your work might you use Stephanie's piece as a basis for discussion?

_____

_____

_____

Gloria Brazell: A Middle School Art Teacher

Gloria Brazell is a veteran middle school art teacher in a large suburban district with a diverse student population, including a large number of students from Bosnia. She is a former school board member who taught in the inner city, and she recently completed a second master's degree in culturally diverse learners from Fontbonne University.

The following is her lesson plan based on the work she did with literacy strategies using the novel _Betsey Brown_ (Shange, 1985).

Shange's _Betsey Brown_
An Inspiration for Mind Mapping and Story Quilting

Goal 1: To develop students' understanding of the interrelationship between literature and visual arts.

Objectives: Students will demonstrate their understanding of passages of _Betsey Brown_ by creating a mind map of their own experiences.

Students will demonstrate an understanding of the style of Faith Ringgold, an artist, by creating a story quilt based upon their mind map.

Students' story quilt will demonstrate an understanding of the principles and elements of design.

Note: Teachers must show in their lesson plans where they meet specific state standards.

Missouri Show-Me Standards Met by This Lesson

Goal 2: Students in Missouri public schools will acquire the knowledge and skills to communicate effectively within and beyond the classroom.

Students will demonstrate within and integrate across all content areas the ability to perform or produce works in the fine and practical arts.

Fine Arts

In Fine Arts, students in Missouri public schools will acquire a solid foundation that includes knowledge of interrelationships of visual and performing arts and the relationships of the arts to other disciplines.

(Continued)

(Continued)

Communication Arts

In Communication Arts, students in Missouri public schools will acquire a solid foundation that includes knowledge of and proficiency in reading and evaluating fiction, poetry, and drama.

Materials Needed

- Class set of *Betsey Brown* by Ntozake Shange (1985)
- *Faith Ringgold, The Last Story Quilt* (2001) VHS.
- Posters of Faith Ringgold's work
- Student examples
- Mind mapping handout—Gateway Writing Project, Mehlville School District, 2005
- Paper, markers, construction paper, fabric, scissors, pencils, pens
- Computer access: www.faithringgold.com

Learning Activities

1. Make the statement that everyone has a story. Explain that getting an idea, whether for writing a story or for creating an art project, is difficult for everyone.

2. Present the mind mapping handout. Sit down with students gathered around and request that they write their stories using one of the mind mapping layouts I modeled for students. I explained the mind map and drew a map of the house where I grew up. I went on to talk about people in our neighborhood, the confectionary (they had no idea what this was!) at the top of the hill, and walking to the school playground. I told them about alleys and hiding in ash pits when we played hide and seek. They were so attentive and wanted to hear more and more. I expanded the story and showed them how to draw it on their mind maps. My story extended to city bus stops and taking the bus downtown.

3. I read descriptive passages from *Betsey Brown* to the class. There are passages describing the neighborhood at the beginning of the book. We also talked about relatives and how they intertwine in each person's story. I provided copies of the book to use as a resource.

4. Students accessed www.faithringgold.com. While they were surfing the Web site, I read aloud from *Betsey Brown.* We compared the artist's visual work with the descriptive passages of the author.

5. I showed previous examples of student-created story quilts. We watched the movie *Faith Ringgold, the Last Story Quilt.* I stopped the movie at critical intervals to point out her style of using borders and writing within the artwork. We then viewed posters of her work.

6. Students created their own mind maps from their individual stories.

7. From their stories, students designed quilt-like wall hangings in the style of Faith Ringgold. Their subject matter involved their neighborhoods and people who are involved in their lives—as in *Betsey Brown.*

Assessment

Assessment will consist of a gallery walk with student-generated questions regarding the story line of *Betsey Brown* and the art style of Faith Ringgold as they relate to each student's story quilt. Students will use Post-it notes to direct their comments (must be positive) about their classmates' work. The teacher will use the Post-it notes to generate discussion.

Assessment will also include meeting criteria of a scoring guide that was explained at the beginning of the unit.

Extended Activities

1. Team with a social studies teacher for a unit on civil rights in St. Louis.

2. Use the Web to research the history of quilts in America from colonial times to contemporary times.

3. Team with a math teacher to plan layouts of geometric shapes to make a quilt.

4. Team with a communication arts teacher to read the poetry of Langston Hughes.

5. Study the architecture of St. Louis, its Victorian neighborhoods and schools.

6. Plan a cooperative exhibit of the class story quilts. Have students decide if they want to hang the quilts as neighborhoods, put together to form a large block, or individually. Have them explain their choice.

7. Have students interview elderly relatives and neighbors of their choice. Include the interviews in the story quilts.

8. Create a book. Have students write chapters of their lives. Illustrate the chapters. Teach them simple bookbinding techniques.

Reprinted with permission from Gloria Brazell.

These writings are just a sampling of the work we receive from the middle and high school teachers who join us for the MOHum Project. As you can see, they often contain provocative, heart-rending portraits of the worlds our teachers and students inhabit. Because of these realities, we must offer professional and collegial support with both our minds and our hearts. It is our professional responsibility to provide it. MOHum exemplifies what the research states must happen: long-term professional development using a collegial model that offers teachers an opportunity to examine their practice and improve their instruction.

Dennis Lubeck, the executive director of the program, sums up the work:

Missouri Humanities (MOHum) is a project that has endured because it represents what is best about professional development when it works. Activities are led by master teachers who weave the best research about reading and writing into all activities. When teachers read essays, poetry or literature, the presenters weave pedagogical content (pedagogy that flows from the academic discipline of literature or history) and the ideas expressed by the author.

This project has become a professional learning community on two levels: first, teachers come in teams and work together to solve student achievement challenges; second, the teams from 8 to 10 schools (depending upon the year) have become a large learning community representing several school districts. Finally, the teacher leaders and the teacher participants are all interested in addressing what has become the most challenging issue in public education—addressing the gap in achievement between White students and students of Color. Bonnie Davis, along with Sue Heggarty, the two master teachers responsible for coordinating this project, have become invaluable resources to the St. Louis project, as well as to schools across Missouri and the country on strategies for addressing the achievement gap.

Finally, this project works because, unlike so many far more expensive professional development projects, the teacher leaders do not over promise. Goals are only achievable with hard work and sustained growth over a long period of time. The "quick fix" is anathema to this project.

Reprinted with permission from Dennis Lubeck, PhD, Executive Director of the International Education Consortium, a professional development division of Cooperating School Districts, St. Louis, Missouri.

The following evaluations attest to the success of the MOHum Project.

International Education Consortium

Cooperating School Districts

MOHum RETREAT

March 30–31, 2006

EVALUATION REPORT

Approximately 35 teachers attended the last retreat of the year for the MOHum project. Twenty-seven participants returned the evaluation questionnaire. Following are the results.

1. **The time to work in teams was**

Profitable				Not profitable
(21)	(3)	(2)	(0)	(0)

No answer: (1)

2. **The presentations by guest lecturers/field trips were**

Informative				Not informative
(25)	(2)	(0)	(0)	(0)

3. **The opportunity to design a school/class project has been**

Valuable				Not valuable
(21)	(1)	(2)	(0)	(0)

No answer: (3)

4. **The opportunity to meet with colleagues on a regular basis was**

Valuable   Not valuable

(25)   (2)   (0)   (0)   (0)

5. **The resources provided by the project have been**

Helpful   Not helpful

(26)   (1)   (0)   (0)   (0)

6. **The action research project was**

Valuable   Not valuable

(23)   (2)   (0)   (0)   (0)

No answer: (2)

7. **This final retreat was**

Beneficial   Waste of time

(25)   (2)   (0)   (0)   (0)

Comments:

Awesome.

8. **Overall comments about the project this year, including how it could have been improved:**

All projects have been great. I feel so blessed to have an opportunity to be a part of MOHum.

The *Building Background Knowledge* book has been very helpful in areas that I truly needed ideas for. Improvements-Final Retreat after MAP.

Great!!! More workshop days during the school year (at least two more).

Poignant topic this session—thank you. We have been ignoring it too long.

Love it! MOHum has made me a better teacher without a doubt/missed Mary Kim Schreck at the retreat.

As always I have enjoyed the Missouri Humanities programs, especially w/ the addition of Willy Wood.

Lots of good ideas for *practical* application in the classroom.

I appreciate really using the time together for important discussion and sharing of best practices.

As usual the year was very beneficial. Trying out the reading strategies in my class for building vocabulary in the class. The race issue put the topping on the cake. I had always been aware that there was an issue but my White colleagues brushed me off.

Even though I was not able to attend all sessions this year, due to jury duty and administrative project assistance, I did receive all materials issued and I think the project was well organized and helpful. I would have loved to attend and could give an objective response to how improvement could be made (if needed).

The timing for the final retreat over spring breaks is not ideal.

Time to write and share—super. The work with Bonnie's book—super.

Didn't love *Betsey Brown* (sorry!).

Always wonderful and enjoyable.

The sharing time today was wonderful! I wish we'd shared more practical ideas from *Betsey Brown* and other uses of MOHum in the classroom.

Refreshing, relaxing, makes me able to go back and finish up the year!

Send topics (agenda) before we come.

I didn't like *B. Brown.* More exposure to each other from different teams. Great reflective activities—vocabulary study was great. How about study of Jeff Wilhelm strategies? The race discussions were powerful.

(Continued)

(Continued)

More sharing and writing!

The support from colleagues and their sharing how they apply concepts from MOHum creates a dynamic learning environment.

9. **What did you learn this year that will be helpful to you in your classroom? Also, please give examples if you used any project activities in your classroom.**

Sue Heggarty and Bonnie Davis illustrate through their leadership how an open, stimulating atmosphere fosters growth.

Vocabulary instruction has been absolutely amazing. Teaching it in context has been revolutionary and has brought life to classes where I have had trouble getting them motivated.

Vocabulary strategies—Willy Wood—Willy's advice helped me begin some different vocab experiments in my class. Vocab strategies mostly.

I learned many things from colleagues and others. I always have a strategy for "Monday morning." I learned how life and experiences change your perspective, but no matter what, don't give up.

Betsey Brown is a good resource. It can be tied into the curriculum very easily—social studies, language arts, and so on. It will make a great interdisciplinary unit next year. This year I used vocabulary strategies given to us by Willy Wood.

I learned that I am not the only one who has a journey like me. I really enjoyed reading the racial history. Nan's information on Johns Hopkins was great (mind mapping). The discussion on racism was powerful.

Vocabulary, writing exercise/activities. Bonnie's book!

Vocab activities that Willy Wood shared are practical and useful.

Vocab strategies that got me excited with the kids. As well as a chance to incorporate Marzano into my lessons deliberately.

I *allow time* to listen to my students.

The discussion on race relations is a topic in today's world. Being open about it can be helpful in the future.

I have used a lot of Willy's vocab strategies in my classroom. The tea party worked great as a prereading strategy. I also did the vocab prereading of putting nouns/verbs/adjectives into sentences, and that was really effective at getting my students to think about the word usage.

The Willy Wood vocabulary and reading strategies are most useful.

Willy Wood's vocab strategies, mind mapping, others. *How to Teach . . . You,* Bonnie's book. I can't wait to get into this book.

A couple of the vocabulary exercises Willy Wood showed us I used in my class. We did the exercise where you found other meanings of the word by posing different questions. Express to self (encouragement) from *Betsey Brown* book. Teaching the poem and allowing the students to determine meaning as well as writing responses as if to write back to the writer.

Specific strategies from Willy Wood. I have used vocab activities in my room to great success.

Willy Wood vocab. exercises have been quite helpful.

I've learned many things this year that have been helpful in my classroom; my students have enjoyed these: (1) direct vocabulary instruction, (2) tea party, (3) mind mapping, (4) *Betsey Brown* activity.

Wow . . . I've used so many activities from this year. The *Background Knowledge* book activities include word play, roots/word part activities, nonlinguistic representations, and developing a wider vocabulary base. I also used activities from the fall poetry session.

I plan to use all information that I learned in my classroom from MOHum. Next year will be when I put this in place.

10. **Do you have any student achievement data that would support the idea that this project impacted student performance? If so, please describe and say how IEC can access it.**

I used *Witness* again this year, but did not use *Betsey Brown* yet.

I should be able to provide something in a stipend to write up. Yes, I have student work that I can e-mail to you.

Students have practiced Willy Wood's techniques in vocab and constructive response.

I think I might have some vocab and reading data that I will incorporate into my writing project.

Student data in progress.

Not solid data—the "light bulb moments" I've seen have greatly increased this year. Unfortunately that is not measurable.

I can only say that the exercises increased comprehension as is evident in daily work. I don't really have "formal" documentation.

I'm continuously reinforcing students to use new vocabulary words in their writing prompts.

I have not collected data specifically related to this project and its impact on student achievement. Most of the activities have been intertwined with science activities but it's something for me to think about for next year.

11. **Other comments about this project, especially how it impacted you:**

When teachers from diverse districts interact with each other, they expand their competencies.

It inspires me to do better every time I come. It motivates me to keep on doing good for kids!! Thanks for providing opportunities for me to grow.

This project always enriches my practice in powerful ways. This year in particular I have concentrated on vocabulary strategies and some of the critical testing strategies we used.

This has helped me to be more creative and to help bring out the creativity of my students.

This project really stimulates good ideas from teachers. Its best impact is from what we take to the classroom from other teachers and the bonding we make with them to be able to communicate with them—extend relationships as well as continue using them for more resources.

MOHum retreat is always informative.

Love the time for professional support/community.

Helping me to write down my reflections so that I put in print my audio voice in my head has been powerful. Let's keep this going!

The project has been a positive experience for me and it has given me more supportive teaching materials to use with students and share with fellow staff members. Looking forward to next school year.

My favorite part is the valuable teaching conversations that I have with other professionals, especially Bonnie and Sue. As a new teacher coming into this program last year, I was strongly impacted by the development I was able to receive from model teachers who are actively working to close the achievement gap. I cannot express in words how much I value this opportunity.

This is a wonderful, enriching project.

Hopefully, MOHum will continue next year, as it's the most valuable professional development I've had.

As a whole I enjoy the action research approach to improving instruction in class as well as improving staff reflections. Networking with other schools as well as providing a forum to improve as a professional.

I have more confidence in trying new strategies with my kids. I don't overlook my kids' strategies because of my fear; I address them head on because I know I can.

This is my second year in the program, and the knowledge materials and relationships I've gained have been invaluable. I see myself growing as a teacher and expanding my "teacher tool kit." I am becoming independent and confident enough to find ways to teach reading and writing in my science classroom.

MOHum pushes me to become an "Educator," not just a "Teacher."

(Continued)

(Continued)

SUMMARY

Again this year, the participants rated their overall MOHum experience highly as well as this final retreat. The teachers reported that they gained a great deal of knowledge that they are either using in their classrooms or will use. As one teacher stated, "I see myself growing as a teacher and expanding my 'teacher tool kit.'" The teachers frequently mentioned their increased knowledge of how to teach vocabulary and knowledge of new literature as a result of their participation in MOHum. They also stated that they appreciated the work of the leaders and presenters and that all of them were excellent. In short, MOHum was a successful experience for the participants and for IEC.

Reprinted with permission from independent evaluator Professor Michael Grady, PhD, St. Louis University, St. Louis, Missouri.

Note: MOHum is grant-based project that is part of the professional development division of Cooperating School Districts. The executive director of this professional development division is Dennis Lubeck. If not for Dennis's administrative style, this program would not have been developed and evolved into the successful project it is. Dennis believes in integrating the research into successful practice, focusing heavily upon content while enveloping it within the finest of pedagogy. Along with Sheila Onuska, the outstanding grant writer for this program and the associate director of the division, Dennis set the standard for professional development long before there were terms like "professional learning communities." In order to receive the grant year after year for this project, Dennis needed an extensive evaluation process and accountability piece. This is accomplished through the work of Dr. Michael Grady of St. Louis University, an expert in evaluation. If you are interested in reviewing these evaluations, they are available from Dennis Lubeck, dlubeck@csd.org, at the International Education Consortium (IEC), a division of Cooperating School Districts, www.csd.org. At the state level, Dr. Doug Miller of the Department of Elementary and Secondary Education (DESE) has been our supporter, mentor, and visionary for this project for the past decade.

SUMMARY

This chapter outlined a successful coaching project that has existed for more than a decade and included the specific work done to ensure its continued success. The project described involved multiple teams of teachers (some who think like us and some who don't) from multiple districts coming together four times per year to examine their instruction. As a result of this project, student achievement has improved in their classrooms because their teacher instruction has improved.

❖   ❖   ❖

In Chapter 10 you will read the account of a literacy coach as she supports teachers to write reflections about their classroom instruction. One teacher's written reflection about reading instruction was turned into an article for publication in *English Journal* and received the NCTE writing award for the best article of the year.

10

Coaching Teachers to Write and Reflect Upon Their Instructional Practices

The master teacher that lurks within each of us is likelier to burst forth within the intellectual atmosphere that collegiality can create.

—Author Unknown

This chapter focuses on how to coach teachers to improve instruction through individual teacher writing. Growing teachers as writers often involves challenging teachers who don't think like you to reexamine their mental models. This is a process and content chapter, emphasizing the how-to do the work as well as the what-if of the content. You might use the process in this chapter for the following kinds of professional development:

- Coaching teachers in a single department or across disciplines
- Coaching teachers in different buildings within a district
- Coaching teachers from different regions of a city or state

- Coaching teachers with university collaboration
- Coaching teachers using a research model such as the Teachers' Academy model described in this chapter

The content of the coaching in this chapter may transfer to your coaching in the following ways:

- Writing instruction for action research
- Writing instruction for teachers to use with students
- Questions for teacher reflection
- Passionate question: how to develop one for teacher reflection
- Student choice and student surveys: how to build choice and surveys into student learning
- Involving parents in teacher instruction
- Book talks and how to generate student dialogue
- Additional concrete strategies and effective methods to share with teachers to improve instruction

In this chapter, coach Sue Heggarty shares how to coach teachers to examine their practice and to formulate a question about it to research in their classroom. Sue shares her journey with Kim Gutchewsky, a young English teacher who welcomed Sue as her coach in a structured professional development format titled Teachers' Academy.

SUE HEGGARTY

Sue Heggarty is an educator with more than 40 years of experience. She taught English for 31 years and was an English department head for 22 of those years. She teaches English education courses at local universities, and for the past eight years she directed the Missouri Humanities Project for the Cooperating School Districts, housed at the University of Missouri-St. Louis. An avid reader and writer, she is currently writing a history of Lafayette Square, the historic district in which she has lived since 1974. Her areas of expertise include action research, literacy coaching, and interdisciplinary instruction with an emphasis on art and writing.

By Sue Heggarty

For four years I directed the Teachers' Academy for Cooperating School Districts, a consortium of school districts in the St. Louis area. After 31 years of middle and high school English, I retired from the classroom and began work in staff development. The Teachers' Academy was my first job in staff development, and it allowed me to use what I had learned about writing and about writing action research, or teacher reflection.

I had been department chair of our suburban school district English department, and I had designed and run writing projects in the summer with district teachers. I had watched the transformation of teachers so many times when they wrote and then shared their writing. I had watched them struggle, agonize, and labor over a personal narrative. I had witnessed the electricity in the room when teachers shared their writing with colleagues and immediately supported, praised, and encouraged each other.

The struggle and support carry over into each classroom. Every teacher is reminded of how important the process of writing and the struggle to compose are to every writer. Teachers return to their own classrooms with new sensitivity and a new arsenal of writing ideas taken from the summer trenches and their own experience.

While personal writing is a place to start, action research asks teachers to focus their attention on their own practice. Action research is defined as "a disciplined process of inquiry conducted by and for those taking the action. The primary reason for engaging in action research is to assist the actor in improving and refining his or her actions" (Sagor, 2000, p. 3). Sagor identifies a seven-step action research process: (1) selecting a focus, (2) clarifying theories, (3) identifying research questions, (4) collecting data, (5) analyzing data, (6) reporting results, and (7) taking informed action. While action research may have an academic structure, it is also an efficacious vehicle for learning about our own work. When we write, we learn what we think.

How can I tell what I think until I see what I say?

—E. M. Forster

Action Research

The term "action research" floated through educational communities in the late 1980s and early 1990s. Reflecting upon our teaching, in action, while we teach is the heart of this process. While teaching we find ways to gather data about our teaching and our students' learning. Finally, we give ourselves the time and structure to write about this process. We need to make time for reflection and to give ourselves time to write down those reflections. We really do not know what we think until we write it down.

Teachers' Academy Model

The Teachers' Academy model for staff development sprang up in many parts of the country in the 1990s. Financed by school districts and private philanthropies, this staff development model brought together university faculty and secondary and elementary school faculty to study the process of teaching and learning. Teachers from different departments, different school buildings, or even different districts were chosen to spend a year in study. The study was designed by the participating teachers. What did they want to learn? What had they heard about in educational circles, noticed in a glance at a professional magazine, heard mentioned in the teachers' lounge, or scanned on a Listserv? Seldom do teachers feel they have the time to stop and dig out the pertinent information. The Teachers' Academy model gives teachers the permission and the time to explore what will work in their classrooms.

The model begins and ends with a retreat of a day or an evening away from the school district for a group of about 25 teachers, university faculty, and staff developers. While time is precious, the time to build trusting

(Continued)

(Continued)

relationships is crucial. Time to talk about teaching in a safe environment ensures that the group of educators will learn to respect and listen to each other. There are many activities that encourage conversation. We used Tom Jackson's *Activities That Teach*, which is filled with short ideas for conversations. These same activities build conversation in the classroom as well. Whatever the method, time must be spent on learning about each other in the academy. We used the following questions to provoke conversation, first having the teachers write down their answers and then use them to engage in dialogue.

- When do you have conversations about your profession that bring growth and affirmation?
- When do you give yourself the time to reflect and discuss what happens in your classroom?
- When was the last time you realized that you can learn about your own teaching from listening and sharing with colleagues?

Questioning

Questioning is a centerpiece of the Teachers' Academy model. Once the group of teachers has spent time discussing their individual teaching situations and philosophies, they design a plan of study for the year. The study might include attending conferences or workshops or simply having resources available to learn more about technology, cooperative learning, or guided reading. Teachers choose their own topics and adapt their schedules to meet time constraints. They need release time from their classes as well as time for evening sessions with university faculty and facilitators.

University Connection

The university connection is a strength of this teacher development model. The graduate class model does not consistently offer conversation and coaching that is not tied to a grade and credit. In this academy setting, the university faculty person can offer expertise, the bigger picture, while not directly grading or rating the classroom teacher. The university faculty person offers understanding the depth of both practical and philosophical information. Last, the university faculty guides the teacher on his or her personal journey of reflection in action.

ACTION RESEARCH, OR HOW TO LEAD THE EXAMINED LIFE

Formal descriptions of action research abound, but basically it is you, the teacher, experimenting with a question about your teaching while you teach. Teachers are aware that they make hundreds of decisions each class period, on their feet, as they teach. With some planning and discussion with colleagues, it is possible to explore a question about your teaching without compounding an already stressful job.

Through university work we are aware of the form of traditional research. We associate it with those "hard" sciences: physics, chemistry, biology. But teachers also know that most of what goes on in any classroom comes down to a craft and an art.

Traditional Research

- Quantitative
- Objective (removing all bias)
- Experimental studies and correlational studies with control groups and experimental groups
- Tests, theories, hypotheses
- Reports of statistical significance
- Stems from "hard" sciences

Action Research

- Subjective
- Studies from living culture, the classroom
- Methods are observations, participation, interview journals, documents, analysis
- Findings: insights, concepts, understanding of culture and perspectives of participants
- Stems from anthropology

Action research is a reflective practice that gives teachers a framework for research in their own classroom. The reflection gives rise to innovation, experimentation, and collaboration, with both students and other teachers. So where does one begin? Begin with a question about your teaching. What do you wonder, passionately, about your teaching? What is your Passionate Question?

PASSIONATE QUESTIONS

Here are some questions teachers used. The question should be honest enough so that there is the possibility of discovery.

- How do I hear from every member of my class each day on the topic of the novel?
- Are there benefits to service-learning projects in a biology class?
- How can we create an outdoor classroom for interdisciplinary lessons?
- Will teaching writing and design (art) together enhance student understanding or appreciation of both subjects?
- Will touching each student each day, physically and verbally, increase student achievement?
- Can student-led group discussions on racism improve the climate in the classroom?

(Continued)

(Continued)

> - What are the benefits to classroom discipline of having live animals in the classroom?
> - Can students evaluate their own work and learn more by doing this?
> - What are the benefits to reading aloud in the high school English classroom?
> - What interventions will most significantly improve the attitudes and academic progress of at-risk students?

Kim Gutchewsky's Passionate Question

Kim Gutchewsky of Webster Groves, Missouri, began with a question: How can a high school English teacher change the attitudes of reluctant readers? She begins with a confession:

I've found that one of the most unnerving moments in professional development occurs when I'm asked "to share," especially when I have nothing to say. Such a moment occurred last year, during the first meeting of our district language arts team focused on improving reading scores. Right off the bat, the coordinator wanted to know what we were currently reading for fun and asked us each to share our reaction to the book. As I ran through my summer activities, I couldn't think of anything I'd really read for fun, so I dove into the archives of the past school year, past summer, previous school year. . . . Imagine my horror, then, when I realized that I would be forced to admit to my colleagues—English teachers, for heaven's sake—that I hadn't read anything for fun in as long as I could remember. I was so far removed from noncanonical literature that I couldn't even make up a workable lie. The "sharing" worked its way around to my side of the table, and in a fit of perspiration, I spilled my guts: "I'm afraid I just don't have time to read for enjoyment. You know student essays always come first, and reviewing the novels in the curriculum takes time, and you all know that I've just begun my master's degree in literature. Did I mention that I am newly married and have other priorities? And then there's that darn library card issue that I can't seem to get resolved. . . ."

Although I seemed to survive the morning's inquisition, I was left unnerved by what I had realized about myself, and the occasion provided much reason for professional and personal introspection.

Kim has an epiphany:

What do our kids usually say when we ask them if they like to read? The most common reactions are variations of the following:

1. I don't have time to read.

2. I've never read anything I liked.

3. Reading is hard.

So discovering that I use many of the same excuses helped me to develop empathy for my kids. Even the most conscientious students legitimately have a hard time prioritizing reading; they go home to five or six classes of homework, jobs, and the all-important social life. So who has time to read?

Kim examined her students and the many obstacles to their reading, both diagnosed and not diagnosed, and she comes to her passionate question:

Kim's Question Expanded

With so many roadblocks in front of students and teachers, how can we help students become better readers? Thus I began my action research. I decided that the focus of my next school year would be reading. Because I did not begin and end the year on reading test scores, I'll never be able to assert this action research as objective or scientific. However, I found through articles and research that helping a reluctant reader to be less afraid of the task is a huge step toward helping him or her become a better reader, and it is on this theory that I based my action research.

STUDENT CHOICE

Kim scanned magazine and newspaper articles about low reading scores and proposed solutions. One commonality seemed to be student choice. Letting students choose what they read helps engage even the most reluctant reader. She decided to explore this motivation, but how and when to do it was a struggle. A prescribed curriculum in a suburban high school is rigorous and requires time. This leaves little time for choices.

Student Surveys

Kim surveyed her students for their attitudes toward reading.

Out of nearly 100 students, only 1 brave soul claimed that she enjoys reading, but she admitted that she never has time to do so. The remaining students were broken down into categories: 59% said that they do not read because they "hate it," "it's stupid," or something similar; 24% said they do not read because "it's hard." The remaining students varied: some said they didn't read because they've "never found anything worth reading."

Sadly, the majority of our classroom consists of nonreaders; yet we all can't throw in the towel on reading.

Involving the Parents

Kim found places in the curriculum when her freshman students were not reading an assigned novel together, and she could require them to choose a novel to read outside of class. She created the list of 30 choices so that kids could not choose a book too easy for them. She involved the parents with permission slips for outside readings and introduced the unit at a parent open house.

(Continued)

(Continued)

STUDENT-TO-STUDENT BOOK TALKS

Kim found a successful strategy: student-to-student book talks.

About once a week throughout this unit, I put students in groups to discuss what they were reading. . . . Since I had modeled a book talk for them, I felt comfortable giving the students very few and general guidelines for theirs. During their talks, I roamed around the room and eavesdropped, asking them questions if the talks slowed to a halt, but trying not to interfere so as to keep their discussions as sincere as possible. When we returned to whole-group discussion, I called on students to tell the class about their partner's book; this was a sneaky way of keeping them accountable for the group time and making sure they politely listened to each other.

Some of the best teacher moments of the year occurred during these weeks because I heard some quality dialogue:

Mrs. Gutchewsky:	Mark, could you tell the class about the book that Larry is reading?
Mark:	I'd like to, but I really don't think that Larry has read much since last week. He's reading *Hiroshima*, and he didn't tell us anything new about the book this time.
Larry:	Nuh-un! I have so read a little. I've got soccer this week, so I didn't have time to read too much.
Michelle (random interjector):	Come on, Larry, we've all got stuff going on. You better learn to keep up or else you're not going to make it through your book.

Another group:

Shenelle (to her character):	I tell you what. My girl's got it going on! She's not putting up group, about her with no man's stuff. She knows when she is not treatedmain female right, so she's got self-respect enough to say "good-bye" to his sorry behind.
Chaniqua:	Your girl sounds just like you. I bet you like your book.
Shenelle:	You know I do.

Mike's group did not realize I was in earshot:

Mike:	I can't believe you guys are actually reading your books. Why didn't you just do what I did and pick a book that I know has a movie. I'm just going to watch the movie when she has the stuff due.
Kevin:	Don't you know how to read? Besides, I heard the *Tom Sawyer* movie isn't like the book.
Mike:	Of course I know how to read. I just don't want to.

| Kevin: | Then you're a moron. High school isn't like middle school; you've got to read all the time for real here. You're also missing out. I like my book a lot and it's better than any movie they'd make about it. |
| Mike: | What's your book? |

Additional Strategies to Motivate Students to Read

Kim also tries extra credit reading, silent sustained reading, and teacher conferencing one-on-one. Understandably, she discovers a problem for teachers when we haven't read the book the student chooses to read. She discovers that the student is willing to share much more when the teacher admits not having read the book but is interested in knowing about the book. Knowing how and when to relinquish some control and authority is a major lesson for any teacher.

Kim's lesson: "It is unnatural for a teacher to put herself in a situation where she is unprepared; I've never felt at ease professionally in the situations where I didn't know as much as my students, especially when they are being graded on that knowledge. But the dilemma remains: if I'm trying to engage my students by allowing them to pursue their own reading interests, how can I limit them to what I know?"

REFLECTION

That is what action research is about. We ask questions about our teaching and we see where that question takes us. The data we collect take us on this journey. Data should be at least threefold. Triangulation, bringing at least three methods of data collection together, is the goal.

Effective methods to use:

- Classroom observation, teacher journal. Record your thoughts. Take the time to write it down. Use the margin of lesson plan book or any form that works for you.
- Students' written or interview responses. Ask your students what they think about their learning and your teaching. Be fearless. Include them in the research.
- Student products, student work. What can you learn from their work about your teaching?
- Videotape. Tape your teaching and student interactions.
- Audiotape. Set the recorder on your chair and forget about it. Record the discussion and/or your lesson.
- Test results. Look at tests over time. Compare types of tests and student successes. When students do well on a test, why do they? Why do they do less well on other types of tests? What type of tests do you give? One type? Many kinds?
- Anecdotal records of student interactions. Stand back and watch their interactions. Take the time to write it down.
- Attendance records, discipline referrals. What do these records show about a particular student or several in a single class?

(Continued)

(Continued)

- Observations of colleagues or students from another class. Enlist the help of a colleague or an older student. Invite their observation and their feedback.
- Parental feedback. Informal interactions or survey for a formal piece of feedback.
- Structured interviews or questionnaires. Construct a set of questions to give students, parents, and colleagues.

Kim's Reflection

Kim employed more than three of these methods and she relied on her students to let her know her effectiveness.

My end-of-the-year survey asked students to anonymously respond to the question, "I asked you at the beginning of the year about your opinion of reading. After a year, has anything changed? Do enjoy reading now? Why or why not?"

Seventy percent of students said they liked to read now or have always liked to read as long as they're reading what they like. (When I compare this to the one child at the beginning of the year who said she liked to read, I see a positive.)

Twenty-six percent said they hate to read.

The rest had ambiguous responses.

Kim admitted that none of her techniques were new or failsafe.

This study has been an awakening in that I have been reminded of the importance of just generally talking about reading; because I'm in the middle of my master's in literature program, I often just spent a few minutes of class time telling my students about the book I currently have to read and what I think of it. Very simple, but it helped maintain the reading focus of the class atmosphere. I was also reminded of the importance of close-reading skills; requiring text-based support will only help students become good readers, writers, and thinkers, which will also help prepare them for English at higher levels.

A tremendous help to my findings was actually just doing the research. This process required that I choose one aspect of my teaching on which to improve, and by keeping a journal and careful notes of students' performances and my personal reactions, the year was a time of constant introspection, which can help any professional.

Because Kim was a member of Teachers' Academy when she did this research, she followed a suggested form and then worked with the form until it fit the question she had chosen and the kinds of data she collected. Kim, with encouragement from me, took the action research and turned it into an article for *English Journal.* For her efforts, Kim's writing was not only published, but her article won the Paul and Kate Farmer *English Journal* Writing Award for the Outstanding Article published in *English Journal* for 2002.

PARTS AND PIECES

Action research should include the following in some logical order:
  Most will be included, but not all pieces may apply to your question.

- A statement of the passionate question and rationale for addressing it
- A summary or overview of actions the researcher took to address the question
- A description of the context, setting, or background of the study
- An explanation of the research methods and types of data collected
- A descriptive account or narrative of what happened in the study
- An interpretation or analysis of the data collected or the findings
- Conclusions, recommendations, suggestions for future actions
- Connections to existing research (an option)

Journals

In our journals, we write to see what we know. Each year I taught, I bought a "book of days," usually filled with works of art or bits of poetry in which the days of the month are spread out without attention to the year. September 1st may be a Wednesday or a Thursday, and each year I noted what my students were like that year and where I wanted to take them. Sometimes bits of my family's life would float through or feelings about work and life, but each year was a new beginning. An entry in 1998 sits beside an entry in 2000, and in a glance I could see change and growth. That is the best element of teaching, each year a new beginning and a new chance to get it right. In 31 years I never really got it right, but the journey was wondrous. We have an obligation as professionals to record that journey, and we further the profession as we do.

Not all action research needs a formal publishing goal, but putting thoughts, epiphanies, and revelations into writing is its own reward. In his 2003 *Unspeakable Acts, Unnatural Practices*, Frank Smith says, "Writing provides the additional power to create our own characters, express our feelings and develop our ideas, and submit them to our own private inspection. Long before any piece of writing influences a reader—if it ever gets that far—it symbiotically affects the person who writes it" (p. 87).

We write and read to know what we know and what we need to know, and that is what we want for our students. Teachers want their students to be thinkers, readers, researchers, writers, and speakers. Teachers must be what they want their students to be.

You may contact Sue at sheggarty@csd.org for information about Teachers' Academy, action research, and consulting.

SUMMARY

To walk the talk and model what our students need to see, hear, and feel, we must become writers. This chapter gave you an example for using reflective writing in the form of action research with the teachers you coach. Kim's writing shows us why even strong teachers need to question their pedagogy and model for students what they want them to do and be. Kim reflected, wrote, published, and improved her instruction! This chapter described that process along with ways to transfer the strategies and methods to your coaching work.

❖   ❖   ❖

Chapter 11 brings us full circle as it describes a summer writing project that can be the beginning of your work as a literacy coach in a district, the interim work, or the culmination.

11

Coaching Teachers as Writers

A Writing Workshop Model

Thoughts are created in the act of writing, which changes the writer and changes emerging text.

—Frank Smith

In order to teach writing, teachers must be writers themselves. Teachers usually don't see themselves as writers, and when they walk into a writing workshop, often they are *not* going to think like the coach presenting the workshop. This presents a challenge. For teachers to see themselves first as writers, then as teachers of writing, no matter what their discipline, often requires a huge paradigm shift. One way to accomplish this paradigm shift is to immerse teachers in a multiday experience of writing. This might be a school, district, state, or national writers' workshop or writing project. This chapter describes the process and the content (the how-to and the what-if) of a writing workshop where teachers learn how to be writers themselves as well as how to immerse their students in writing experiences to improve student achievement. This workshop model was used successfully with staffs in several diverse school districts. These included:

- A middle school staff in the inner city (6–8)
- A district staff (K–12) in an affluent suburban district
- A staff in a middle class suburban district (K–12)
- A staff in an outer suburban school district (K–12)
- A small rural school district staff (K–5)

How does this chapter translate to your work as a coach? You may not have the opportunity to implement a writing workshop as described in this chapter; however, many of the strategies discussed may be helpful in your work as a coach. You'll find the following:

- Questions to assess your comfort level as a writer
- Models for writing experiences
- A flyer for a writing workshop
- Agendas for writing workshops
- Strategies to use during a writing experience with teachers
- Activities to use during a writing experience with teachers and/or students
- Participants' comments about the writing workshop
- Teacher's comments about application in her classroom

WHAT IS THE WRITING WORKSHOP?

The writing workshop is a favorite part of the professional development experience because it focuses on the belief systems of participants engaged in deep reflection and writing as they shift paradigms. Teachers join the workshop thinking of themselves as teachers of writing—or not—but seldom do they enter thinking of themselves as writers. As Frank Smith (1983) tells us, we must be writers ourselves in order to teach students how to write.

The following describes a writing workshop we facilitated numerous times in several districts. In no way does this workshop take the place of formalized writing projects such as the Bay Area Writing Project, the Gateway Writing Project, and the Iowa Writing Project. If you have the opportunity, consider attending one of these national writing project (NWP) opportunities. However, if you are working in a district as a literacy coach and want to offer the staff an extended writing experience, the following may work for you. When an NWP four- to six-week-long writing project is not feasible for reasons of time, distance, cost, and so on, consider an in-district writing workshop based on the following model, which is valuable for teachers in all content areas.

Evaluations

The evaluations of writing workshops are uniformly excellent, and teachers comment that this workshop challenges and changes their former paradigms about what students are capable of writing as well as what teachers themselves are capable of writing. Teachers and administrators, K–12, who take part in the writing workshop begin to see themselves as "real" writers and to understand the power of writing. As they struggle and write as real writers do, they learn more about themselves and the struggles their students face as they use writing to learn.

DO YOU SEE YOURSELF AS A WRITER?

I did not think of myself as a writer until I took the Clayton Writing Project (a district-based writing project held in the Clayton School District in Clayton, Missouri). In the summer of 1991, I learned to trust my writing voice and share it with colleagues. Your teachers will do the same when you offer them the opportunity to write as real writers in a community of safety.

How comfortable with writing are the teachers you coach? Why, or why not?

_____

_____

_____

_____

How comfortable are you with writing?

_____

_____

_____

_____

Are you as comfortable with writing as you are with reading? Why, or why not?

_____

_____

_____

_____

What activities do you set up to encourage teachers to write and model "real writers"?

_____

_____

_____

What do you do for yourself to improve and practice your own writing?

_____

_____

_____

_____

SAMPLE FLYER/AGENDA FOR A WRITING PROJECT

Below is a sample flyer and agenda. In addition, there are tips for conducting a writing workshop, followed by actual comments from participants as to how their writing workshop experience changed their writing instruction and their use of writing in their content area.

Once you know the names of the participants for the writing workshop, send them a couple of articles to stimulate interest. Arrange to meet with them to give them an overview of the workshop. Use the time to meet and learn something about the participants.

Flyer for the Workshop

Summer Writing Workshop

Audience: K–12 teachers and administrators
Where: Administration Building
Open to All Staff
Instructor: Dr. Bonnie Davis
Time: 8:00 A.M.–3:30 P.M. daily
Length: 5 Days

Begin your summer with a workshop experience like no other! Come join your colleagues for the Summer Writing Project. During our five days together, we will explore the potential of writing to expand our inner voice, build community, and deepen our learning. This workshop blends pedagogy and personal expression with plenty of time for writing, reading, and discussing literacy application across the curriculum. You will leave energized with lots of ideas for your personal writing and your classroom (not to mention many new friends).

Goals
- Participants (classroom teachers and administrators) will write and read about writing for five full days.
- Participants will exit this workshop better understanding the writing process and what their students experience when they are assigned writing across the disciplines.
- Participants will exit the workshop with finished pieces of their writing.
- Participants will exit the workshop with numerous concrete strategies that motivate and support student writing that they may implement in their classrooms during the next school year.

Agenda

Day 1
8:00   Coffee/conversation
8:30   "Our Writing Journey"
10:00   Writing pedagogy: what the research tells us
11:00   How to begin the process
Noon   Lunch on your own
1:00   Writing time
2:00   How we share our writing
2:30   Sharing
3:30   Adjourn

Homework: Write for a time in the evening and bring drafts for the next day.

Day 2
8:00   Coffee/conversation
8:30   Writing pedagogy (cont.)
9:30   Sharing in small groups
10:30   Large group reflection/processing
11:00   Reading about writing
Noon   Lunch on your own
1:00   Writing time
2:30   Sharing
3:30   Adjourn

Homework: Continue writing.

Day 3
8:00   Coffee/conversation
8:30   Stretching our writing muscles
10:00   Reading about writing pedagogy: writing across the disciplines
11:00   Small group sharing
Noon   Lunch on your own
1:00   Sharing our stories
2:00   Writing on your own
3:00   Revision strategies
3:30   Adjourn

Homework: Choose some of your writing for revision. Practice revision strategies on a part of your writing. Choose one short piece to share on our final day together.

Day 4
8:00   Coffee/conversation
8:30   For the Good of the Group (see asterisk below)
9:00   Reading/writing on your own
11:15   Sharing
Noon   Lunch on your own
1:00   Reading/writing on your own
2:30   Sharing
3:30   Adjourn

Day 5
8:00   Coffee/conversation
8:30   Pedagogy: How has this Writing Workshop informed our classroom instruction?

(Continued)

(Continued)

10:30	Final time to write
11:30	Reflections on the workshop
Noon	Lunch together
1:00	Sharing our stories, poems, essays, memoirs: celebrating our collegiality
3:30	Adjourn; evaluations

University Credit: Two hours university credit available through Webster University

For those participants taking the Writing Project for university credit:

Assignments:

- Participants will write and revise approximately 15 pages of typed original writing.
- Participants will read books on writing pedagogy throughout the workshop and discuss them with colleagues, emphasizing application in their classrooms for the coming school year.

Grade: The participant's grade will be based on the following:

- **Daily Participation Required**. No absences allowed for credit.
- **Written pages**: To be assessed by instructor.
- **Oral Participation**: Daily oral participation in large and small groups.

Supplies: Poster paper, markers

---

*For the Good of the Group

Directions: Begin each morning after coffee/conversation with a "For the Good of the Group." Ask participants if anyone has anything to say "for the good of the group." After you ask the question, remain silent until someone responds, no matter how long you must remain silent. This stimulates conversation based on the insights gained by focusing on writing during the workshop. It also builds community, airs concerns, generates ideas, and sets the tone for the day's work. I first learned the For the Good of the Group strategy from Lola Mapes (Des Moines, Iowa) and have used it successfully in multiday workshops, no matter the topic.

ACTIVITIES TO USE IN A WRITING PROJECT

Note: Many of these activities can be used in the regular classroom. Modify them to suit your needs.

1. On the first morning, ask participants to jot down all the things they have written during the past week. Respond aloud. You usually receive responses such as lists, e-mail, IEPs, journals, thank-you notes, letters, cards, and so on. Process the responses by stating that we are all writers who write throughout our daily lives.

2. Do three-minute freewrites about a topic you choose. Ask participants to share. Use wait time (sit quietly until someone volunteers), and you will always have someone who shares. After three or so shares, read your own.

   Example: We used this freewrite on the first day: Describe the summers you used to have.

This is what I wrote and shared:

> *I loved the heat, the sweating, sweltering, sopping heat, walking with a cold bottle of water, a wet wash cloth around my neck, up and down the hills under the big trees that blanketed the neighborhood. I loved the blanket in the backyard where I would lie for hours in the sun, bathed in baby oil before skin cancer was christened a reality, and read my day's choice of fiction with a glass of unsweetened strong ice tea propped at my elbow under the clothesline of white sheets hanging limply in the stillness of summer.*

By sharing my freewrite after others have shared theirs, I accomplish the following:

- Show openness and vulnerability
- Model and take part in the process
- Allow participants to see me as both a writer and a human being
- When all the participants write together, it builds the writing community, whether they share or not

3. Read Frank Smith's (1983) article "Myths of Writing." Participants discuss.

4. Practice sustained silent reading (SSR), using books on writing pedagogy.

5. Use free time to read and write.

6. Ask participants to change seats each day to experience the workshop from a new perspective.

7. As participants find quotes in their reading or in the writing, post them on the quote page (a poster board or area in the room). These can be a long quote or a single word. This activity builds community and stimulates ideas for future writing.

8. Post words to pilfer and use in your writing.

9. Show the participants opportunities for publication. Bring in journals and other publication materials.

10. Bring in dozens of books and do book talks on the books. Ask participants to post titles/authors of their favorite books, professional and personal choices.

11. Do a book walk around the tables of the books and point out books that might interest individual participants.

12. Have several books on hand that you can give away to stimulate interest.

13. Use a styles inventory to illustrate that each participant is an individual who learns in a unique way.

14. Use humor.

15. Begin each day by reading a poem to the group. Ask participants to read the poems.

16. Use questions to serve as writing prompts.

17. Ask participants to share their "writing journey." Give participants 15 minutes and a full sheet of poster paper with choice of markers and pens. Tell them to use words and nonlinguistic representations. When completed, share in groups of three, giving each participant three minutes to share his or her journey with the group. This time builds community, shares commonalities, reinforces how much we have written during our lives, displays our persona for the public, and builds a shared writing journey for the group. After the sharing, hang the posters throughout the area and do a journey walk to view all participants' writing journeys.

After teachers overcome their fears and produce some writing, their next big fear sets in when they share it with their colleagues. The following is a vehicle for response that ensures only positive specific feedback that supports powerful revision.

PARTICIPANT SHARING

(Workshop facilitators need to first model the participant sharing in order to avoid confusion.)

1. Participants sit in a circle.

2. Depending upon the amount of time allowed, participants share their writing. Participants volunteer to share. There is *no* mandatory sharing in a writing workshop. For example, during the first sharing, two to three participants may share their writing.

3. The first volunteer reads his or her piece out loud to the group.

4. During the reading, the others practice good listening skills, such as attentive body language, writing down key phrases, and not interrupting the reader.

5. When the reader finishes, the entire group gives the reader applause, then sits quietly for approximately seven seconds.

6. After the silent wait time, during which participants collect their thoughts, the responses begin.

7. Listeners respond with specific, positive comments to what they have heard. Listeners make no negative statements and avoid generalized statements, such as "I liked your piece." Instead, listeners respond with specific comments about the writing. For example, they may read back

specific phrases from the piece that they jotted while listening, then comment on them. Or they may say something such as "I like the way you introduced your piece with the anecdote about your mother. It grabbed my attention immediately."

Note: Listeners may not include *any* personal information in their comments. Nothing may be added to the comment that did not arise out of the piece. For example, listeners may *not* say, "I like the way you introduced your piece with an anecdote about your mother. Your mom is just like my mom." This shifts the focus from the writer to the listener. If listeners take care to avoid anything in their comments that was not in the writing, they will avoid this trap. The response is all about the writer, not about the listener.

This is often confusing to participants because they may think that a personal comment, such as the one stated above where the listener says, "It grabbed my attention immediately," is about them. No, it is their opinion, but it does not detract from the piece or add additional personal information that was not included in the piece. They may state their opinion; they may not add personal information to expand and detract from the writer's piece.

8. After several listeners comment, the facilitator cues for the next kind of response, which is an "I wonder" response. Now listeners respond to the writer, beginning their sentences with "I wonder . . . ." For example, they may say, "I wonder what your piece would sound like if it were written from the viewpoint of your mother." The reader/writer may *not* respond to these "I wonder" statements. These give the writer additional ideas to use during revision, if he or she desires to do so. The facilitator explains to the group how "not answering" these queries actually promotes thinking for the writer/reader; whereas if the writer/reader gave an answer, that might end the thinking about the query. This also adds an element of curiosity and suspense to t he readings as listeners as well as the writer/reader leave with open questions.

9. Finally, everyone looks around the group, making eye contact and thanking all who participated in the sharing. (Adapted from Linda Henke, 1991–1997, *The Clayton Writing Project*)

As you might imagine, this activity is a tremendous community builder. Participants bond quickly during a writing workshop because they share their personal selves with each other in a community willing to be silent, noncritical, and receptive. It is a powerful experience!

Left to their own decisions about when to share, all participants eventually share. In 15 years of writing workshops, not one participant has refused to share by the end of the workshop.

Why do participants enjoy writing workshops so much?

- Facilitators work hard to ensure that each participant's voice is listened to—both the spoken voice and the written voice.
- Facilitators use brain-compatible delivery of content material.
- Facilitators make themselves available to participants throughout the workshop.
- Facilitators do all activities with participants. They write with participants and share their writing with the group. They model what good writers and good teachers do in their classrooms.
- Facilitators ensure that the sharing is safe, nonthreatening, and productive.
- Facilitators use provocative writing prompts and engaging activities throughout the workshop.
- Facilitators ensure that the workshops are held in a peaceful setting where amenities, such as good food and drink, laptop computers, comfortable chairs and nooks for privacy, time and space considerations, access to nature, and so on are available.
- Facilitators present the writing workshop as a "spa for the mind" during which participants focus on themselves, not their neighbors, not their students, not their families, but themselves. They are truly on an inward writing journey, where one takes the gift of time in a retreat-like setting and writes inward to discover and learn more about oneself.

PARTICIPANTS' COMMENTS TAKEN FROM WRITTEN EVALUATIONS

At the end of each writing workshop, we ask for evaluations from the participants. As stated earlier, these are uniformly positive. Some samples are below.

My participation in the writing project left me with a desire, a very strong desire, to continue writing and to get my students to discover the joys of writing. I have discovered the joy of writing my heart, taking my pain, frustrations, love, and expressing them on paper, not hiding them in my male-centric heart. I now relish the time I have for writing and I am on a quest to share this discovery with my math students.

—John Hefflinger, Math Teacher

It was tremendously beneficial for self-renewal and stress release and for sharing with students who can learn to do the same. Pedagogy and creativity were combined in a practical and accepting way.

—Jan Dineen, Reading Specialist

Time to write and read and think is a gift. As teachers, or maybe even just adults, finding the time for ourselves and to cultivate our creative talents is difficult. I honestly was looking forward to having time to read this week, but found myself spending most of the work time writing. Therapeutic, relaxing, invigorating, frustrating, inspiring—all of these words describe the last week. Thank you for all of the time and reminding me how much writing is part of my life.

—Jennifer Bange, English Teacher

At the end of the Writers' Project, I feel a weight lifted off my shoulders. Each time I return to my notebook to add more thoughts to paper, my mind expands. I look at the world with a writer's eyes, something I don't usually do.

—Angie Dickson, History Teacher

The Writing Project is like a wonderful gift that arrives totally unexpected. It is a gift of time—time to reflect, read and write. It is a gift of sharing of ideas, of feelings, of books, of friendship. It is a gift of laughter and tears. It is an experience that will help us as teachers to better help students be successful—in the classroom and in life, and help us as human beings in our life's journey. We will nurture students to be writers and readers. We will nurture ourselves to be writers and readers.

—Mary Lou Montgomery, Science Teacher

This week has been invaluable to my writing soul. I used to write all the time, especially when I needed to confront difficult situations or emotions, but I really had gotten away from it over the past several years. It took a while even this week, but I'm back to cleansing my soul through my own written word. Now that I've reconnected with writing, I'm eager to implement what I've learned in my own classroom. I know my students have a lot to say!

—April Horst, English Teacher

These comments came from a few teachers who took part in a workshop given in the summer of 2006; however, each year the reflections mirror these no matter when the workshop occurs. Since 1992, when I began facilitating writing workshops, I have found that they are truly a spa for the mind and soul that offer educators time to reconnect with their writing lives.

Does the writing workshop experience translate to the classroom? The answer is nearly always yes. Teachers take back their newfound writing confidence and implement "writing to learn" in various forms in their classroom. After Robyn took the writing workshop, she transformed how she taught English.

Robyn's comments:

I looked around the classroom and saw them all. They were writers. My students were real writers. I thought to myself how far I've come. . . .

When I started in the classroom, writing was the most difficult subject to address with students. Now, it is a favorite! I had read books about Writer's Workshop, but I had nothing real to hang the information on. Thanks to one week in the summer spent with Dr. Bonnie Davis and several pioneer teachers setting out to find their own voice, I found my hook. In that week of the first ever St. Charles Writing Project, I also found my voice, my spirit, and my vision for the classroom.

(Continued)

(Continued)

> *Before being coached by fellow teachers, I found writing almost as dull and boring as my students did. Now we all look forward to "turn-in day." It is a ritual in the classroom. We not only share our projects, we share our life stories, our creativity, and our personality. Each six weeks we kick back, eat candy (I am a teacher and know the value of a treat!), and read our projects aloud. Students share on a voluntary basis, but we always manage to fill an entire class period just sharing our finished work and celebrating our success. We also share on other days of writing workshop to get a glimpse into the road a student is traveling toward a finished piece of work, but the turn-in days allow me to learn more about my students than anything else we do throughout the year. I might mention, as well, that Writing Workshop projects have the highest turn-in percentage of any other project we do. The freedom to choose . . . the creativity expressed . . . the lives revealed in each session of writing workshop makes it a rewarding program for my students.*
>
> *More than a successful writing program, however, Writer's Workshop is an opening into the lives and minds of my students. We all work with students that do not look and behave as we do. How powerful for us to be able to see into those lives through writing. We, as educators and individuals who value the power of writing, must learn from each other and guide each other through the high mountains and deep caverns of our profession.*

Robyn's comments attest to the fact that the writing workshop experience brings about changes in classroom instruction. It's true that Robyn is an English teacher, yet teachers across the content areas leave writing workshop experiences better equipped to incorporate daily writing activities in their classroom instruction. John wrote this comment after he implemented what he had learned in the writing workshop:

> *My practice after having attended the writing workshop: I now have my math class write two or three times a week. I encourage the "reluctant" writers to write what's in their hearts, to pour out their frustrations, or love, of math on their paper. The benefits of this are awesome: I am not the recipient of their frustrations, and they feel better after doing so. My students actually look forward to writing in math class.*
>
> —John Hefflinger, Math Teacher

Often, that is not the only change that occurs. Many teachers use their newfound confidence in their writing to form writing groups in their schools. These groups often meet monthly to continue the writing and sharing teachers did during their summer experience.

The writing workshop offers coaches a valuable tool to facilitate change, both in teacher instruction and school climate. In addition, the writing workshop is a valuable method to build community across schools in a district, to improve school culture, and to continue long-term professional development and teacher growth.

SUMMARY

This chapter outlined the process and content of a writing workshop used with teachers. Included are agendas, activities, strategies, and suggestions for implementing writing experiences that allow teachers to discover themselves as writers and to learn how to better support their students as writers.

❖　❖　❖

The appendices include frequently asked questions about coaching, coaching strategies, and additional resources.

SUGGESTED WRITING PROMPTS

1. Write about one of the most frustrating days in your life.

2. If you knew you were going to die tomorrow, to whom would you write tonight and what would you say?

3. What is your favorite vehicle and why? You don't have to own it.

4. If you could have free tickets to any event in history, what would it be and why?

5. With what three historical figures would you most like to share a dinner and why?

6. If you could take a vacation with any literary character, which would it be?

7. Create a list of 100 things you would not do.

8. Create a list of 100 things you would like to do in your lifetime.

9. Describe your perfect dream vacation.

10. Write about the five books/authors that most influenced you in your life.

11. Write about the faults you most hate in others. How do you avoid these faults in yourself?

12. Describe how you think your life might be if you were born the opposite sex: who would be your partner, what would be your profession, accomplishments, and so on.

13. Describe what your 10 most precious possessions (not people) have been throughout your lifetime.

14. What are your peak times of day? How do you use your peak times to your advantage?

15. Write about how you organize your life.

(Continued)

(Continued)

16. Describe your parade of holidays: which do you celebrate most heartily, dislike, ignore, wish you could celebrate, and so on.

17. Which are your favorite numbers and why?

18. Would you rather travel in a space ship or a submarine and why?

19. What forms of exercise and/or sports do you most enjoy and why?

20. Write about the colors of your world.

21. What are your favorite animals and why?

22. What mysteries in life would you most like revealed during your lifetime?

23. What facets of you have changed during the past decade; what facets have remained the same?

24. If you could, for what aspects/people/challenges of your life would you hold a requiem service?

25. Write about your gift to the universe.

Final Words

A young teacher recently told me she takes a picture of each of her fifth-grade students in the cap and gown she wore when she graduated from college. She then posts the photos on her classroom walls. For the entire year, her students "see" themselves as college graduates as they continue their journey toward this goal. As you read this book, hopefully you visualized how you "look" as a coach. If it worked, you learned some tips to navigate the maze of details involved in coaching, you found some strategies to implement when you coach teachers, and you discovered new resources to expand your coaching repertoire. You heard the writing "voices" of expert coaches who shared their failures and their successes in the hope of providing you with the vision you need to fulfill your dream of being the best coach you can be.

Thank you for joining us on our journey. We hope to hear about yours! Please contact me at a4achievement@earthlink.net.

Appendix A

Frequently Asked Questions

Below are questions that were asked at a gathering of language arts coordinators and coaches.

1. Are there specific strategies for coaching that you think are applicable to most classrooms that are especially effective? If so, what are they?

Reading and writing strategies that work across the disciplines are especially effective. Before reading, during reading, and after reading strategies work in every classroom. We especially like the strategies found in Robert Marzano's books (see Bibliography) and in Janet Allen's (2004) book *Tools for Teaching Content Literacy*. When demonstrating lessons in reading and writing workshops, we use books by Nancie Atwell (1998), Ralph Fletcher (1998), Fountas and Pinnel (2001), Jim Burke (1999, 2000, 2003, 2006), Donald Graves (1989), and others (see Bibliography).

2. How do you "coach" a teacher who doesn't want to be coached? Example: she uses excuses all the time or has already tried everything you suggest.

You can do several things. First, understand that the teacher has a reason for feeling the way she does. Honor her feelings by giving her respect. You may want to ask her a question to help you understand why she feels the way she does. Read about reluctant teachers in Chapter 3.

3. How do you motivate burned-out teachers to reach out to their students' needs?

Burned-out teachers can't reach out to their students' needs because they feel their needs are not being met. First, you must find how you can meet some of the needs of the teachers with whom you work. Try to reach out to your teachers with kindness. Listen to them and listen quietly without trying to fix them. Stay quiet in your listening. Be open in your body language. Try meeting with the teachers and offer them something that will make their lives just a bit nicer. This might be food. This might be a strategy for them to use in their classrooms. This might be a quiet ear. This might be a hug.

4. Literacy coaching sounds good. What do we do about high school students who read on a fourth-grade level and have no access to any kind of remedial reading instruction?

You can offer some help even if you are not a remedial reading instructor! Read the chapters in my book *How to Teach Students Who Don't Look Like You* (Davis, 2006) on creating a reading culture in your schools. Coach your teachers to build libraries in their rooms—suggest books that attract high school students reading below grade level such as the Bluford series from Townsend Press (www.townsend.com). Institute a sustained silent reading (SSR) program in your school based on the research and suggestions of Robert Marzano (2004).

5. How do you motivate teachers to learn all they can to improve teaching?

You have to tap into what each teacher needs in order to support change. Begin by being your authentic self and reach out to the teachers. Most important, *listen* to them and their concerns. Offer them something concrete and doable in their classrooms. Make yourself available. Demonstrate lessons, if they ask for them. Give nonevaluative feedback, if they ask for it. Follow up with more listening, more strategies, more patience, and more belief in their ability to "fix" themselves.

6. I'm interested in motivating teachers to embrace (well, at least show interest in) professional development in differentiating instruction. How do I do that?

Offer a workshop that is differentiated to prove the worth of differentiating. Discuss the importance of both relationship building and instructional best practices when working as a coach with teachers.

7. How does your literacy coaching differ with more resistant teachers than with gung-ho teachers?

You have to work harder, be more patient, listen better, and lengthen the time of your learning curve.

8. How has your knowledge of teaching "students who don't look like you" affected or influenced your approaches to teaching literacy?

I know now that first I must connect to the student (or the teacher) who does not look like me before I begin to teach the content. Read the strategies to build relationships and connections in *How to Teach Students Who Don't Look Like You* and in this book. I also need to remember that each human is a unique brain who learns in a unique way. I will fail if I stereotype students or teachers rather than approach each one as a unique individual. That said, there are some cultural homogeneities I need to be aware of before I work with any cultural group; therefore, I must learn as much as possible about those with whom I work.

9. **How do you get into every teacher's classroom?**

If you mean logistically, I schedule observations. I spend less time than you might think. Fifteen to 20 minutes gives me ample time, usually, to give nonevaluative feedback on the question the teacher wants addressed. If you are referring to reluctant teachers, I begin with the volunteers, and then after the "good word" spreads, and it usually spreads quickly, others request your services. It is important to create an atmosphere where teachers do not feel pressured. If teachers feel they have a choice, usually they will invite you in to observe.

10. **How do you deal with teachers (a teacher) who would like to sabotage the positive school spirit?**

Here are a few suggestions: seek to understand them by listening to their concerns. Ask the negative teacher to do something that emphasizes his or her strengths. For example, one time we planned a week that emphasized teacher stories and strengths. Teachers shared their achievements, and it built solidarity among the staff. We went to the reluctant teachers first and asked for their buy-in; they became the stars of the event.

11. **Self-reflection is inherent in your first book. How will you incorporate that kind of reflection in your next book?**

This book also emphasizes reflection. Read and reflect away!

12. **Is flexibility an option regarding literacy coaching, or should all of the classrooms look and sound alike?**

Classrooms are taught by individuals and filled with individuals, so each classroom is an individual classroom and will not look and sound alike. However, as a coach you can offer research-based strategies to all the teachers you coach; the implementation will differ according to the personality and makeup of each classroom.

13. **What are some tips for giving criticism?**

Don't give criticism. Instead, focus on the strengths of the teachers you are coaching. What we focus on, we get more of. Continue to give specific positive feedback. Ask the teacher you are coaching and observing to give you a focus for feedback. I ask for a specific question from the teacher. For example, What do you want me to look for when I come into your classroom? The teacher may say that he or she wants me to observe the way the students are working in groups. I focus on that and give specific, concrete feedback on how the student groups are working. Then if I can suggest something that might ameliorate the teacher's group instruction, I offer a suggestion. For example, let's say that the students in groups have assigned roles, but they appear to not be assuming their roles. I might suggest that the teacher use several strategies to increase the likelihood that the students will assume their assigned roles. One suggestion might be that the students create hats with their roles displayed on them and wear them if they want. Should they choose not to wear them (always give choice), they may place them on the desk for others to see. This is one simple visual strategy to increase participation.

14. How do you move a group of reluctant literacy specialists toward the coaching model and implementation?

The term "literacy specialists" raises a red flag for me. If you are getting resistance from your "specialists," you may be encountering resistance because you are trying to push educators who feel they should be the ones who are doing the pushing. You may be "trying to herd cats" and pushing those who feel they inherently are in charge and should be calling the shots. It sounds as though you first need to get the buy-in from the literacy specialists. Some steps to get the buy-in might be the following:

- Consider having a retreat where every literacy specialist is treated as an important member of the team.
- Respect the feedback from each individual.
- Ask for specific feedback and insights from all involved.
- Integrate the specific suggestions that the literacy coordinators offer into your plans.
- Assign specific responsibilities to each literacy coordinator and make them responsible for reporting back on the progress achieved each time you meet.
- Do goal setting and long-term planning with the literacy coordinators and make them feel and be a part of the process.

15. What do you do when your literacy coaching program has gotten off track in terms of changing direction with the teachers who are comfortable with how things currently work?

Break your literacy coaching program down into small, concrete steps. Go back to the beginning. For example, when I coach middle school teams and support their instituting Robert Marzano's strategies, I simply begin with one and move on to the others. However, when teachers revert to old habits, I reteach and we revisit the strategy that should have been implemented by that time. Another important factor to remember is to always honor the work that teachers have done in the past as well as the work they are attempting to implement. If we fail to honor the work previously done by the teachers, they may be less likely to join us in the new work.

Appendix B

Teacher Data Sheet

Your Name: _____

School: _____

School Address: _____

School Phone Number: _____

Voice Mail Extension: _____

Preferred E-mail Address: _____

Other Contact Info You Want to Share: _____

_____

_____

Team Name: _____

Subject Taught: _____

Grade Level: _____

Your Instructional Goal for the School Year: _____

_____

_____

Please share some things about yourself so that we can get to know you better. You can share about your family, your dreams, your avocations, the books you love to read, and so on. (Continue writing on the back.)

_____

_____

Please write any questions you have for us on the back, and we will respond. THANKS!

Appendix C

Suggestions for Nonevaluative Teacher Observations

1. Find an inconspicuous place to sit, a corner perhaps, where you can observe all or most of the students. Remember, you are really here to observe the learning occurring in the classroom.

2. Take a deep breath. Relax and make a goal to focus on the class.

3. Notice the "feel" of the class. What is the "tone" of the class? Do the students seem happy to be in the room? Does the teacher appear relaxed and excited about teaching the class? Do the students and teachers appear to care and accept each other? Do you sense a community of learners in the classroom?

4. Where is the teacher when students enter the classroom? Is she or he smiling? Interacting with students? Is there a procedure in place to welcome and engage students as they enter the room?

5. Does the teacher do the following during the class: Establish proximity (shoulder length) to each student in the class at least once? Use the students' names throughout the lesson? Call on students equitably, not calling on one gender or ethnic group more than the others? Mark on your observation sheet each time the teacher calls on a student. Keep track to make sure no student is called on more than others and each student is called on at least once or twice during the lesson.

6. Does the teacher use an opening activity to build classroom community?

7. Does the teacher share the goal of the lesson before they begin the work?

8. Does the teacher give *one* direction at a time, rather than several directions at once that confuse listeners?

9. Does the teacher do a "state change" every six to eight minutes?

10. Does the teacher teach to different modalities during the lesson?

11. Does the teacher dominate the talking?

12. Are students visibly engaged with the lesson? Are students working with others? Are students doing student talk to move their thinking to higher levels? Are teachers asking higher-level questions? Once again, mark each time the teacher asks a question and evaluate whether it is a factual question (lower level) or an analytical or evaluative question, and so on.

13. Notice how many minutes the teacher uses whole class instruction. Observe how well the students engage with the whole group instruction.

14. Other observations?

Appendix D

Student Interview Template for Teacher Feedback

In some districts, there is a disconnect between what the teacher believes, what the students think, and what the students think the teachers believe. Or we could just call it "what we don't know—we don't know" about each other. In one school, some teachers volunteered their students for interviews in order to get inside their students' minds. We used the following to obtain the students' mental picture. It worked exceedingly well. Students were honest and gave valuable feedback for the teachers.

Teacher Feedback for Improved Instruction

Note: You may modify this activity to fit your style and students. This is a suggested framework for the activity.

1. Inform the class that you will be interviewing six students as part of a project you are doing to improve instruction. Let the students know that the chosen students are not in any trouble nor are they receiving special privileges.

2. Choose six students from one of your classes. Choose two top-performing students, two average-performing students, and two failing students.

3. Hand out a question sheet to the six students at the beginning of class and ask that they think about the questions and fill in their answers on the sheet.

4. Ask a colleague to cover your class for the last 20 minutes so you can find a private place to interview students. If you cannot find someone to cover your class, find a quiet corner to interview the student while your class is engaged in a lesson at their desks.

5. Arrange two student desks facing each other and invite the first student to sit opposite you, facing you. Mix up the order in which you call on the students so that others are not aware that you have chosen low-, middle-, and high-performing students.

6. Ask the students the following questions:
   a. How do you think you learn best?
   b. What helps you learn best in this class?

    c. What keeps you from learning and doing your best in this class?

    d. What do I do as a teacher that helps you learn and do your best in this class?

    e. What do I do that might keep you from doing your best?

    f. If I could change one thing in this class to improve it, what would that change be?

7. Thank the student for taking part. You may want to shake the student's hand and formally thank him or her.

8. Reflect upon the student feedback and bring your thoughts/results to your next department/faculty meeting.

You may also want a coach to interview more than one student from your class. For example, in one middle school math class, the teacher failed to understand why three boys were doing so poorly. She was a caring teacher who provided competent math instruction. But the attitudes of these boys did not reflect what she desired for them to succeed at math. She asked me to interview the boys.

Usually students like positive attention. I began these student interviews by thanking the boys for meeting and talking with me. I formally introduced myself and shook each boy's hand with a firm handshake, looking into the eyes of each boy. The boys were seated in a small circle with me to remove the hierarchy of my standing and towering above them.

I made a few comments to relax the boys, then I began to ask them the questions (listed above in #6), telling them that they should refer to their math teacher when answering the questions. All of the boys agreed that the math teacher respected them and wanted them to learn. Their common concern was not that she didn't give her directions clearly but that she gave them only once. Each of the boys felt he needed the directions to be repeated in order to clearly understand the task. This was so simple.

As soon as the teacher heard the feedback from the boys, she changed the way she gave directions. Her direction-giving improved, the boys' attention improved, and ultimately their achievement improved. A couple of things happened. The boys felt that the teacher cared enough about them to get their feedback, and the boys really did need to hear the directions more than once in order for instruction to improve.

Describe how you learn best.

_____

_____

_____

What helps you learn best in this class?

_____

_____

_____

What keeps you from learning and doing your best in this class?

_____

_____

_____

What do I do as a teacher that helps you learn and do your best in this class?

_____

_____

_____

What do I do that might keep you from doing your best?

_____

_____

_____

If I could change one thing in this class to improve it, what would that change be?

_____

_____

_____

Appendix E

Template for a Parent Conference

In our experience, we find that teachers want strategies that reach parents and build positive relationships with them. The following is an example of a positive teacher conference. This is a skeletal outline; however, it offers suggestions for bridging differences.

1. **Sincerely greet the parents.**

   "Hello, Mr. and Mrs._____. I am _____. How are you?"

   Use the parents' formal names and use your formal name. Do not call the parents by their first names unless they invite you.

   Shake hands with the parents, looking them in the eyes, and take a cue from their handshakes how firm to shake back. Do not begin until you receive a nonverbal signal from the parents that they are ready to listen (this will probably be in the form of some kind of relaxing of the body: setting the purse on the floor, unfolding the arms from the chest, smiling, etc.).

   "Please sit down."

2. **Begin with a *positive* comment about their child to the parents.**

   John is such a caring child. He always wants to help the other kids.

   Mary is such a positive child. She always has a smile for everyone.

   Joe is so friendly. He waits outside my door each day to say hello.

   Jane is so polite. She always says thank you.

3. **Explain the issues/grades in "nondeficit" language.**

   Example: Let's look at John's class work. This folder contains samples of his work from all of his classes.

   Continuing: In class, John often does well in _____. However, he needs to complete three homework assignments, which will raise his grade significantly.

4. **Ask for parent input. What are their goals for their child?**

5. **Make a general goal statement for the student.**

   My goal is for John to be successful in my class, and I am going to do everything I can to support him. I care too much about him to watch him fail.

6. **Make a specific content goal.**

Reflection: Imagine a perfect parent conference of 5–10 minutes. What happens during that conference?

_____

_____

_____

_____

_____

_____

_____

How can you improve your parent conferences?

_____

_____

_____

_____

_____

_____

_____

_____

_____

Appendix F

High School Teachers: Morning Meetings to Improve Instruction

For one semester, a group of high school teachers volunteered to meet weekly with a coach to discuss pedagogy. They met on Friday mornings before school from 7:20 to 7:55 a.m. in the library of the school to discuss ways they could improve their classroom instruction.

At a general meeting they discussed their greatest challenges over which they had control. They made a list and decided to assign a topic a week to discuss. Below are the topics:

- Beginning of class issues; tardies and attendance
- Class community
- Makeup work; absences
- Long-term projects
- End-of-class issues
- Discipline; classroom management
- Parents
- Recruiting students to advanced placement (AP) classes
- Student expectations
- Celebrations
- Grading; rubrics

They spent a semester meeting and discussing these topics. The group generated these ideas, among others:

- Survey students at the end of the year. Find out what they like and dislike. Write the top three dislikes of the students on paper and tape it up in your classroom (for example, above your coat rack) so that you see the list each morning. Attempt to alleviate them. Teachers found that students didn't like the following: too much lecture, not enough humor, boring worksheets and other seat work, calling on the same students repeatedly, no movement during the class, among others.
- Call on each student at least two times per class. Use cards with names on them to check yourself.
- Use a strategy called "story time." Tell the students, "What do you want to tell me?" and give them 3 minutes a day to talk before you begin the lesson or give them 10 minutes each Monday to talk about their weekend.

- Have a joke time for students to tell appropriate jokes.
- Build something in as a transition to the next day's lesson.
- Use this question at the end of your lesson: "Is there any question you have that you won't go to sleep tonight without having the answer?"
- Use a trivia game related to content.
- Tardies: have a clipboard at your door where students sign themselves in, saving face and not interrupting your lesson.
- Begin with this question: "What has happened since yesterday?" Allot five minutes to discuss.
- Use a particular hand signal to begin class. Then for 30 seconds discuss a good dynamic question central to the lesson that draws on previous knowledge. Use an analogy from the texts to connect with student lives.

The teachers offered the following comments about their participation in the group. They said the meetings allowed them to

- Narrow the focus
- Go deeper
- Come together and talk about kids
- Share different methodologies
- Have a forum to be heard and receive feedback
- Find out what other people are doing in general
- Fill themselves up with adult talk, energizing them
- Force themselves to analyze what they do that works and why it works
- Provide a spiritual fix as well

These simple Friday morning meetings were free, fun, informative.

Could the above format work for the teachers you coach? Why or why not?

_____

_____

_____

Thanks to the following teachers who participated in this group (spring 2004) at Webster Groves High School in Webster Groves, Missouri: Donald Johnson, Pam Carmell, Kathy Laufersweiler, Pat Schea, Lisa McDowell, Adam Conway, Terry Verstraete.

Appendix G

How to Start a Middle School Writing Group

By John Hefflinger

During the summers of 2005 and 2006 I attended the St. Charles Writing Project, a workshop with Dr. Bonnie Davis as the presenter. It was during this workshop that my love for writing was rekindled. We spent the majority of our time writing and listening to how to get our students to not only write but to enjoy writing. During the 2005–2006 school year, I implemented several strategies I learned with great results.

With Bonnie's coaching, I began the Jefferson Middle School Writing Club. The club is open to all students at all levels. I began and ended with sixth and eighth graders, mostly girls. Many students attended the first few meetings, but we ended up with 9 or 10 regulars. Some were already very good writers and others wanted to grow. The students decided they didn't want this to be like all the other clubs, with officers and "stuff like that." They just wanted to come in and write. So they did.

On a few occasions I would offer writing prompts and/or pictures to inspire them. The club members were excited about being published, even if it was just for us. With the leadership of the eighth graders, the club decided to focus their writings on "teachers and teaching," with the goal of publishing a book for the faculty. The students worked hard and very well together.

As the deadline approached, I saw students offering advice and encouragement to one another. The only male student still in the group had a difficult time separating himself from his love of writing horror stories and focusing on teachers. He wrote a wonderful poem about how teachers can be a source of peace and encouragement or a horror story to their students. During National Education Week several club members read what they wrote to the faculty at a special meeting. Each faculty member received a copy of our published book. As the year came to a close, some of the eighth graders expressed a desire to come back next year even though they will be in high school and in a different building. With all that high school has to offer, we will see if they do indeed return.

The following two poems were written by students in the club and are included in the book published as *Teachers*.

Teachers

By Alex Blodgett

Some teachers are really nice.

Some are so mean that it cuts like a knife.

Like a dart penetrating my heart.

Some are like flowers with great healing powers.

But some are like planes destroying Twin Towers.

Bonnie's note: Alex was ecstatic when I asked him if I could publish this poem. His mother came to school to sign a permission slip and said she had never seen him so excited. One small act can be the origin of one giant step to becoming a writer.

Thoughts During Class

By Megan Illy

Sitting in this cold, plastic seat,

Amusing myself by examining my feet

There is only so much a size eight can do,

Especially while confined into a Nike shoe.

There must be something interesting in this room,

Other than this boring lecture, the entirety of my doom.

Is it even humanly possible to talk in a monotone for an hour?

A quick glance at the clock confirms my question:

the battery must be dead with no power.

It seems the big hand will not budge.

Wait . . . never mind, it advanced a smudge.

Hmmm, I wonder if I stare long enough at the boy's back in front of me a hole will appear.

Nope, guess not, I hope I won't die of boredom, my biggest fear.

My thoughts drift, going into a zone

Of my own

A place past chalk dust,

Pencil rust,

Wooden desks

Boring books filled with minuscule text.

(Continued)

(Continued)

And most of all far, far away,

From this "teacher" talking my day away.

Unfortunately, I'm stuck in the second row,

Where the question of my sanity defiantly takes a tow.

I am forced with two choices at hand,

I can either daydream some more, or pay attention and not visit my la-la land.

I know that the right thing to do is the latter,

But sometimes I really wonder about this teacher, whom to my entertainment certainly does not cater.

What's her favorite book?

It could be a grim adventure of Captain Hook

Where she gets lost in the riveting text,

Turning quickly from one page to the next.

Or it could be a romance, like Romeo and Juliet?

I know little enough of my teacher to even guess.

I've never really thought of her as a real human being,

I've only seen her day to day in classroom scenes.

Day to day, months and months,

And I don't know the least about her as a person, never talked to her about life, not once.

I've never asked how the kids are doing, if they are in good health or over the flu,

Actually I don't even know if she has children,

Before now that is a part of her life I never care or knew.

I've never asked her to spill her troubles and tell me what's wrong,

I didn't realize she even had feelings, only thought of her lectures, boring and long.

Only when I think about it, those lectures aren't boring,

She's trying to teach me something important that could help me,

something that I should not be ignoring.

It would take a lot of guts to walk in her shoes,

Trying to impact someone's life,

> Which is somewhat hard to do when that someone is taking
> a snooze.
>
> I should try to pay attention to what she has to say,
>
> Because she's a person with thoughts and feelings,
>
> Just like me, trying to live life to its fullest day to day.

Megan's note: Here are the sentences explaining why I wrote "Thoughts During Class." One day in class, I was very bored and wanted to write something that reflected the way I felt, so I wrote the first part of "Thoughts During Class." When I got home later that night, I found the poem in my notebook, reread it, and started to think, Why did I write this so negative? Teachers are people just like me, as hard as that is to believe. So I started to write the second half, about everything I didn't know about my teacher, things that make her real and easier to relate to.

Bonnie's note: Megan's poem illustrates what Frank Smith says about writing: we write to create our thoughts. Megan created her thoughts in a poem. Later, she reflected upon her writing and wrote more. Finally, she reflected upon her process in writing. What an exciting process!

This club offers students an opportunity to see themselves as writers. I work in a nonevaluative, constructive environment that takes student writers from talking about their writing to final publication.

Reprinted with permission from John Hefflinger.

Bibliography and Recommended Web Sites

Alexie, S. (1993). *The Lone Ranger and Tonto fistfight in heaven.* New York: Harper.

Allen, J. (1995). *It's never too late: Leading adolescents to lifelong literacy.* Portsmouth, NH: Heinemann.

Allen, J. (1999). *Words, words, words.* Portland, ME: Stenhouse.

Allen, J. (2004). *Tools for teaching content literacy.* Portland, ME: Stenhouse.

Allen, R. (2002). *Impact teaching.* New York: Allyn & Bacon.

Annenberg Protocols. (1997). *Looking at student work.* Retrieved June 1, 2006, from http://www.lasw.org/protocols.html

Applebee, A., & Langer, J. (1987). *How writing shapes thinking: A study of teaching and learning.* Urbana, IL: National Council of Teachers of English.

Atwell, N. (1998). *In the middle: New understandings about writing, reading, and learning.* Portsmouth, NH: Heinemann.

Bailey, B. (2000). *Conscious discipline: 7 basic skills for brainsmart classroom management.* Oviendo, FL: Loving Guidance.

Barkley, S. G. (2005). *Quality teaching in a culture of coaching.* New York: Rowman & Littlefield.

Birchak, B., Connor, C., Crawford, K. M., Kahn, L. H., Kaser, S., Turner, S., et al. (1998). *Teacher study groups: Building community through dialogue and reflection.* Urbana, IL: National Council of Teachers of English.

Birman, B., Desimone, L., Porter, A., & Garet, M. (2000). Designing professional development that works. *Educational Leadership, 57*(8), 28–33.

Bishop, J. (2003). *Goal setting for students.* St. Louis, MO: Accent on Success.

Bloom, G., Castagna, C., Moir, E., & Warren, B. (2005). *Blended coaching: Skills and strategies to support principal development.* Thousand Oaks, CA: Corwin Press.

Bomer, R. (1995). *Time for meaning: Crafting literate lives in middle and high school.* Portsmouth, NH: Heinemann.

Burke, J. (1999). *The English teacher's companion: A complete guide to classroom, curriculum, and the profession.* Portsmouth, NH: Boynton/Cook.

Burke, J. (2000). *Reading reminders: Tools, tips, and techniques.* Portsmouth, NH: Boynton/Cook.

Burke, J. (2003). *Writing reminders: Tools, tips, and techniques.* Portsmouth, NH: Heinemann.

Burke, J. (2006). *Letters to a new teacher: A month-by-month guide to the year ahead.* Portsmouth, NH: Heinemann.

Calkins, L. (1986). *The art of teaching writing.* Portsmouth, NH: Heinemann.

Carlson, L. (Ed.). (1994). *Cool salsa: Bilingual poems on growing up Latino in the United States.* New York: Henry Holt.

Carr, J., Herman, N., & Harris, D. (2005). *Creating dynamic schools through mentoring, coaching, and collaboration.* Alexandria, VA: Association for Supervision and Curriculum Development.

Carson, B. (1996). *Gifted hands.* Grand Rapids, MI: Zondervan.

Casey, K. (2006). *Literacy coaching: The essentials.* Portsmouth, NH: Heinemann.

Charles A. Dana Center, University of Texas at Austin. (1999). *Hope for urban education: A study of nine high performing high-poverty urban elementary schools.* Washington, DC: U.S. Department of Education, Planning and Evaluation Service. Retrieved June 1, 2006, from http://www.ed.gov/pubs/urbanhope/index.html

Cisneros, S. (1989). *The house on Mango Street.* New York: Random House.

Costa, A., & Garmston, R. (2002). *Cognitive coaching: A foundation for renaissance schools.* Norwood, MA: Christopher-Gordon.

Davis, B. (Ed.). (1990). *Anthology from college composition class.* Missouri Eastern Correctional Center. St. Louis, MO: Author.

Davis, B. (2006). *How to teach students who don't look like you: Culturally relevant teaching strategies.* Thousand Oaks, CA: Corwin Press.

Davis, S., Jenkins, G., & Hunt, R. (2002). *The pact.* New York: Riverhead Books.

Diaz-Maggioli, G. (2004). *Teacher-centered professional development.* Alexandria, VA: Association for Supervision and Curriculum Development.

Dorn, L., French, C., & Jones, T. (1998). *Apprenticeship in literacy: Transitions across reading and writing.* Portland, ME: Stenhouse.

Draper, S. (1997). *Forged by fire.* New York: Simon Pulse.

DuFour, R., & Eaker, R. (1998). *Professional learning communities at work: Best practices for enhancing student achievement.* Alexandria, VA: Association for Supervision and Curriculum Development.

DuFour, R., Eaker, R., & DuFour R. (2005). *On common ground: The power of professional learning communities.* Bloomington, IN: National Educational Service.

Ekman, P. (2001). *Telling lies.* New York: W. W. Norton.

Ekman, P. (2003). *Emotions revealed.* New York: Henry Holt.

Ellison, J., & Hayes, C. (2003). *Cognitive coaching: Weaving threads of learning and change into the culture of an organization.* Norwood, MA: Christopher-Gordon.

Elmore, R. (2002). *Building a new structure for school leadership.* Washington, DC: Albert Shanker Institute.

Fletcher, R., & Portalupi, J. (1998). *Craft lessons: Teaching writing K–8.* York, ME: Stenhouse.

Fountas, I., & Pinnell, G. S. (2001). *Guiding readers and writers, grades 3–6: Teaching comprehension, genre, and content literacy.* Portsmouth, NH: Heinemann.

Freeman, L. (Producer), & Irving, D. (Writer/Director). (1999). *Faith Ringgold: The last story quilt* [Video]. (Available from L & S Video Incorporated, 45 Stornowaye Street, Chappaqua, NY 10514)

Fullan, M. (1996). Turning systemic thinking on its head. *Phi Delta Kappan, 77*(6), 420.

Fullan, M. (2000). The three stories of education reform. *Phi Delta Kappan, 81*(8), 581–584.

Fullan, M. (2001). *Leading in a culture of change.* San Francisco: Jossey-Bass.

Fullan, M. (2005, March 2). Tri-level development. *Education Week, 24*(25), 32–35.

Fullan, M., & Hargreaves, A. (1996). *What's worth fighting for in your school?* New York: Teachers College Press.

Fulwiler, T. (Ed.). (1987). *The journal book.* Portsmouth, NH: Heinemann.

Goff, L., Colton, A., & Langer, G. (2000). Power of the portfolio. *Journal of Staff Development, 21*(4), 44–48.

Graff, G. (2003). *Clueless in academe.* New Haven, CT: Yale University Press.

Graves, D. (1989). *Experiment with fiction.* Portsmouth, NH: Heinemann.

Graves, D. (2003). *Writing: Teachers and children at work.* Portsmouth, NH: Heinemann.

Gregory, G., & Chapman, C. (2002). *Differentiated instructional strategies: One size doesn't fit all.* Thousand Oaks, CA: Corwin Press.

Guy, R. (1981). *The friends.* New York: Laurel Leaf Press.

Hall, E. (1990). *The silent language.* New York: Random House.

Hall, G. E., & Hord, S. M. (2001). *Implementing change: Patterns, principles, and potholes.* Boston: Allyn & Bacon.

Hansen, J. (2001). *When writers read.* Portsmouth, NH: Heinemann.

Harp, B. (2002). *The mentor's handbook: Practical suggestions for collaborative reflection and analysis.* Norwood, MA: Christopher-Gordon.

Harris, Eddy (1998). *Mississippi solo: A river quest.* New York: Henry Holt and Company, Inc.

Henke, L. (1991–1997). *The Clayton writing project model.* St. Louis, MO: Clayton School District.

Hord, S. M. (1997). *Professional learning communities: Communities of continuous inquiry and improvement.* Austin, TX: Southwest Educational Development Laboratory.

Husby, V. (2005). *Individualized professional development: A framework for meeting school and district goals.* Thousand Oaks, CA: Corwin Press.

Intrator, S., & Scribner, M. (Eds.). (2003). *Teaching with fire: Poetry that sustains the courage to teach.* San Francisco: Jossey-Bass.

Irwin, J. (1997). *Reading and the middle school student: Strategies to enhance literacy.* Boston: Allyn & Bacon.

Jago, C. (2002). *Cohesive writing: Why concept is not enough.* Portsmouth, NH: Heinemann.

Jensen, E. (1998). *Teaching with the brain in mind.* Alexandria, VA: Association of Supervision and Curriculum Development.

Johnson, R. (2002). *Using data to close the achievement gap: How to measure equity in our schools.* Thousand Oaks, CA: Corwin Press.

Joyce, B., & Showers, B. (1997). *Student achievement through staff development* (2nd ed.). White Plains, NY: Longman.

Kise, J. (2006). *Differentiated coaching: A framework for helping teachers change.* Thousand Oaks, CA: Corwin Press.

Kohm, B., & Nance, B. (2007). *Principals who learn: Asking the right questions, seeking the best solutions.* Alexandria, VA: Association for Supervision of Curriculum and Development.

Lamott, A. (1994). *Bird by bird.* New York: Pantheon.

Langer, G., Colton, A., & Goff, L. (2003). *Collaborative analysis of student work: Improving teaching and learning.* Alexandria, VA: Association for Supervision of Curriculum and Development.

Langer, J. (2002). *Effective literacy instruction: Building successful reading and writing programs.* Urbana, IL: National Council of Teachers of English.

Lindsey, R. B., Nuri Robins, K., & Terrell, R. D. (2003). *Cultural proficiency: A manual for school leaders* (2nd ed.). Thousand Oaks, CA: Corwin Press.

Lindsey, R. B., Roberts, L., & CampbellJones, F. (2005). *The culturally proficient school: An implementation for school leaders.* Thousand Oaks, CA: Corwin Press.

Little, J. W. (1987). Teachers as colleagues. In V. Richardson-Koehler (Ed.), *Educator's handbook.* White Plains, NY: Longman.

Little, J. W. (1990). The persistence of privacy: Autonomy and initiative in teachers' professional relations. *Teachers College Record, 91*(4), 509–536.

Little, J. W., Gearhart, M., Curry, M., & Kafka, J. (2003). Looking at student work for teacher learning, teacher community, and school reform. *Phi Delta Kappan, 85*(3), 185–192.

Lyons, C. A., & Pinnell, G. S. (2001). *Systems for change in literacy education.* Portsmouth, NH: Heinemann.

Marczely, B. (2001). *Supervision in education: A differentiated approach with legal perspectives.* Gaithersburg, MD: Aspen.

Marzano, R. (2003a). *Classroom management that works.* Alexandria, VA: Association for Supervision and Curriculum Development.

Marzano, R. J. (2003b). *What works in schools.* Alexandria, VA: Association for Supervision and Curriculum Development.

Marzano, R. J. (2004). *Building background knowledge for academic achievement.* Alexandria, VA: Association for Supervision and Curriculum Development.

Marzano, R. J., & Pickering, D. (2005). *Building academic vocabulary: Teacher's manual.* Alexandria, VA: Association for Supervision and Curriculum Development.

Marzano, R. J., Pickering, D. J., & Pollock, J. E. (2001). *Classroom instruction that works: Research-based strategies for increasing student achievement.* Alexandria, VA: Association for Supervision and Curriculum Development.

Moxley, D., & Taylor, R. T. (2006). *Literacy coaching: A handbook for school leaders.* Thousand Oaks, CA: Corwin Press.

Murphy, C. (1992). Study groups foster schoolwide learning. *Educational Leadership, 50*(3), 71–74.

Murray, D. (1985). *A writer teaches writing.* Boston: Houghton Mifflin.

Myers, W. D. (2001). *Bad boy: A memoir.* New York: HarperCollins.

National Council of Teachers of English. (2006). Retrieved from http://www.ncte.org

Nuri Robins, K., Lindsey, R. B., Lindsey, D. B., & Terrell, R. D. (2002). *Culturally proficient instruction: A guide for people who teach.* Thousand Oaks, CA: Corwin Press.

Palmer, P. (1997). *The courage to teach.* San Francisco: Jossey-Bass.

Palmer, P. (2004). *A hidden wholeness: The journey toward an undivided life.* San Francisco: Jossey-Bass.

Payne, R. K. (1995). *A framework for understanding poverty.* Highland, TX: Aha! Process.

Payne, R. K. (2001). *A framework for understanding poverty* (Rev. ed.). Highland, TX: Aha! Process.

Pelzer, D. (2000). *A child called it.* New York: Penguin Press.

Putnam, R. T., & Borko, H. (2000). What do new views of knowledge and thinking have to say about research on teacher learning? *Educational Leadership, 29*(1), 4–15.

Reeves, D. B. (2002). *The leader's guide to standards: A blueprint for educational equity and excellence.* San Francisco: Jossey-Bass.

Reeves, D. B. (2006). *The learning leader: How to focus school improvement for better results.* Alexandria, VA: Association for Supervision and Curriculum Development.

Roberts, S., & Pruitt, E. (2003). *Schools as professional learning communities: Collaborative activities and strategies for professional development.* Thousand Oaks, CA: Corwin Press.

Roizen, M., & Oz, M. (2005). *You: The owner's manual: An insider's guide to the body that will make you healthier and younger.* New York: HarperResource.

Russo, A. (2004). School-based coaching: A revolution in professional development— Or just the latest fad? *Harvard Education Letter,* July/August. Retrieved September 2, 2006, from http://www.edletter.org/past/issues/2004-ja/coaching.shtml

Sagor, R. (2000). *Guiding school improvement with action research.* Alexandria, VA: Association for Supervision and Curriculum Development.

Sausner, R. (2005). Making assessments work. *District Administration, 41*(8), 31–34.

Schmoker, M. (1999). *Results: The key to continuous school improvement.* Alexandria, VA: Association for Supervision and Curriculum Development.

Schmoker, M. (2006). *Results now: How we can achieve unprecedented improvements in teaching and learning.* Alexandria, VA: Association for Supervision and Curriculum Development.

School Improvement Network & Linton Productions (Producers). (2005). *Instructional coaching: School-based staff development for improved teacher and student learning* [DVD set]. (Available from School Improvement Network, 8686 South 1300 East, Sandy, UT 84094)

School Improvement Network & Linton Productions (Producers). (2006). *No excuses! How to increase minority student achievement* [DVD set]. (Available from School Improvement Network, 8686 South 1300 East, Sandy, UT 84094)

Schreck, M. K. (2004). *Pulse of the seasons.* Columbia, MO: Tigress Press.

Schreck, M. K. (2005). *The red desk.* Columbia, MO: Tigress Press.

Schreck, M. K. (2006). *Crystal doorknobs.* Columbia, MO: Tigress Press.

Senge, P. (2000). *Schools that learn: A fifth discipline fieldbook for educators, parents, and everyone who cares about education.* New York: Doubleday-Currency.

Shange, N. (1985). *Betsy Brown.* New York: Picador.

Showers, B., Joyce, B., & Bennett, B. (1987). Synthesis of research on staff development: A framework for future study and a state-of-the-art analysis. *Educational Leadership, 45*(3), 77–87.

Singleton, G., & Linton, C. (2006). *Courageous conversations about race: A field guide for achieving equity in schools.* Thousand Oaks, CA: Corwin Press.

Smith, F. (1983). *Essays into literacy.* Exeter, NH: Heinemann.

Smith, F. (2003). *Unspeakable acts, unnatural practices.* Portsmouth, NH: Heinemann.

Stapleton, L. (Ed.). (1960). *H. D. Thoreau: A writer's journal.* New York: Dover.

Starbright Foundation. (2001). *Once upon a fairy tale.* New York: Viking.

Steinbeck, J. (1993). *Of mice and men.* New York: Penguin Press. (Original work published 1937)

Sylwester, R. (2000). *A biological brain in a cultural classroom: Applying biological research to classroom management.* Thousand Oaks, CA: Corwin Press.

Tate, M. (2003). *Worksheets don't grow dendrites: Instructional strategies that engage the brain.* Thousand Oaks, CA: Corwin Press.

Tate, M. (2004). *"Sit and get" won't grow dendrites: 20 professional learning strategies that engage the adult brain.* Thousand Oaks, CA: Corwin Press.

Tatum, A. (2005). *Teaching reading to black adolescent males: Closing the achievement gap.* Portland, ME: Stenhouse.

Taylor, R., & Gunter, G. A. (2005). *The K–12 literacy leadership fieldbook.* Thousand Oaks, CA: Corwin Press.

Toll, C. (2005). *The literacy coach's survival guide: Essential questions and practical answers.* Newark, DE: International Reading Association.

Toll, C. (2006). *The literacy coach's desk reference.* Urbana, IL: National Council of Teachers of English.

Tompson, C. L., & Zeuli, J. S. (1999). The frame and the tapestry: Standards-based reform and professional development. In L. Darling-Hammond & G. Sykes (Eds.), *Teaching and learning profession: Handbook of policy and practice* (pp. 341–375). San Francisco: Jossey-Bass.

Tovani, C. (2000). *I read it, but I don't get it: Comprehension strategies for adolescent readers.* Portland, ME: Stenhouse.

Tovani, C. (2004). *Do I really have to teach reading?: Content comprehension, grades 6–12.* Portland, ME: Stenhouse.

Veljkovic, P., & Schwartz, A. (Eds.). (2001). *Writing from the heart: Young people share their wisdom: Best of the laws of life essay contests* (Vol. 1). West Conshohocken, PA: Templeton Foundation Press.

Walpole, S., & McKenna, M. (2004). *The literacy coach's handbook: A guide to research-based practices: Solving problems in teaching of literacy.* New York: Guilford Press.

Wiggens, G., & McTighe, J. (1998). *Understanding by design.* Alexandria, VA: Association for Supervision and Curriculum Development.

Wiggins, G., & McTighe, J. (2006). Examining the teaching life. *ASCD Educational Leadership, 63*(6), 26–29.

Wilhelm, J. (1995). *"You gotta be the book": Teaching engaged and reflective reading with adolescents.* New York: Teachers College Press.

York-Barr, J., Sommers, W. A., Ghere, G. S., & Montie, J. K. (2006). *Reflective practice to improve schools: An action guide for educators.* Thousand Oaks, CA: Corwin Press.

Zeni, J., Krater, J., & Cason, N. (1994). *Mirror images: Teaching writing in black and white.* Portsmouth, NH: Heinemann.

RECOMMENDED WEB SITES

Association for Supervision and Curriculum Development. http://www.ascd.org
National Council of Teachers of English. http://www.ncte.org
National Staff Development Council. http://www.nsdc.org

Index

CORWIN PRESS

DATE DUE